PENGUIN

ARKANA

BE AS YOU ARE

Ramana Maharshi was one of the most significant spiritual teachers to emerge from India during the first half of this century, and remains widely admired. This collection of conversations between him and the many seekers who came to his ashram for guidance contains the essence of his teaching.

David Godman has been studying and practising the teachings of Sri Ramana in India since 1976. He is the past librarian of Sri Ramana's ashram and a former editor of *The Mountain Path*, a journal which propagates Sri Ramana's teachings.

Be As You Are

The Teachings
of
Sri Ramana Maharshi

Edited by David Godman

ARKANA
PENGUIN BOOKS

ARKANA

Published by the Penguin Group
Penguin Books Ltd, 27 Wrights Lane, London W8 5TZ, England
Penguin Putnam Inc., 375 Hudson Street, New York, New York 10014, USA
Penguin Books Australia Ltd, Ringwood, Victoria, Australia
Penguin Books Canada Ltd, 10 Alcorn Avenue, Toronto, Ontario, Canada M4V 3B2
Penguin Books (NZ) Ltd, Private Bag 102902, NSMC, Auckland, New Zealand

Penguin Books Ltd, Registered Offices: Harmondsworth, Middlesex, England

First published by Arkana 1985
7 9 10 8

Printed in England by Clays Ltd, St Ives plc

Contents

CONTENTS

Acknowledgments

To Sri Ramanasramam for permission to reprint extracts from most of the books listed in the bibliography.

To Rider and Co., London, for permission to reprint an extract from *A Search in Secret India*.

To Sadhu Om for permission to reprint material from *The Path of Sri Ramana* and for permission to use and adapt his unpublished translations of the writings of Sri Ramana Maharshi and *Guru Vachaka Kovai*.

To Michael James for assistance in adapting verses from *Guru Vachaka Kovai* and for offering constructive advice throughout the preparation of the book.

Introduction

In 1896 a sixteen-year-old schoolboy walked out on his family and, driven by an inner compulsion, slowly made his way to Arunachala, a holy mountain and pilgrimage centre in South India. On his arrival he threw away all his money and possessions and abandoned himself to a newly-discovered awareness that his real nature was formless, immanent consciousness. His absorption in this awareness was so intense that he was completely oblivious of his body and the world; insects chewed away portions of his legs, his body wasted away because he was rarely conscious enough to eat and his hair and fingernails grew to unmanageable lengths. After two or three years in this state he began a slow return to physical normality, a process that was not finally completed for several years. His awareness of himself as consciousness was unaffected by this physical transition and it remained continuous and undimmed for the rest of his life. In Hindu parlance he had 'realised the Self'; that is to say, he had realised by direct experience that nothing existed apart from an indivisible and universal consciousness which was experienced in its unmanifest form as beingness or awareness and in its manifest form as the appearance of the universe.

Normally this awareness is only generated after a long and arduous period of spiritual practice but in this case it happened spontaneously, without prior effort or desire. Venkataraman, the sixteen-year-old schoolboy, was alone in an upstairs room of his uncle's house in Madurai (near the southern tip of India) when he was suddenly gripped by an intense fear of death. In the following few minutes he went through a simulated death experience during which he became consciously aware for the first time that his real nature was imperishable and that it was unrelated to the body, the mind or the personality. Many people have reported similar unexpected experiences but they are almost invariably temporary. In Venkataraman's case the experience was permanent and irreversible. From that time on his consciousness of being an

1

individual person ceased to exist and it never functioned in him
again.

Venkataraman told no one about his experience and for six
weeks he kept up the appearance of being an ordinary schoolboy.
However, he found it an increasingly difficult posture to maintain
and at the end of this six week period he abandoned his family
and went directly to the holy mountain of Arunachala.

The choice of Arunachala was far from random. Throughout
his brief life he had always associated the name of Arunachala
with God and it was a major revelation to him when he
discovered that it was not some heavenly realm but a tangible
earthly entity. The mountain itself had long been regarded by
Hindus as a manifestation of Siva, a Hindu God, and in later years
Venkataraman often said that it was the spiritual power of
Arunachala which had brought about his Self-realisation. His love
for the mountain was so great that from the day he arrived in
1896 until his death in 1950 he could never be persuaded to go
more than two miles away from its base.

After a few years of living on its slopes his inner awareness
began to manifest as an outer spiritual radiance. This radiance
attracted a small circle of followers and, although he remained
silent for most of the time, he embarked upon a teaching career.
One of his earliest followers, impressed by the evident saintliness
and wisdom of the young man, decided to rename him Bhagavan
Sri Ramana Maharshi – Bhagavan means Lord or God, Sri is an
Indian honorific title, Ramana is a contraction of Venkataraman
and Maharshi means 'great seer' in Sanskrit. The name found
favour with his other followers and it soon became the title by
which he became known to the world.

At this stage of his life Sri Ramana was speaking very little and
so his teachings were transmitted in an unusual fashion. Instead of
giving out verbal instructions he constantly emanated a silent
force or power which stilled the minds of those who were attuned
to it and occasionally even gave them a direct experience of the
state that he himself was perpetually immersed in. In later years he
became more willing to give out verbal teachings, but even then,
the silent teachings were always available to those who were able
to make good use of them. Throughout his life Sri Ramana
insisted that this silent flow of power represented his teachings in
their most direct and concentrated form. The importance he
attached to this is indicated by his frequent statements to the effect

that his verbal teachings were only given out to those who were unable to understand his silence.

As the years passed he became more and more famous. A community grew up around him, thousands of visitors flocked to see him and for the last twenty years of his life he was widely regarded as India's most popular and revered holy man. Some of these thousands were attracted by the peace they felt in his presence, others by the authoritative way in which he guided spiritual seekers and interpreted religious teachings, and some merely came to tell him their problems. Whatever their reasons for coming almost everyone who came into contact with him was impressed by his simplicity and his humbleness. He made himself available to visitors twenty-four hours a day by living and sleeping in a communal hall which was always accessible to everyone, and his only private possessions were a loin-cloth, a water-pot and a walking-stick. Although he was worshipped by thousands as a living God, he refused to allow anyone to treat him as a special person and he always refused to accept anything which could not be shared equally by everyone in his ashram. He shared in the communal work and for many years he rose at 3 a.m. in order to prepare food for the residents of the ashram. His sense of equality was legendary. When visitors came to see him – it made no difference whether they were VIPs, peasants or animals – they would all be treated with equal respect and consideration. His egalitarian concern even extended to the local trees; he discouraged his followers from picking flowers or leaves off them and he tried to ensure that whenever fruit was taken from the ashram trees it was always done in such a way that the tree only suffered a minimum amount of pain.

Throughout this period (1925-50) the centre of ashram life was the small hall where Sri Ramana lived, slept and held court. He spent most of his day sitting in one corner radiating his silent power and simultaneously fielding questions from the constant flow of visitors who descended on him from every corner of the globe. He rarely committed his ideas to paper and so the verbal replies given out during this period (by far the most well-documented of his life) represent the largest surviving source of his teachings.

These verbal teachings flowed authoritatively from his direct knowledge that consciousness was the only existing reality. Consequently, all his explanations and instructions were geared to convincing his followers that this was their true and natural state. Few of his followers were capable of assimilating this truth in its highest and most undiluted form and so he often adapted his teachings to conform to the limited understanding of the people who came to him for advice. Because of this tendency it is possible to distinguish many different levels of his teachings. At the highest level that could be expressed in words he would say that consciousness alone exists. If this was received with scepticism he would say that awareness of this truth is obscured by the self-limiting ideas of the mind and that if these ideas were abandoned then the reality of consciousness would be revealed. Most of his followers found this high-level approach a little too theoretical – they were so immersed in the self-limiting ideas that Sri Ramana was encouraging them to drop that they felt that the truth about consciousness would only be revealed to them if they underwent a long period of spiritual practice. To satisfy such people Sri Ramana prescribed an innovative method of self-attention which he called self-enquiry. He recommended this technique so often and so vigorously that it was regarded by many people as the most distinctive motif in his teachings.

Even then, many people were not satisfied and they would continue to ask for advice about other methods or try to engage him in theoretical philosophical discussions. With such people Sri Ramana would temporarily abandon his absolute standpoint and give appropriate advice on whatever level it was asked. If he appeared on these occasions to accept and endorse many of the misconceptions which his visitors had about themselves it was only to draw their attention to some aspect of his teachings that he felt would help them to better understand his real views.

Inevitably, this policy of modifying his teachings to meet the needs of different people led to many contradictions. He might, for example, tell one person that the individual self is non-existent and then turn to another person and give a detailed description of how the individual self functions, accumulates *karma* and reincarnates. It is possible for an observer to say that such opposing statements may both be true when seen from different standpoints, but the former statement clearly has more validity when it is viewed from the absolute standpoint of Sri Ramana's own experience. This standpoint, summarised by his statement that consciousness alone exists, is ultimately the only yardstick by which one can realistically assess the relative truth of his widely differing and contradictory statements. To whatever extent his other statements deviate from this it may be assumed that to that extent they are dilutions of the truth.

Bearing this in mind I have tried to arrange the material in this book in such a way that his highest teachings come first and his least important or most diluted ones last. The only exception is a chapter in which he talks about his silent teachings. It ought to be somewhere near the beginning but I found it more expedient for a variety of reasons to fit it into a section about half-way through the book.

I decided on this overall structure for two reasons. Firstly it gives the reader a chance to gauge the relative importance of the various ideas presented, and secondly, and more importantly, it was Sri Ramana's own preferred method of teaching. When visitors came to see him he would always try to convince them of the truth of his higher teachings and only if they seemed unwilling to accept them would he tone down his answers and speak from a more relative level.

The teachings have been presented in the form of a series of questions and answers in which Sri Ramana outlines his views on various subjects. Each chapter is devoted to a different topic and each topic is prefaced by a few introductory or explanatory remarks. The questions and answers which form the bulk of each chapter have been taken from many sources and assembled in such a way that they give the appearance of being a continuous conversation. I was forced to adopt this method because there are no continuous lengthy conversations available which cover the full spectrum of his views on any particular subject. For those who are interested, the sources of the quotations which make up the conversations are all listed at the end of the book.

Sri Ramana usually answered questions in one of the three vernacular languages of South India: Tamil, Telugu and Malayalam. No tape-recordings were ever made and most of his answers were hurriedly written down in English by his official interpreters. Because some of the interpreters were not completely fluent in English some of the transcriptions were either ungrammatical or written in a kind of stilted English which occasionally makes Sri Ramana sound like a pompous Victorian. I have deviated from the published texts by correcting a few of the worst examples of this kind; in such cases the meaning has not been tampered with, only the mode of expression. I have also contracted some of the questions and answers in order to eliminate material which digressed too far from the subject under discussion. Throughout the book the questions are prefaced by a 'Q:' and Sri Ramana's answers by an 'A:'.

The original texts from which these conversations are taken are characterised by a luxuriant profusion of capital letters. I have eliminated most of them, leaving only three terms, Guru, Self and Heart, consistently capitalised. Sri Ramana often used these terms as synonyms for consciousness and wherever this meaning is implied I have retained the capitalisation to avoid confusion.

A complete glossary of Sanskrit words which are not translated in the text can be found at the end of the book. The same glossary also includes brief descriptions of unfamiliar people, places and scriptural works which are mentioned in the text. Sri Ramana occasionally used Sanskrit terms in unconventional ways. On the few occasions that he does so in this book I have ignored the standard dictionary definitions and have instead given a definition which more accurately reflects the intended meaning.

PART ONE

The Self

That in which all these worlds seem to exist steadily, that of
which all these worlds are a possession, that from which all
these worlds rise, that for which all these exist, that by
which all these worlds come into existence and that which is
indeed all these – that alone is the existing reality. Let us
cherish that Self, which is the reality, in the Heart.[1]

CHAPTER 1
The nature of the Self

The essence of Sri Ramana's teachings is conveyed in his frequent assertions that there is a single immanent reality, directly experienced by everyone, which is simultaneously the source, the substance and the real nature of everything that exists. He gave it a number of different names, each one signifying a different aspect of the same indivisible reality. The following classification includes all of his more common synonyms and explains the implications of the various terms used.

1 *The Self* This is the term that he used the most frequently. He defined it by saying that the real Self or real 'I' is, contrary to perceptible experience, not an experience of individuality but a non-personal, all-inclusive awareness. It is not to be confused with the individual self which he said was essentially non-existent, being a fabrication of the mind which obscures the true experience of the real Self. He maintained that the real Self is always present and always experienced but he emphasised that one is only consciously aware of it as it really is when the self-limiting tendencies of the mind have ceased. Permanent and continuous Self-awareness is known as Self-realisation.

2 *Sat-chit-ananda* This is a Sanskrit term which translates as being-consciousness-bliss. Sri Ramana taught that the Self is pure being, a subjective awareness of 'I am' which is completely devoid of the feeling 'I am this' or 'I am that'. There are no subjects or objects in the Self, there is only an awareness of being. Because this awareness is conscious it is also known as consciousness. The direct experience of this consciousness is, according to Sri Ramana, a state of unbroken happiness and so the term *ananda* or bliss is also used to describe it. These three aspects, being, consciousness and bliss, are experienced as a unitary whole and not as

separate attributes of the Self. They are inseparable in the same way that wetness, transparency and liquidity are inseparable properties of water.

3 *God* Sri Ramana maintained that the universe is sustained by the power of the Self. Since theists normally attribute this power to God he often used the word God as a synonym for the Self. He also used the words *Brahman*, the supreme being of Hinduism, and Siva, a Hindu name for God, in the same way. Sri Ramana's God is not a personal God, he is the formless being which sustains the universe. He is not the creator of the universe, the universe is merely a manifestation of his inherent power; he is inseparable from it, but he is not affected by its appearance or its disappearance.

4 *The Heart* Sri Ramana frequently used the Sanskrit word *hridayam* when he was talking about the Self. It is usually translated as 'the Heart' but a more literal translation would be 'this is the centre'. In using this particular term he was not implying that there was a particular location or centre for the Self, he was merely indicating that the Self was the source from which all appearances manifested.

5 *Jnana* The experience of the Self is sometimes called *jnana* or knowledge. This term should not be taken to mean that there is a person who has knowledge of the Self, because in the state of Self-awareness there is no localised knower and there is nothing that is separate from the Self that can be known. True knowledge, or *jnana*, is not an object of experience, nor is it an understanding of a state which is different and apart from the subject knower; it is a direct and knowing awareness of the one reality in which subjects and objects have ceased to exist. One who is established in this state is known as a *jnani*.

6 *Turiya and turyatita* Hindu philosophy postulates three alternating levels of relative consciousness – waking, dream and deep sleep. Sri Ramana stated that the Self was the underlying reality which supported the appearance of the other three temporary states. Because of this he sometimes

called the Self *turiya avastha* or the fourth state. He also occasionally used the word *turiyatita*, meaning 'transcending the fourth', to indicate that there are not really four states but only one real transcendental state.

7 *Other terms*   Three other terms for the Self are worth noting. Sri Ramana often emphasised that the Self was one's real and natural state of being, and for this reason, he occasionally employed the terms *sahaja sthiti*, meaning the natural state, and *swarupa*, meaning real form or real nature. He also used the word 'silence' to indicate that the Self was a silent thought-free state of undisturbed peace and total stillness.

Q: *What is reality?*
A: Reality must be always real. It is not with forms and names. That which underlies these is the reality. It underlies limitations, being itself limitless. It is not bound. It underlies unrealities, itself being real. Reality is that which is. It is as it is. It transcends speech. It is beyond the expressions 'existence, non-existence', etc.[1]

The reality which is the mere consciousness that remains when ignorance is destroyed along with knowledge of objects, alone is the Self [*atma*]. In that *Brahma-swarupa* [real form of *Brahman*], which is abundant Self-awareness, there is not the least ignorance.

The reality which shines fully, without misery and without a body, not only when the world is known but also when the world is not known, is your real form [*nija-swarupa*].

The radiance of consciousness-bliss, in the form of one awareness shining equally within and without, is the supreme and blissful primal reality. Its form is silence and it is declared by *jnanis* to be the final and unobstructable state of true knowledge [*jnana*].

Know that *jnana* alone is non-attachment; *jnana* alone is purity; *jnana* is the attainment of God; *jnana* which is devoid of forgetfulness of Self alone is immortality; *jnana* alone is everything.[2]

Q: *What is this awareness and how can one obtain and cultivate it?*
A: You are awareness. Awareness is another name for you.

Since you are awareness there is no need to attain or cultivate it. All that you have to do is to give up being aware of other things, that is of the not-Self. If one gives up being aware of them then pure awareness alone remains, and that is the Self.[3]

Q: *If the Self is itself aware, why am I not aware of it even now?*

A: There is no duality. Your present knowledge is due to the ego and is only relative. Relative knowledge requires a subject and an object, whereas the awareness of the Self is absolute and requires no object.

Remembrance also is similarly relative, requiring an object to be remembered and a subject to remember. When there is no duality, who is to remember whom?[4]

The Self is ever-present. Each one wants to know the Self. What kind of help does one require to know oneself? People want to see the Self as something new. But it is eternal and remains the same all along. They desire to see it as a blazing light etc. How can it be so? It is not light, not darkness. It is only as it is. It cannot be defined. The best definition is 'I am that I am'. The *srutis* [scriptures] speak of the Self as being the size of one's thumb, the tip of the hair, an electric spark, vast, subtler than the subtlest, etc. They have no foundation in fact. It is only being, but different from the real and the unreal; it is knowledge, but different from knowledge and ignorance. How can it be defined at all? It is simply being.[5]

Q: *When a man realises the Self, what will he see?*

A: There is no seeing. Seeing is only being. The state of Self-realisation, as we call it, is not attaining something new or reaching some goal which is far away, but simply being that which you always are and which you always have been. All that is needed is that you give up your realisation of the not-true as true. All of us are regarding as real that which is not real. We have only to give up this practice on our part. Then we shall realise the Self as the Self; in other words, 'Be the Self'. At one stage you will laugh at yourself for trying to discover the Self which is so self-evident. So, what can we say to this question?

That stage transcends the seer and the seen. There is no seer there to see anything. The seer who is seeing all this now ceases to exist and the Self alone remains.[6]

Q: *How to know this by direct experience?*

A: If We talk of knowing the Self, there must be two selves,

one a knowing self, another the self which is known, and the
process of knowing. The state we call realisation is simply being
oneself, not knowing anything or becoming anything. If one has
realised, one is that which alone is and which alone has always
been. One cannot describe that state. One can only be that. Of
course, we loosely talk of Self-realisation, for want of a better
term. How to 'real-ise' or make real that which alone is real?[7]

Q: *You sometimes say the Self is silence. Why is this?*

A: For those who live in Self as the beauty devoid of thought,
there is nothing which should be thought of. That which should
be adhered to is only the experience of silence, because in that
supreme state nothing exists to be attained other than oneself.[8]

Q: *What is* mouna *[silence]?*

A: That state which transcends speech and thought is *mouna*.[9]
That which is, is *mouna*. How can *mouna* be explained in
words?[10]

Sages say that the state in which the thought 'I' [the ego] does
not rise even in the least, alone is Self [*swarupa*] which is silence
[*mouna*]. That silent Self alone is God; Self alone is the *jiva*
[individual soul]. Self alone is this ancient world.

All other knowledges are only petty and trivial knowledges; the
experience of silence alone is the real and perfect knowledge.
Know that the many objective differences are not real but are
mere superimpositions on Self, which is the form of true
knowledge.[11]

Q: *As the bodies and the selves animating them are everywhere
actually observed to be innumerable how can it be said that the
Self is only one?*

A: If the idea 'I am the body' is accepted, the selves are
multiple. The state in which this idea vanishes is the Self since in
that state there are no other objects. It is for this reason that the
Self is regarded as one only.[12]

Since the body itself does not exist in the natural outlook of the
real Self, but only in the extroverted outlook of the mind which is
deluded by the power of illusion, to call Self, the space of
consciousness, *dehi* [the possessor of the body] is wrong.

The world does not exist without the body, the body never
exists without the mind, the mind never exists without consciousness and consciousness never exists without the reality.

For the wise one who has known Self by diving within
himself, there is nothing other than Self to be known. Why?

Because since the ego which identifies the form of a body as 'I' has perished, he [the wise one] is the formless existence-consciousness.[13]

The *jnani* [one who has realised the Self] knows he is the Self and that nothing, neither his body nor anything else, exists but the Self. To such a one what difference could the presence or absence of a body make?

It is false to speak of realisation. What is there to realise? The real is as it is always. We are not creating anything new or achieving something which we did not have before. The illustration given in books is this. We dig a well and create a huge pit. The space in the pit or well has not been created by us. We have just removed the earth which was filling the space there. The space was there then and is also there now. Similarly we have simply to throw out all the age-long *samskaras* [innate tendencies] which are inside us. When all of them have been given up, the Self will shine alone.[14]

Q: *But how to do this and attain liberation?*

A: Liberation is our very nature. We are that. The very fact that we wish for liberation shows that freedom from all bondage is our real nature. It is not to be freshly acquired. All that is necessary is to get rid of the false notion that we are bound. When we achieve that, there will be no desire or thought of any sort. So long as one desires liberation, so long, you may take it, one is in bondage.[15]

Q: *For one who has realized his Self, it is said that he will not have the three states of wakefulness, dream and deep sleep. Is that a fact?*

A: What makes you say that they do not have the three states? In saying 'I had a dream; I was in deep sleep; I am awake', you must admit that you were there in all the three states. That makes it clear that you were there all the time. If you remain as you are now, you are in the wakeful state; this becomes hidden in the dream state; and the dream state disappears when you are in deep sleep. You were there then, you are there now, and you are there at all times. The three states come and go, but you are always there. It is like a cinema. The screen is always there but several types of pictures appear on the screen and then disappear. Nothing sticks to the screen, it remains a screen. Similarly, you remain your own Self in all the three states. If you know that, the three states will not trouble you, just as the pictures which appear on the screen do not stick to it. On the screen, you sometimes see a huge ocean with endless waves; that disappears. Another time, you see fire spreading all around; that too disappears. The screen is there on both occasions. Did the screen get wet with the water or did it get burned by the fire? Nothing affected the screen. In the same way, the things that happen during the wakeful, dream and sleep states do not affect you at all; you remain your own Self.

Q: *Does that mean that, although people have all three states, wakefulness, dream and deep sleep, these do not affect them?*

A: Yes, that is it. All these states come and go. The Self is not bothered; it has only one state.

Q: *Does that mean that such a person will be in this world merely as a witness?*

A: That is so; for this very thing, Vidyaranya, in the tenth chapter of the *Panchadasi*, gives as example the light that is kept on the stage of a theatre. When a drama is being played, the light is there, which illuminates, without any distinction, all the actors, whether they be kings or servants or dancers, and also all the audience. That light will be there before the drama begins, during the performance and also after the performance is over. Similarly, the light within, that is, the Self, gives light to the ego, the intellect, the memory and the mind without itself being subject to processes of growth and decay. Although during deep sleep and other states there is no feeling of the ego, that Self remains attributeless, and continues to shine of itself.[16]

Actually, the idea of the Self being the witness is only in the mind; it is not the absolute truth of the Self. Witnessing is relative to objects witnessed. Both the witness and his object are mental creations.[17]

Q: *How are the three states of consciousness inferior in degree of reality to the fourth [turiya]? What is the actual relation between these three states and the fourth?*

A: There is only one state, that of consciousness or awareness or existence. The three states of waking, dream and sleep cannot be real. They simply come and go. The real will always exist. The 'I' or existence that alone persists in all the three states is real. The other three are not real and so it is not possible to say they have such and such a degree of reality. We may roughly put it like this. Existence or consciousness is the only reality. Consciousness plus waking, we call waking. Consciousness plus sleep, we call sleep. Consciousness plus dream, we call dream. Consciousness is the screen on which all the pictures come and go. The screen is real,

the pictures are mere shadows on it. Because by long habit we
have been regarding these three states as real, we call the state of
mere awareness or consciousness the fourth. There is however no
fourth state, but only one state.[18]

There is no difference between dream and the waking state
except that the dream is short and the waking long. Both are the
result of the mind. Because the waking state is long, we imagine
that it is our real state. But, as a matter of fact, our real state is
turiya or the fourth state which is always as it is and knows
nothing of the three states of waking, dream or sleep. Because we
call these three *avasthas* [states] we call the fourth state also *turiya
avastha*. But is it not an *avastha*, but the real and natural state of
the Self. When this is realised, we know it is not a *turiya* or fourth
state, for a fourth state is only relative, but *turiyatita*, the
transcendent state.[19]

Q: *But why should these three states come and go on the real
state or the screen of the Self?*

A: Who puts this question? Does the Self say these states come
and go? It is the seer who says these come and go. The seer and
the seen together constitute the mind. See if there is such a thing as
the mind. Then, the mind merges in the Self, and there is neither
the seer nor the seen. So the real answer to your question is, 'They
neither come nor go.' The Self alone remains as it ever is. The
three states owe their existence to non-enquiry and enquiry puts
an end to them. However much one may explain, the fact will not
become clear till one attains Self-realisation and wonders how
one was blind to the self-evident and only existence so long.

Q: *What is the difference between the mind and the Self?*

A: There is no difference. The mind turned inwards is the Self;
turned outwards, it becomes the ego and all the world. Cotton
made into various clothes we call by various names. Gold made
into various ornaments, we call by various names. But all the
clothes are cotton and all the ornaments gold. The one is real, the
many are mere names and forms.

But the mind does not exist apart from the Self, that is, it has
no independent existence. The Self exists without the mind, never
the mind without the Self.[20]

Q: Brahman *is said to be* sat-chit-ananda. *What does that
mean?*

A: Yes. That is so. That which is, is only *sat*. That is called
Brahman. The lustre of *sat* is *chit* and its nature is *ananda*. These

are not different from *sat*. All the three together are known as *sat-chit-ananda*.[21]

Q: *As the Self is existence* [sat] *and consciousness* [chit] *what is the reason for describing it as different from the existent and the non-existent, the sentient and the insentient?*

A: Although the Self is real, as it comprises everything, it does not give room for questions involving duality about its reality or unreality. Therefore it is said to be different from the real and the unreal. Similarly, even though it is consciousness, since there is nothing for it to know or to make itself known to, it is said to be different from the sentient and the insentient.[22]

Sat-chit-ananda is said to indicate that the supreme is not *asat* [different from being], not *achit* [different from consciousness] and not an *ananda* [different from happiness]. Because we are in the phenomenal world we speak of the Self as *sat-chit-ananda*.[23]

Q: *In what sense is happiness or bliss* [ananda] *our real nature?*

A: Perfect bliss is *Brahman*. Perfect peace is of the Self. That alone exists and is consciousness.[24] That which is called happiness is only the nature of Self; Self is not other than perfect happiness. That which is called happiness alone exists. Knowing that fact and abiding in the state of Self, enjoy bliss eternally.[25]

If a man thinks that his happiness is due to external causes and his possessions, it is reasonable to conclude that his happiness must increase with the increase of possessions and diminish in proportion to their diminution. Therefore if he is devoid of possessions, his happiness should be nil. What is the real experience of man? Does it conform to this view?

In deep sleep man is devoid of possessions, including his own body. Instead of being unhappy he is quite happy. Everyone desires to sleep soundly. The conclusion is that happiness is inherent in man and is not due to external causes. One must realise the Self in order to open the store of unalloyed happiness.[26]

Q: *Sri Bhagavan speaks of the Heart as the seat of consciousness and as identical with the Self. What does the Heart exactly signify?*

A: Call it by any name, God, Self, the Heart or the seat of consciousness, it is all the same. The point to be grasped is this, that Heart means the very core of one's being, the centre, without which there is nothing whatever.[27]

The Heart is not physical, it is spiritual. *Hridayam* equals *hrit* plus *ayam*; it means 'this is the centre'. It is that from which thoughts arise, on which they subsist and where they are resolved. The thoughts are the content of the mind and they shape the universe. The Heart is the centre of all. That from which beings come into existence is said to be *Brahman* in the *Upanishads*. That is the Heart. *Brahman* is the Heart.[28]

Q: *How to realise the Heart?*

A: There is no one who even for a moment fails to experience the Self. For no one admits that he ever stands apart from the Self. He is the Self. The Self is the Heart.[29]

The Heart is the centre from which everything springs. Because you see the world, the body and so on, it is said that there is a centre for these, which is called the Heart. When you are in the Heart, the Heart is known to be neither the centre nor the circumference. There is nothing else apart from it.[30]

The consciousness which is the real existence and which does not go out to know those things which are other than Self, alone is the Heart. Since the truth of Self is known only to that consciousness, which is devoid of activity, that consciousness which always remains attending to Self alone is the shining of clear knowledge.[31]

CHAPTER 2
Self-awareness and Self-ignorance

Sri Ramana occasionally indicated that there were three classes of spiritual aspirants. The most advanced realise the Self as soon as they are told about its real nature. Those in the second class need to reflect on it for some time before Self-awareness becomes firmly established. Those in the third category are less fortunate since they usually need many years of intensive spiritual practice to achieve the goal of Self-realisation. Sri Ramana sometimes used a metaphor of combustion to describe the three levels: gunpowder ignites with a single spark, charcoal needs the application of heat for a short time, and wet coal needs to dry out and heat up over a long period of time before it will begin to burn.

For the benefit of those in the top two categories Sri Ramana taught that the Self alone exists and that it can be directly and consciously experienced merely by ceasing to pay attention to the wrong ideas we have about ourselves. These wrong ideas he collectively called the 'not-Self' since they are an imaginary accretion of wrong notions and misperceptions which effectively veil the true experience of the real Self. The principal misperception is the idea that the Self is limited to the body and the mind. As soon as one ceases to imagine that one is an individual person, inhabiting a particular body, the whole superstructure of wrong ideas collapses and is replaced by a conscious and permanent awareness of the real Self.

At this level of the teaching there is no question of effort or practice. All that is required is an understanding that the Self is not a goal to be attained, it is merely the awareness that prevails when all the limiting ideas about the not-Self have been discarded.

Q: *How can I attain Self-realisation?*
A: Realisation is nothing to be gained afresh; it is already there. All that is necessary is to get rid of the thought 'I have not realised'.

Stillness or peace is realisation. There is no moment when the Self is not. So long as there is doubt or the feeling of non-realisation, the attempt should be made to rid oneself of these thoughts. They are due to the identification of the Self with the not-Self. When the not-Self disappears, the Self alone remains. To make room, it is enough that objects be removed. Room is not brought in from elsewhere.

Q: *Since realisation is not possible without* vasana-kshaya *[destruction of mental tendencies], how am I to realise that state in which the tendencies are effectively destroyed?*

A: You are in that state now.

Q: *Does it mean that by holding on to the Self, the* vasanas *[mental tendencies] should be destroyed as and when they emerge?*

A: They will themselves be destroyed if you remain as you are.

Q: *How shall I reach the Self?*

A: There is no reaching the Self. If Self were to be reached, it would mean that the Self is not here and now and that it is yet to be obtained. What is got afresh will also be lost. So it will be impermanent. What is not permanent is not worth striving for. So I say the Self is not reached. You are the Self, you are already that.

The fact is, you are ignorant of your blissful state. Ignorance supervenes and draws a veil over the pure Self which is bliss. Attempts are directed only to remove this veil of ignorance which is merely wrong knowledge. The wrong knowledge is the false identification of the Self with the body and the mind. This false identification must go, and then the Self alone remains.

Therefore realisation is for everyone; realisation makes no difference between the aspirants. This very doubt, whether you can realise, and the notion 'I-have-not-realised' are themselves the obstacles. Be free from these obstacles also.[1]

Q: *How long does it take to reach* mukti *[liberation]?*

A: *Mukti* is not to be gained in the future. It is there for ever, here and now.

Q: *I agree, but I do not experience it.*

A: The experience is here and now. One cannot deny one's own Self.

Q: *That means existence and not happiness.*

A: Existence is the same as happiness and happiness is the same as being. The word *mukti* is so provoking. Why should one seek it? One believes that there is bondage and therefore seeks liberation. But the fact is that there is no bondage but only liberation. Why call it by a name and seek it?

Q: *True – but we are ignorant.*

A: Only remove ignorance. That is all there is to be done.

All questions relating to *mukti* are inadmissible. *Mukti* means release from bondage which implies the present existence of bondage. There is no bondage and therefore no *mukti* either.[2]

Q: *Of what nature is the realisation of westerners who relate that they have had flashes of cosmic consciousness?*

A: It came as a flash and disappeared as such. That which has a beginning must also end. Only when the ever-present consciousness is realised will it be permanent. Consciousness is indeed always with us. Everyone knows 'I am'. No one can deny his own being. The man in deep sleep is not aware; while awake he seems to be aware. But it is the same person. There is no change in the one who slept and the one who is now awake. In deep sleep he was not aware of his body and so there was no body-consciousness. In the wakeful state he is aware of his body and so there is body-consciousness. Therefore the difference lies in the emergence of body-consciousness and not in any change in the real consciousness.

The body and body-consciousness arise together and sink together. All this amounts to saying that there are no limitations in deep sleep, whereas there are limitations in the waking state. These limitations are the bondage. The feeling 'The body is I' is the error. This false sense of 'I' must go. The real 'I' is always there. It is here and now. It never appears anew and disappears again. That which is must also persist for ever. That which appears anew will also be lost. Compare deep sleep and waking. The body appears in one state but not in the other. Therefore the body will be lost. The consciousness was pre-existent and will survive the body.

There is no one who does not say 'I am'. The wrong knowledge of 'I am the body' is the cause of all the mischief. This wrong knowledge must go. That is realisation. Realisation is not acquisition of anything new nor is it a new faculty. It is only removal of all camouflage.

The ultimate truth is so simple. It is nothing more than being in the pristine state. This is all that need be said.[3]

Q: *Is one nearer to pure consciousness in deep sleep than in the waking state?*

A: The sleep, dream and waking states are mere phenomena

appearing on the Self which is itself stationary. It is also a state of simple awareness. Can anyone remain away from the Self at any moment? This question can arise only if that were possible.

Q: *Is it not often said that one is nearer pure consciousness in deep sleep than in the waking state?*

A: The question may as well be 'Am I nearer to myself in my sleep than in my waking state?'

The Self is pure consciousness. No one can ever be away from the Self. The question is possible only if there is duality. But there is no duality in the state of pure consciousness.

The same person sleeps, dreams and wakes up. The waking state is considered to be full of beautiful and interesting things. The absence of such experience makes one say that the sleep state is dull. Before we proceed further let us make this point clear. Do you not admit that you exist in your sleep?

Q: *Yes, I do.*

A: You are the same person that is now awake. Is it not so?

Q: *Yes.*

A: So there is a continuity in the sleep and the waking states. What is that continuity? It is only the state of pure being.

There is a difference in the two states. What is that difference? The incidents, namely, the body, the world and objects appear in the waking state but they disappear in sleep.

Q: *But I am not aware in my sleep.*

A: True, there is no awareness of the body or of the world. But you must exist in your sleep in order to say now 'I was not aware in my sleep'. Who says so now? It is the wakeful person. The sleeper cannot say so. That is to say, the individual who is now identifying the Self with the body says that such awareness did not exist in sleep.

Because you identify yourself with the body, you see the world around you and say that the waking state is filled with beautiful and interesting things. The sleep state appears dull because you were not there as an individual and therefore these things were not. But what is the fact? There is the continuity of being in all the three states, but no continuity of the individual and the objects.

Q: *Yes.*

A: That which is continuous is also enduring, that is permanent. That which is discontinuous is transitory.

Q: *Yes.*

A: Therefore the state of being is permanent and the body and the world are not. They are fleeting phenomena passing on the screen of being-consciousness which is eternal and stationary.

Q: *Relatively speaking, is not the sleep state nearer to pure consciousness than the waking state?*

A: Yes, in this sense: when passing from sleep to waking the 'I'-thought [individual self] must start and the mind must come into play. Then thoughts arise and the functions of the body come into operation. All these together make us say that we are awake. The absence of all this evolution is the characteristic of sleep and therefore it is nearer to pure consciousness than the waking state.

But one should not therefore desire to be always in sleep. In the first place it is impossible, for it will necessarily alternate with the other states. Secondly it cannot be the state of bliss in which the *jnani* is, for his state is permanent and not alternating. Moreover, the sleep state is not recognised to be one of awareness by people, but the sage is always aware. Thus the sleep state differs from the state in which the sage is established.

Still more, the sleep state is free from thoughts and their impression on the individual. It cannot be altered by one's will because effort is impossible in that condition. Although nearer to pure consciousness, it is not fit for efforts to realise the Self.[4]

Q: *Is not the realisation of one's absolute being, that is,* Brahma-jnana, *something quite unattainable for a layman like me?*

A: *Brahma-jnana* is not a knowledge to be acquired, so that acquiring it one may obtain happiness. It is one's ignorant outlook that one should give up. The Self you seek to know is truly yourself. Your supposed ignorance causes you needless grief like that of the ten foolish men who grieved at the loss of the tenth man who was never lost.

The ten foolish men in the parable forded a stream and on reaching the other shore wanted to make sure that all of them had in fact safely crossed the stream. One of the ten began to count, but while counting the others left himself out. 'I see only nine; sure enough, we have lost one. Who can it be?' he said. 'Did you count correctly?' asked another, and did the counting himself. But he too counted only nine. One after the other each of the ten counted only nine, missing himself. 'We are only nine', they all agreed, 'but who is the missing one?' they asked themselves. Every effort they made to discover the 'missing' individual failed. 'Whoever he is that is drowned', said the most sentimental of the ren fools, 'we have lost him.' So saying he burst into tears, and the others followed suit.

Seeing them weeping on the river bank, a sympathetic wayfarer enquired about the cause. They related what had happened and said that even after counting themselves several times they could find no more than nine. On hearing the story, but seeing all the ten before him, the wayfarer guessed what had happened. In order to make them know for themselves they were really ten, that all of them had survived the crossing, he told them, 'Let each of you count for himself but one after the other serially, one, two, three and so on, while I shall give you each a blow so that all of you may be sure of having been included in the count, and included only once. The tenth missing man will then be found.' Hearing this they rejoiced at the prospect of finding their 'lost' comrade and accepted the method suggested by the wayfarer.

While the kind wayfarer gave a blow to each of the ten in turn, he that got the blow counted himself aloud. 'Ten,' said the last man as he got the last blow in his turn. Bewildered they looked at one another, 'We are ten,' they said with one voice and thanked the wayfarer for having removed their grief.

That is the parable. From where was the tenth man brought in? Was he ever lost? By knowing that he had been there all the while, did they learn anything new? The cause of their grief was not the real loss of anyone, it was their own ignorance, or rather, their mere supposition that one of them was lost.

Such is the case with you. Truly there is no cause for you to be miserable and unhappy. You yourself impose limitations on your true nature of infinite being, and then weep that you are but a finite creature. Then you take up this or that spiritual practice to transcend the non-existent limitations. But if your spiritual practice itself assumes the existence of the limitations, how can it help you to transcend them?

Hence I say know that you are really the infinite pure being, the Self. You are always that Self and nothing but that Self. Therefore, you can never be really ignorant of the Self. Your ignorance is merely an imaginary ignorance, like the ignorance of the ten fools about the lost tenth man. It is this ignorance that caused them grief.

Know then that true knowledge does not create a new being for you, it only removes your ignorant ignorance. Bliss is not added to your nature, it is merely revealed as your true natural state, eternal and imperishable. The only way to be rid of your grief is to know and be the Self. How can this be unattainable?[5]

Q: *However often Bhagavan teaches us, we are not able to understand.*

A: People say that they are not able to know the Self that is all pervading. What can I do? Even the smallest child says, 'I exist; I do; this is mine.' So, everyone understands that the thing 'I' is always existent. It is only when that 'I' is there that there is the feeling that you are the body, he is Venkanna, this is Ramanna and so on. To know that the one that is always visible is one's own Self, is it necessary to search with a candle? To say that we do not know the *atma swarupa* [the real nature of the Self] which is not different but which is in one's own Self is like saying, 'I do not know myself.'[6]

Q: *But how is one to reach this state?*

A: There is no goal to be reached. There is nothing to be attained. You are the Self. You exist always. Nothing more can be predicated of the Self than that it exists. Seeing God or the Self is only being the Self or yourself. Seeing is being. You, being the Self, want to know how to attain the Self. It is something like a man being at Ramanasramam asking how many ways there are to reach Ramanasramam and which is the best way for him. All that is required of you is to give up the thought that you are this body and to give up all thoughts of the external things or the not-Self.[7]

Q: *What is the ego-self? How is it related to the real Self?*

A: The ego-Self appears and disappears and is transitory, whereas the real Self is permanent. Though you are actually the true Self you wrongly identify the real Self with the ego-self.

Q: *How does the mistake come about?*

A: See if it has come about.

Q: *One has to sublimate the ego-self into the true Self.*

A: The ego-self does not exist at all.

Q: *Why does it give us trouble?*

A: To whom is the trouble? The trouble also is imagined. Trouble and pleasure are only for the ego.

Q: *Why is the world so wrapped up in ignorance?*

A: Take care of yourself. Let the world take care of itself. See your Self. If you are the body there is the gross world also. If you are spirit all is spirit alone.

Q: *It will hold good for the individual, but what of the rest?*

A: Do it first and then see if the question arises afterwards.

Q: *Is there* avidya *[ignorance]?*

A: For whom is it?

Q: *For the ego-self.*

A: Yes, for the ego. Remove the ego and *avidya* is gone. Look for it, the ego vanishes and the real Self alone remains. The ego professing *avidya* is not to be seen. There is no *avidya* in reality. All *sastras* [scriptures] are meant to disprove the existence of *avidya*.

Q: *How did the ego arise?*

A: Ego is not. Otherwise do you admit of two selves? How can there be *avidya* in the absence of the ego? If you begin to enquire, the *avidya*, which is already non-existent, will be found not to be, or you will say it has fled away.

Ignorance pertains to the ego. Why do you think of the ego and also suffer? What is ignorance again? It is that which is non-existent. However the worldly life requires the hypothesis of *avidya*. *Avidya* is only our ignorance and nothing more. It is ignorance or forgetfulness of the Self. Can there be darkness before the sun? Similarly, can there be ignorance before the self-evident and self-luminous Self? If you know the Self there will be no darkness, no ignorance and no misery.

It is the mind which feels the trouble and the misery. Darkness never comes nor goes. See the sun and there is no darkness. Similarly, see the Self and *avidya* will be found not to exist.[8]

Q: *How has the unreal come? Can the unreal spring from the real?*

A: See if it has sprung. There is no such thing as the unreal, from another standpoint. The Self alone exists. When you try to trace the ego, which is the basis of the perception of the world and everything else, you find the ego does not exist at all and neither does all this creation that you see.[9]

Q: *It is cruel of God's leela [play] to make the knowledge of the Self so hard.*

A: Knowing the Self is being the Self, and being means existence, one's own existence. No one denies one's existence any more than one denies one's eyes, although one cannot see them. The trouble lies with your desire to objectify the Self, in the same way as you objectify your eyes when you place a mirror before them. You have been so accustomed to objectivity that you have lost the knowledge of yourself, simply because the Self cannot be objectified. Who is to know the Self? Can the insentient body know it? All the time you speak and think of your 'I', yet when questioned you deny knowledge of it. You are the Self, yet you ask how to know the Self. Where then is God's *leela* and where is its cruelty? Because of this denial of the Self by people the *sastras* speak of *maya, leela*, etc.[10]

Q: *Does my realisation help others?*

A: Yes, certainly. It is the best help possible. But there are no others to be helped. For a realised being sees only the Self, just like a goldsmith estimating the gold in various items of jewellery sees only gold. When you identify yourself with the body then only the forms and shapes are there. But when you transcend your body the others disappear along with your body-consciousness.

Q: *Is it so with plants, trees, etc.?*

A: Do they exist at all apart from the Self? Find it out. You think that you see them. The thought is projected out from the Self. Find out from where it rises. Thoughts will cease to rise and the Self alone will remain.

Q: *I understand theoretically. But they are still there.*

A: Yes. It is like a cinema-show. There is the light on the screen and the shadows flitting across it impress the audience as the enactment of some piece. If in the same play an audience also is shown on the screen as part of the performance, the seer and the seen will then both be on the screen. Apply it to yourself. You are the screen, the Self has created the ego, the ego has its accretions of thoughts which are displayed as the world, the trees and the plants of which you are asking. In reality, all these are nothing but the Self. If you see the Self, the same will be found to be all, everywhere and always. Nothing but the Self exists.

Q: *Yes, I still understand only theoretically. Yet the answers are simple, beautiful and convincing.*

A: Even the thought 'I do not realise' is a hindrance. In fact, the Self alone is.[11]

Our real nature is *mukti*. But we are imagining we are bound and are making various, strenuous attempts to become free, while we are all the while free. This will be understood only when we reach that stage. We will be surprised that we were frantically trying to attain something which we have always been and are. An illustration will make this clear. A man goes to sleep in this hall. He dreams he has gone on a world tour, is roaming over hill and dale, forest and country, desert and sea, across various continents and after many years of weary and strenuous travel, returns to this country, reaches Tiruvannamalai, enters the ashram and walks into the hall. Just at that moment he wakes up and finds he has not moved an inch but was sleeping where he lay down. He has not returned after great effort to this hall, but is and always has been in the hall. It is exactly like that. If it is asked, 'Why being free do we imagine that we are bound?' I answer, 'Why being in the hall did you imagine you were on a world adventure, crossing hill and dale, desert and sea? It is all mind or *maya* [illusion].'[12]

Q: *How then does ignorance of this one and only reality unhappily arise in the case of the* ajnani *[one who has not realised the Self]?*

A: The *ajnani* sees only the mind which is a mere reflection of the light of pure consciousness arising from the Heart. Of the Heart itself he is ignorant. Why? Because his mind is extroverted and has never sought its source.

Q: *What prevents the infinite, undifferentiated light of consciousness arising from the Heart from revealing itself to the* ajnani?

A: Just as water in a pot reflects the enormous sun within the narrow limits of the pot, even so the *vasanas* or latent tendencies of the mind of the individual, acting as the reflecting medium, catch the all-pervading, infinite light of consciousness arising from the Heart. The form of this reflection is the phenomenon called the mind. Seeing only this reflection, the *ajnani* is deluded into the belief that he is a finite being, the *jiva*, the individual self.[13]

Q: *What are the obstacles which hinder realisation of the Self?*

A: They are habits of mind [*vasanas*].

Q: *How to overcome the mental habits [*vasanas*]?*

A: By realising the Self.

Q: *This is a vicious circle.*

A: It is the ego which raises such difficulties, creating obstacles and then suffering from the perplexity of apparent paradoxes. Find out who makes the enquiries and the Self will be found.[14]

Q: *Why is this mental bondage so persistent?*

A: The nature of bondage is merely the rising, ruinous thought 'I am different from the reality'. Since one surely cannot remain separate from the reality, reject that thought whenever it rises.[15]

Q: *Why do I never remember that I am the Self?*

A: People speak of memory and oblivion of the fullness of the Self. Oblivion and memory are only thought-forms. They will alternate so long as there are thoughts. But reality lies beyond these. Memory or oblivion must be dependent on something. That something must be foreign to the Self as well, otherwise there would not be oblivion. That upon which memory and oblivion depend is the idea of the individual self. When one looks for it, this individual 'I' is not found because it is not real. Hence this 'I' is synonymous with illusion or ignorance (*maya*, *avidya* or *ajnana*]. To know that there never was ignorance is the goal of all the spiritual teachings. Ignorance must be of one who is aware. Awareness is *jnana*. *Jnana* is eternal and natural, *ajnana* is unnatural and unreal.

Q: *Having heard this truth, why does not one remain content?*

A: Because *samskaras* [innate mental tendencies] have not been destroyed. Unless the *samskaras* cease to exist, there will always be doubt and confusion. All efforts are directed to destroying doubt and confusion. To do so their roots must be cut. Their roots are the *samskaras*. These are rendered ineffective by practice as prescribed by the Guru. The Guru leaves it to the seeker to do this much so that he might himself find out that there is no ignorance. Hearing the truth [*sravana*] is the first stage. If the understanding is not firm one has to practise reflection [*manana*] and uninterrupted contemplation [*nididhyasana*] on it. These two processes scorch the seeds of *samskaras* so that they are rendered ineffective.

Some extraordinary people get unshakable *jnana* after hearing the truth only once. These are the advanced seekers. Beginners take longer to gain it.

Q: *How did ignorance [avidya] arise at all?*

A: Ignorance never arose. It has no real being. That which is, is only *vidya* [knowledge].

Q: *Why then do I not realise it?*

A: Because of the *samskaras*. However, find out who does not realise and what he does not realise. Then it will be clear that there is no *avidya*.[16]

Q: *So, it is wrong to begin with a goal, is it?*

A: If there is a goal to be reached it cannot be permanent. The goal must already be there. We seek to reach the goal with the ego, but the goal exists before the ego. What is in the goal is even prior to our birth, that is, to the birth of the ego. Because we exist the ego appears to exist too.

If we look on the Self as the ego then we become the ego, if as the mind we become the mind, if as the body we become the body.

It is the thought which builds up sheaths in so many ways. The shadow on the water is found to be shaking. Can anyone stop the shaking of the shadow? If it would cease to shake you would not notice the water but only the light. Similarly take no notice of the ego and its activities, but see only the light behind. The ego is the thought 'I'. The true 'I' is the Self.

Q: *If it is just a question of giving up ideas then it is only one step to realisation.*

A: Realisation is already there. The state free from thoughts is the only real state. There is no such action as realisation. Is there anyone who is not realising the Self? Does anyone deny his own existence? Speaking of realisation, it implies two selves – the one to realise, the other to be realised. What is not already realised is sought to be realised. Once we admit our existence, how is it that we do not know our Self?

Q: *Because of the thoughts, the mind.*

A: Quite so. It is the mind that veils our happiness. How do we know that we exist? If you say because of the world around us, then how do you know that you existed in deep sleep?

Q: *How to get rid of the mind?*

A: Is it the mind that wants to kill itself? The mind cannot kill itself. So your business is to find the real nature of the mind. Then you will know that there is no mind. When the Self is sought, the mind is nowhere. Abiding in the Self, one need not worry about the mind.[17]

Q: *Is mukti the same as realisation?*

A: *Mukti* or liberation is our nature. It is another name for us. Our wanting *mukti* is a very funny thing. It is like a man who is in the shade, voluntarily leaving the shade, going into the sun, feeling the severity of the heat there, making great efforts to get back into the shade and then rejoicing, 'How sweet is the shade! I have reached the shade at last!' We are all doing exactly the same. We are not different from the reality. We imagine we are different, that is we create the *bheda bhava* [the feeling of difference] and then undergo great *sadhana* [spiritual practices] to get rid of the *bheda bhava* and realise the oneness. Why imagine or create *bheda bhava* and then destroy it?[18]

Q: *This can be realised only by the grace of the master. I was reading* Sri Bhagavata. *It says that bliss can be had only by the dust of the master's feet. I pray for grace.*

A: What is bliss but your own being? You are not apart from

being which is the same as bliss. You are now thinking that you are the mind or the body which are both changing and transient. But you are unchanging and eternal. That is what you should know.

Q: *It is darkness and I am ignorant.*

A: This ignorance must go. Again, who says 'I am ignorant'? He must be the witness of ignorance. That is what you are. Socrates said, 'I know that I do not know.' Can it be ignorance? It is wisdom.

Q: *Why then do I feel unhappy when I am in Vellore and feel peace in your presence?*

A: Can the feeling in this place be bliss? When you leave this place you say you are unhappy. Therefore this peace is not permanent, it is mixed with unhappiness which is felt in another place. Therefore you cannot find bliss in places and in periods of time. It must be permanent in order that it may be useful. It is your own being which is permanent. Be the Self and that is bliss. You are always that.[19]

The Self is always realised. It is not necessary to seek to realise what is already and always realised. For you cannot deny your own existence. That existence is consciousness, the Self.

Unless you exist you cannot ask questions. So you must admit your own existence. That existence is the Self. It is already realised. Therefore the effort to realise results only in your realising your present mistake – that you have not realised your Self. There is no fresh realisation. The Self becomes revealed.

Q: *That will take some years.*

A: Why years? The idea of time is only in your mind. It is not in the Self. There is no time for the Self. Time arises as an idea after the ego arises. But you are the Self beyond time and space. You exist even in the absence of time and space.[20]

Were it true that you realise it later it means that you are not realised now. Absence of realisation in the present moment may be repeated at any moment in the future, for time is infinite. So too, such realisation is impermanent. But that is not true. It is wrong to consider realisation to be impermanent. It is the true eternal state which cannot change.

Q: *Yes, I shall understand it in course of time.*

A: You are already that. Time and space cannot affect the Self. They are in you. So also all that you see around you is in you. There is a story to illustrate this point. A lady had a precious necklace round her neck. Once in her excitement she forgot it and thought that the necklace was lost. She became anxious and looked for it in her home but could not find it. She asked her friends and neighbours if they knew anything about the necklace. They did not. At last a kind friend of hers told her to feel the necklace round her neck. She found that it had all along been round her neck and she was happy. When others asked her later if she had found the necklace which was lost, she said, 'Yes, I have found it.' She still felt that she had recovered a lost jewel.

Now did she lose it at all? It was all along round her neck. But judge her feelings. She was as happy as if she had recovered a lost jewel. Similarly with us, we imagine that we will realise that Self some time, whereas we are never anything but the Self.[21]

Q: *There must be something that I can do to reach this state.*

A: The conception that there is a goal and a path to it is wrong. We are the goal or peace always. To get rid of the notion that we are not peace is all that is required.

Q: *All books say that the guidance of a Guru is necessary.*

A: The Guru will say only what I am saying now. He will not give you anything you have not already got. It is impossible for anyone to get what he has not got already. Even if he gets any such thing, it will go as it came. What comes will also go. What always is will alone remain. The Guru cannot give you anything new, which you don't have already. Removal of the notion that we have not realised the Self is all that is required. We are always the Self only we don't realise it.[22]

We go round and round in search of *atma* [Self] saying, 'Where is *atma*? Where is it? till at last the dawn of *jnana drishti* [vision of knowledge] is reached, and we say, 'This is *atma* this is me.' We should acquire that vision. When once that vision is reached, there will be no attachments even if one mixes with the world and moves about in it. When once you put on shoes your feet do not feel the pain of walking on any number of stones or thorns on the way. You walk about without fear or care, even if there are mountains on the way. In the same way, everything will be natural to those who have attained *jnana drishti*. What is there apart from one's own Self?

Q: *The natural state can be known only after all this worldly vision subsides. But how is it to subside?*

A: If the mind subsides, the whole world subsides. Mind is the cause of all this. If that subsides, the natural state presents itself.

The Self proclaims itself at all times as 'I, I'. It is self-luminous. It is here. All this is that. We are in that only. Being in it, why search for it? The ancients say: 'Making the vision absorbed in *jnana* one sees the world as *Brahman*.'[23]

CHAPTER 3
The jnani

Many of the Sri Ramana's visitors appeared to have an insatiable curiosity about the state of Self-realisation and they were particularly interested to know how a *jnani* experienced himself and the world around him. Some of the questions he was asked on the subject reflected the bizarre notions that many people had about this state, but most of them tended to be variations of one of the four following questions:

1 How can a *jnani* function without any individual awareness of consciousness?
2 How can he say that he 'does nothing' (a statement which Sri Ramana often made) when others see him active in the world?
3 How does he perceive the world? Does he perceive the world at all?
4 How does the *jnani*'s awareness of pure consciousness relate to the alternating states of body and mind consciousness experienced in waking, dreaming and sleeping?

The hidden premise behind all such questions is the belief that there is a person (the *jnani*) who experiences a state he calls the Self. This assumption is not true. It is merely a mental construct devised by those who have not realised the Self (*ajnanis*) to make sense of the *jnani*'s experience. Even the use of the word *jnani* is indicative of this erroneous belief since it literally means a knower of *jnana*, the reality. The *ajnani* uses this term because he imagines that the world is made up of seekers of reality and knowers of reality; the truth of the Self is that there are neither *jnanis* nor *ajnanis*, there is only *jnana*.

Sri Ramana pointed this out both directly and indirectly on many occasions, but few of his questioners were able to grasp, even conceptually, the implications of such a statement. Because of this he usually adapted his ideas in such a way that they conformed to the prejudices of his listeners. In most of the conversations in this chapter he accepts that his questioners perceive a distinction between the *jnani* and the *ajnani*, and, without challenging the basis of that assumption, he assumes the role of the *jnani* and attempts to explain the implications of being in that state.

Q: *Then what is the difference between the* baddha *and the* mukta, *the bound man and the one liberated?*

A: The ordinary man lives in the brain unaware of himself in the Heart. The *jnana siddha* [*jnani*] lives in the Heart. When he moves about and deals with men and things, he knows that what he sees is not separate from the one supreme reality, the *Brahman* which he realised in the Heart as his own Self, the real.

Q: *What about the ordinary man?*

A: I have just said that he sees things outside himself. He is separate from the world, from his own deeper truth, from the truth that supports him and what he sees. The man who has realised the supreme truth of his own existence realises that it is the one supreme reality that is there behind him, behind the world. In fact, he is aware of the one, as the real, the Self in all selves, in all things, eternal and immutable, in all that is impermanent and mutable.[1]

Q: *What is the relation between the pure consciousness realised by the* jnani *and the 'I am'-ness which is accepted as the primary datum of experience?*

A: The undifferentiated consciousness of pure being is the Heart or *hridayam*, which is what you really are. From the Heart arises the 'I am'-ness as the primary datum of one's experience. By itself it is completely pure [*suddha-sattva*] in character. It is in this form of pristine purity [*suddha-sattva-swarupa*], uncontaminated by *rajas* and *tamas* [activity and inertia], that the 'I' appears to subsist in the *jnani*.

Q: *In the* jnani *the ego subsists in the pure form and therefore it appears as something real. Am I right?*

A: The appearance of the ego in any form, either in the *jnani* or *ajnani*, is itself an experience. But to the *ajnani* who is deluded into thinking that the waking state and the world are real, the ego also appears to be real. Since he sees the *jnani* act like other individuals, he feels constrained to posit some notion of individuality with reference to the *jnani* also.

Q: *How then does the* aham-vritti *['I'-thought, the sense of individuality] function in the* jnani?

A: It does not function in him at all. The *jnani*'s real nature is the Heart itself, because he is one and identical with the undifferentiated, pure consciousness referred to by the *Upanishads* as the *prajnana* [full consciousness]. *Prajnana* is truly *Brahman*, the absolute, and there is no *Brahman* other than *prajnana*.[2]

Q: *Does a* jnani *have* sankalpas *[desires]*?

A: The main qualities of the ordinary mind are *tamas* and *rajas* [sloth and excitement]; hence it is full of egoistic desires and weaknesses. But the *jnani*'s mind is *suddha-sattva* [pure harmony] and formless, functioning in the subtle *vijnanamayakosha* [the sheath of knowledge], through which he keeps contact with the world. His desires are therefore also pure.[3]

Q: *I am trying to understand the* jnani's *point of view about the world. Is the world perceived after Self-realisation?*

A: Why worry yourself about the world and what happens to it after Self-realisation? First realise the Self. What does it matter if the world is perceived or not? Do you gain anything to help you in your quest by the non-perception of the world during sleep? Conversely, what would you lose now by the perception of the world? It is quite immaterial to the *jnani* or *ajnani* if he perceives the world or not. It is seen by both, but their view-points differ.

Q: *If the* jnani *and the* ajnani *perceive the world in like manner, where is the difference between them?*

A: Seeing the world, the *jnani* sees the Self which is the substratum of all that is seen; the *ajnani*, whether he sees the world or not, is ignorant of his true being, the Self.

Take the instance of moving pictures on the screen in the cinema-show. What is there in front of you before the play begins? Merely the screen. On that screen you see the entire show, and for all appearances the pictures are real. But go and try to take hold of them. What do you take hold of? Merely the screen on which the pictures appeared. After the play, when the pictures disappear, what remains? The screen again.

So with the Self. That alone exists, the pictures come and go. If you hold on to the Self, you will not be deceived by the appearance of the pictures. Nor does it matter at all if the pictures appear or disappear. Ignoring the Self the *ajnani* thinks the world is real, just as ignoring the screen he sees merely the pictures, as if they existed apart from it. If one knows that without the seer there is nothing to be seen, just as there are no pictures without the screen, one is not deluded. The *jnani* knows that the screen and the pictures are only the Self. With the pictures the Self is in its manifest form; without the pictures it remains in the unmanifest form. To the *jnani* it is quite immaterial if the Self is in the one form or the other. He is always the Self. But the *ajnani* seeing the *jnani* active gets confounded.[4]

Q: *Does Bhagavan see the world as part and parcel of himself? How does he see the world?*

A: The Self alone is and nothing else. However, it is differentiated owing to ignorance. Differentiation is threefold:

(1) of the same kind;
(2) of a different kind; and
(3) as parts in itself.

The world is not another Self similar to the Self. It is not different from the Self; nor is it part of the Self.

Q: *Is not the world reflected on the Self?*

A: For reflection there must be an object and an image. But the Self does not admit of these differences.[5]

Q: *Does a* jnani *have dreams?*

A: Yes, he does dream, but he knows it to be a dream, in the same way as he knows the waking state to be a dream. You may call them dream no.1 and dream no.2. The *jnani* being established in the fourth state – *turiya*, the supreme reality – he detachedly witnesses the three other states, waking, dreaming and dreamless sleep, as pictures superimposed on it.[6]

For those who experience waking, dream and sleep, the state of wakeful sleep, which is beyond those three states, is named *turiya* [the fourth]. But since that *turiya* alone exists and since the seeming three states do not exist, know for certain that *turiya* is itself *turiyatita* [that which transcends the fourth].[7]

Q: *For the* jnani *then, there is no distinction between the three states of mind?*

A: How can there be, when the mind itself is dissolved and lost in the light of consciousness?

For the *jnani* all the three states are equally unreal. But the *ajnani* is unable to comprehend this, because for him the standard of reality is the waking state, whereas for the *jnani* the standard of reality is reality itself. This reality of pure consciousness is eternal

by its nature and therefore subsists equally during what you call
waking, dreaming and sleep. To him who is one with that reality
there is neither the mind nor its three states and, therefore, neither
introversion nor extroversion.

His is the ever-waking state, because he is awake to the eternal
Self; his is the ever-dreaming state, because to him the world is no
better than a repeatedly presented dream phenomenon; his is the
ever-sleeping state, because he is at all times without the 'body-
am-I' consciousness.[8]

Q: *Is there no* dehatma buddhi *[I-am-the-body idea] for the*
jnani? *If, for instance, Sri Bhagavan is bitten by an insect, is there
no sensation?*

A: There is the sensation and there is also the *dehatma buddhi*.
The latter is common to both *jnani* and *ajnani* with this difference,
that the *ajnani* thinks only the body is myself, whereas the *jnani*
knows all is of the Self, or all this is *Brahman*. If there be pain let
it be. It is also part of the Self. The Self is *poorna* [perfect].

After transcending *dehatma buddhi* one becomes a *jnani*. In the
absence of that idea there cannot be either *kartritva* [doership] or
karta [doer]. So a *jnani* has no *karma* [that is, a *jnani* performs no
actions]. That is his experience. Otherwise he is not a *jnani*.
However the *ajnani* identifies the *jnani* with his body, which the
jnani does not do.[9]

Q: *I see you doing things. How can you say that you never
perform actions?*

A: The radio sings and speaks, but if you open it you will find
no one inside. Similarly, my existence is like the space; though
this body speaks like the radio, there is no one inside as a doer.[10]

Q: *I find this hard to understand. Could you please elaborate
on this?*

A: Various illustrations are given in books to enable us to
understand how the *jnani* can live and act without the mind,
although living and acting require the use of the mind. The
potter's wheel goes on turning round even after the potter has
ceased to turn it because the pot is finished. In the same way, the
electric fan goes on revolving for some minutes after we switch off
the current. The *prarabdha* [predestined *karma*] which created the
body will make it go through whatever activities it was meant for.
But the *jnani* goes through all these activities without the notion
that he is the doer of them. It is hard to understand how this is
possible. The illustration generally given is that the *jnani* performs

actions in some such way as a child that is roused from sleep to eat eats but does not remember next morning that it ate. It has to be remembered that all these explanations are not for the *jnani*. He knows and has no doubts. He knows that he is not the body and he knows that he is not doing anything even though his body may be engaged in some activity. These explanations are for the onlookers who think of the *jnani* as one with a body and cannot help identifying him with his body.

Q: *It is said that the shock of realisation is so great that the body cannot survive it.*

A: There are various controversies or schools of thought as to whether a *jnani* can continue to live in his physical body after realisation. Some hold that one who dies cannot be a *jnani* because his body must vanish into air, or some such thing. They put forward all sorts of funny notions. If a man must at once leave his body when he realises the Self, I wonder how any knowledge of the Self or the state of realisation can come down to other men. And that would mean that all those who have given us the fruits of their Self-realisation in books cannot be considered *jnanis* because they went on living after realisation. And if it is held that a man cannot be considered a *jnani* so long as he performs actions in the world (and action is impossible without the mind), then not only the great sages who carried on various kinds of work after attaining *jnana* must be considered *ajnanis* but the gods also, and *Iswara* [the supreme personal God of Hinduism] himself, since he continues looking after the world. The fact is that any amount of action can be performed, and performed quite well, by the *jnani*, without his identifying himself with it in any way or ever imagining that he is the doer. Some power acts through his body and uses his body to get the work done.[11]

Q: *Is a* jnani *capable of or likely to commit sins?*

A: An *ajnani* sees someone as a *jnani* and identifies him with the body. Because he does not know the Self and mistakes his body for the Self, he extends the same mistake to the state of the *jnani*. The *jnani* is therefore considered to be the physical frame.

Again since the *ajnani*, though he is not the doer, imagines himself to be the doer and considers the actions of the body his own, he thinks the *jnani* to be similarly acting when the body is active. But the *jnani* himself knows the truth and is not confounded. The state of a *jnani* cannot be determined by the *ajnani* and therefore the question troubles only the *ajnani* and never arises for the *jnani*. If he is a doer he must determine the nature of the actions. The Self cannot be the doer. Find out who is the doer and the Self is revealed.

Q: *So it amounts to this. To see a* jnani *is not to understand him. You see the* jnani's *body and not his* jnana. *One must therefore be a* jnani *to know a* jnani.

A: The *jnani* sees no one as an *ajnani*. All are only *jnanis* in his sight. In the ignorant state one superimposes one's ignorance on a *jnani* and mistakes him for a doer. In the state of *jnana*, the *jnani* sees nothing separate from the Self. The Self is all shining and only pure *jnana*. So there is no *ajnana* in his sight. There is an illustration for this kind of illusion or superimposition. Two friends went to sleep side by side. One of them dreamt that both of them had gone on a long journey and that they had had strange experiences. On waking up he recapitulated them and asked his friend if it was not so. The other one simply ridiculed him saying that it was only his dream and could not affect the other.

So it is with the *ajnani* who superimposes his illusory ideas on others.[12]

Q: *You have said that the* jnani *can be and is active, and deals with men and things. I have no doubt about it now. But you say at the same time that he sees no differences; to him all is one, he is always in the consciousness. If so, how does he deal with differences, with men, with things which are surely different?*

A: He sees these differences as but appearances, he sees them as not separate from the true, the real, with which he is one.

Q: *The* jnani *seems to be more accurate in his expressions, he appreciates the differences better than the ordinary man. If sugar is sweet and wormwood is bitter to me, he too seems to realise it so. In fact, all forms, all sounds, all tastes, etc., are the same to him as they are to others. If so, how can it be said that these are mere appearances? Do they not form part of his life-experience?*

A: I have said that equality is the true sign of *jnana*. The very term equality implies the existence of differences. It is a unity that the *jnani* perceives in all differences, which I call equality. Equality does not mean ignorance of distinctions. When you have the realisation you can see that these differences are very superficial, that they are not at all substantial or permanent, and what is essential in all these appearances is the one truth, the real. That I call unity. You referred to sound, taste, form, smell, etc. True the *jnani* appreciates the distinctions, but he always perceives and experiences the one reality in all of them. That is why he has no preferences. Whether he moves about, or talks, or acts, it is all the one reality in which he acts or moves or talks. He has nothing apart from the one supreme truth.[13]

Q: *They say that the* jnani *conducts himself with absolute equality towards all?*

A: Yes.

Friendship, kindness, happiness and such other *bhavas* [attitudes] become natural to them. Affection towards the good, kindness towards the helpless, happiness in doing good deeds, forgiveness towards the wicked, all such things are natural characteristics of the *jnani* (Patanjali, *Yoga Sutras*, 1:37).[14]

You ask about *jnanis*: they are the same in any state or condition, as they know the reality, the truth. In their daily routine of taking food, moving about and all the rest, they, the *jnanis*, act only for others. Not a single action is done for themselves. I have already told you many times that just as there are people whose profession is to mourn for a fee, so also the *jnanis* do things for the sake of others with detachment, without themselves being affected by them.

The *jnani* weeps with the weeping, laughs with the laughing, plays with the playful, sings with those who sing, keeping time to the song. What does he lose? His presence is like a pure, transparent mirror. It reflects the image exactly as it is. But the *jnani*, who is only a mirror, is unaffected by actions. How can a mirror, or the stand on which it is mounted, be affected by the reflections? Nothing affects them as they are mere supports. On the other hand, the actors in the world – the doers of all acts, the *ajnanis* – must decide for themselves what song and what action is for the welfare of the world, what is in accordance with the *sastras*, and what is practicable.[15]

Q: *There are said to be* sadeha mukta *[liberated while still in the body] and* videha mukta *[liberated at the time of death].*

A: There is no liberation, and where are *muktas*?

Q: *Do not Hindu* sastras *speak of* mukti?

A: *Mukti* is synonymous with the Self. *Jivan mukti* [liberated while still in the body] and *videha mukti* are all for the ignorant. The *jnani* is not conscious of *mukti* or *bandha* [bondage]. Bondage, liberation and orders of *mukti* are all said for an *ajnani* in order that ignorance might be shaken off. There is only *mukti* and nothing else.

Q: *It is all right from the standpoint of Bhagavan. But what about us?*

A: The difference 'he' and 'I' are the obstacles to *jnana*.[16]

Q: *You once said: 'The liberated man is free indeed to act as he pleases, and when he leaves the mortal coil, he attains absolution, but returns not to this birth which is actually death.'*

This statement gives the impression that although the jnani *takes no birth again on this plane, he may continue to work on subtler planes, if he so chooses. Is there any desire left in him to choose?*

A: No, that was not my intention.

Q: *Further, an Indian philosopher, in one of his books, interpreting Sankara, says that there is no such thing as* videha mukti, *for after his death, the* mukta *takes a body of light in which he remains till the whole of humanity becomes liberated.*

A: That cannot be Sankara's view. In verse 566 of *Vivekachudamani* he says that after the dissolution of the physical sheath the liberated man becomes like 'water poured into water and oil into oil'. It is a state in which there is neither bondage nor liberation. Taking another body means throwing a veil, however subtle, upon reality, which is bondage. Liberation is absolute and irrevocable.[17]

Q: *How can we say the* jnani *is not in two planes? He moves about with us in the world and sees the various objects we see. It is not as if he does not see them. For instance he walks along. He sees the path he is treading. Suppose there is a chair or table placed across that path; he sees it, avoids it and goes round. So, have we not to admit he sees the world and the objects there, while of course he sees the Self?*

A: You say the *jnani* sees the path, treads it, comes across obstacles, avoids them, etc. In whose eye-sight is all this, in the *jnani*'s or yours? He sees only the Self and all in the Self.

Q: *Are there not illustrations given in our books to explain this* sahaja *[natural] state clearly to us?*

A: There are. For instance you see a reflection in the mirror and the mirror. You know the mirror to be the reality and the picture in it a mere reflection. Is it necessary that to see the mirror we should cease to see the reflection in it?[18]

Q: *What are the fundamental tests for discovering men of*

*great spirituality, since some are reported to behave like insane
people?*

A: The *jnani*'s mind is known only to the *jnani*. One must be a
jnani oneself in order to understand another *jnani*. However the
peace of mind which permeates the saint's atmosphere is the only
means by which the seeker understands the greatness of the saint.

His words or actions or appearance are no indication of his
greatness, for they are ordinarily beyond the comprehension of
common people.[19]

Q: *Why is it said in scriptures that the sage is like a child?*

A: A child and a *jnani* are similar in a way. Incidents interest a
child only so long as they last. It ceases to think of them after they
have passed away. So then, it is apparent that they do not leave
any impression on the child and it is not affected by them
mentally. So it is with a *jnani*.[20]

Q: *You are Bhagavan. So you should know when I shall get*
jnana. *Tell me when I shall be a* jnani.

A: If I am Bhagavan there is no one besides the Self – therefore
no *jnani* or *ajnani*. If otherwise, I am as good as you are and know
as much as yourself. Either way I cannot answer your question.[21]

Coming here, some people do not ask about themselves. They
ask: 'Does the *jivan mukta* see the world? Is he affected by *karma*?
What is liberation after being disembodied? Is one liberated only
after being disembodied or even while alive in the body? Should
the body of the sage resolve itself in light or disappear from view
in any other manner? Can he be liberated though the body is left
behind as a corpse?'

Their questions are endless. Why worry oneself in so many
ways? Does liberation consist in knowing these things?

Therefore I say to them, 'Leave liberation alone. Is there
bondage? Know this. See yourself first and foremost.'[22]

PART TWO

Enquiry and surrender

'I exist' is the only permanent self-evident experience of everyone. Nothing else is so self-evident as 'I am'. What people call self-evident, that is, the experience they get through the senses, is far from self-evident. The Self alone is that. So to do self-enquiry and be that 'I am' is the only thing to do. 'I am' is reality. I am this or that is unreal. 'I am' is truth, another name for Self.[1]

Devotion is nothing more than knowing oneself.[2]

On scrutiny, supreme devotion and *jnana* are in nature one and the same. To say that one of these two is a means to the other is due to not knowing the nature of either of them. Know that the path of *jnana* and the path of devotion are interrelated. Follow these inseparable two paths without dividing one from the other.[3]

CHAPTER 4
Self-enquiry — theory

It will be remembered that in the chapter on Self-awareness and Self-ignorance Sri Ramana maintained that Self-realisation could be brought about merely by giving up the idea that there is an individual self which functions through the body and the mind. A few of his advanced devotees were able to do this quickly and easily, but the others found it virtually impossible to discard the ingrained habits of a lifetime without undertaking some form of spiritual practice. Sri Ramana sympathised with their predicament and whenever he was asked to prescribe a spiritual practice which would facilitate Self-awareness he would recommend a technique he called self-enquiry. This practice was the cornerstone of his practical philosophy and the next three chapters will be devoted to a detailed presentation of all its aspects.

Before embarking on a description of the technique itself it will be necessary to explain Sri Ramana's views on the nature of the mind since the aim of self-enquiry is to discover, by direct experience, that the mind is non-existent. According to Sri Ramana, every conscious activity of the mind or body revolves around the tacit assumption that there is an 'I' who is doing something. The common factor in 'I think', 'I remember', 'I am acting' is the 'I' who assumes that it is responsible for all these activities. Sri Ramana called this common factor the 'I'-thought (*aham-vritti*). Literally *aham-vritti* means 'mental modification of I'. The Self or real 'I' never imagines that it is doing or thinking anything; the 'I' that imagines all this is a mental fiction and so it is called a mental modification of the Self. Since this is a rather cumbersome translation of *aham-vritti* it is usually translated as 'I'-thought.

Sri Ramana upheld the view that the notion of individuality is only the 'I'-thought manifesting itself in different ways. Instead of regarding the different activities of the mind (such as ego, intellect and memory) as separate functions he preferred to view them all as different forms of the 'I'-thought. Since he equated individuality with the mind and the mind with the 'I'-thought it follows that the disappearance of the sense of individuality (i.e. Self-realisation) implies the disappearance of both the mind and the 'I'-thought. This is confirmed by his frequent statements to the effect that after Self-realisation there is no thinker of thoughts, no performer of actions and no awareness of individual existence.

Since he upheld the notion that the Self is the only existing reality he regarded the 'I'-thought as a mistaken assumption which has no real existence of its own. He explained its appearance by saying that it can only appear to exist by identifying with an object. When thoughts arise the 'I'-thought claims ownership of them – 'I think', 'I believe', 'I want', 'I am acting' – but there is no separate 'I'-thought that exists independently of the objects that it is identifying with. It only appears to exist as a real continuous entity because of the incessant flow of identifications which are continually taking place. Almost all of these identifications can be traced back to an initial assumption that the 'I' is limited to the body, either as an owner-occupant or co-extensive with its physical form. This 'I am the body' idea is the primary source of all subsequent wrong identifications and its dissolution is the principal aim of self-enquiry.

Sri Ramana maintained that this tendency towards self-limiting identifications could be checked by trying to separate the subject 'I' from the objects of thought which it identified with. Since the individual 'I'-thought cannot exist without an object, if attention is focused on the subjective feeling of 'I' or 'I am' with such intensity that the thoughts 'I am this' or 'I am that' do not arise, then the individual 'I' will be unable to connect with objects. If this awareness of 'I' is sustained, the individual 'I' (the 'I'-thought) will disappear and in its place there will be a direct experience of the Self. This constant attention to the inner awareness of 'I' or 'I am' was called self-enquiry (*vichara*) by Sri Ramana and he constantly recommended it as the most efficient and direct way of discovering the unreality of the 'I'-thought.

In Sri Ramana's terminology the 'I'-thought rises from the Self or the Heart and subsides back into the Self when its tendency to identify itself with thought objects ceases. Because of this he often tailored his advice to conform to this image of a rising and subsiding 'I'. He might say 'trace the "I"-thought back to its source', or 'find out where the "I" rises from', but the implication was always the same. Whatever the language used he was advising his devotees to maintain awareness of the 'I'-thought until it dissolved in the source from which it came.

He sometimes mentioned that thinking or repeating 'I' mentally would also lead one in the right direction but it is important to note that this is only a preliminary stage of the practice. The repetition of 'I' still involves a subject (the 'I'-thought) having a perception of an object (the thoughts 'I, I') and while such duality exists the 'I'-thought will continue to thrive. It only finally disappears when the perception of all objects, both physical and mental, ceases. This is not brought about by being aware *of* an 'I', but only by *being* the 'I'. This stage of experiencing the subject rather than being aware of an object is the culminating phase of self-enquiry and it will be explained in greater detail in the following chapter.

This important distinction is the key element which distinguishes self-enquiry from nearly all other spiritual practices and it explains why Sri Ramana consistently maintained that most other practices were ineffective. He often pointed out that traditional meditations and yoga practices necessitate the existence of a subject who meditates on an object and he would usually add that such a relationship sustained the 'I'-thought instead of eliminating it. In his view such practices may effectively quieten the mind, and they may even produce blissful experiences, but they will never culminate in Self-realisation because the 'I'-thought is not being isolated and deprived of its identity.

The conversations which comprise this chapter mostly deal with Sri Ramana's views on the theoretical background of self-enquiry. The practical aspects of the technique will be explained in greater detail in chapter 5.

Q: *What is the nature of the mind?*
A: The mind is nothing other than the 'I'-thought. The mind and the ego are one and the same. The other mental faculties such as the intellect and the memory are only this. Mind [*manas*], intellect [*buddhi*], the storehouse of mental tendencies [*chittam*], and ego [*ahamkara*]; all these are only the one mind itself. This is like different names being given to a man according to his different functions. The individual soul [*jiva*] is nothing but this soul or ego.[1]
Q: *How shall we discover the nature of the mind, that is, its*

ultimate cause, or the noumenon of which it is a manifestation?

A: Arranging thoughts in the order of value, the 'I'-thought is the all-important thought. Personality-idea or thought is also the root or the stem of all other thoughts, since each idea or thought arises only as someone's thought and is not known to exist independently of the ego. The ego therefore exhibits thought-activity. The second and the third persons [he, you, that, etc.] do not appear except to the first person [I]. Therefore they arise only after the first person appears, so all the three persons seem to rise and sink together. Trace, then, the ultimate cause of 'I' or personality.[2]

From where does this 'I' arise? Seek for it within; it then vanishes. This is the pursuit of wisdom. When the mind unceasingly investigates its own nature, it transpires that there is no such thing as mind. This is the direct path for all. The mind is merely thoughts. Of all thoughts the thought 'I' is the root. Therefore the mind is only the thought 'I'.[3]

The birth of the 'I'-thought is one's own birth, its death is the person's death. After the 'I'-thought has arisen, the wrong identity with the body arises. Get rid of the 'I'-thought. So long as 'I' is alive there is grief. When 'I' ceases to exist there is no grief.

Q: *Yes, but when I take to the 'I'-thought, other thoughts arise and disturb me.*

A: See whose thoughts they are. They will vanish. They have their root in the single 'I'-thought. Hold it and they will disappear.[4]

Q: *How can any enquiry initiated by the ego reveal its own unreality?*

A: The ego's phenomenal existence is transcended when you dive into the source from where the 'I'-thought rises.

Q: *But is not the* aham-vritti *only one of the three forms in which the ego manifests itself.* Yoga Vasishtha *and other ancient texts describe the ego as having a threefold form.*

A: It is so. The ego is described as having three bodies, the gross, the subtle and the causal, but that is only for the purpose of analytical exposition. If the method of enquiry were to depend on the ego's form, you may take it that any enquiry would become altogether impossible, because the forms the ego may assume are legion. Therefore, for the purposes of self-enquiry you have to proceed on the basis that the ego has but one form, namely that of *aham-vritti.*

Q: *But it may prove inadequate for realising* jnana.

A: Self-enquiry by following the clue of *aham-vritti* is just like the dog tracing his master by his scent. The master may be at some distant unknown place, but that does not stand in the way of the dog tracing him. The master's scent is an infallible clue for the animal, and nothing else, such as the dress he wears, or his build and stature, etc., counts. To that scent the dog holds on undistractedly while searching for him, and finally it succeeds in tracing him.

Q: *The question still remains why the quest for the source of* aham-vritti, *as distinguished from other* vrittis *[modifications of the mind], should be considered the direct means to Self-realisation.*

A: Although the concept of 'I'-ness or 'I am'-ness is by usage known as *aham-vritti* it is not really a *vritti* [modification] like other *vrittis* of the mind. Because unlike the other *vrittis* which have no essential interrelation, the *aham-vritti* is equally and essentially related to each and every *vritti* of the mind. Without the *aham-vritti* there can be no other *vritti*, but the *aham-vritti* can subsist by itself without depending on any other *vritti* of the mind. The *aham-vritti* is therefore fundamentally different from other *vrittis*.

So then, the search for the source of the *aham-vritti* is not merely the search for the basis of one of the forms of the ego but for the very source itself from which arises the 'I am'-ness. In other words, the quest for and the realisation of the source of the ego in the form of *aham-vritti* necessarily implies the transcendence of the ego in every one of its possible forms.

Q: *Conceding that the* aham-vritti *essentially comprises all the forms of the ego, why should that* vritti *alone be chosen as the means for self-enquiry?*

A: Because it is the one irreducible datum of your experience and because seeking its source is the only practicable course you can adopt to realise the Self. The ego is said to have a causal body [the state of the 'I' during sleep], but how can you make it the subject of your investigation? When the ego adopts that form, you are immersed in the darkness of sleep.

Q: *But is not the ego in its subtle and causal forms too intangible to be tackled through the enquiry into the source of* aham-vritti *conducted while the mind is awake?*

A: No. The enquiry into the source of *aham-vritti* touches the very existence of the ego. Therefore the subtlety of the ego's form is not a material consideration.

Q: *While the one aim is to realise the unconditioned, pure being of the Self, which is in no way dependent on the ego, how can enquiry pertaining to the ego in the form of* aham-vritti *be of any use?*

A: From the functional point of view the ego has one and only one characteristic. The ego functions as the knot between the Self which is pure consciousness and the physical body which is inert and insentient. The ego is therefore called the *chit-jada-granthi* [the knot between consciousness and the inert body]. In your investigation into the source of *aham-vritti*, you take the essential *chit* [consciousness] aspect of the ego. For this reason the enquiry must lead to the realisation of pure consciousness of the Self.[5]

You must distinguish between the 'I', pure in itself, and the 'I'-thought. The latter, being merely a thought, sees subject and object, sleeps, wakes up, eats and thinks, dies and is reborn. But the pure 'I' is the pure being, eternal existence, free from ignorance and thought-illusion. If you stay as the 'I', your being alone, without thought, the 'I'-thought will disappear and the delusion will vanish for ever. In a cinema-show you can see pictures only in a very dim light or in darkness. But when all the lights are switched on, the pictures disappear. So also in the floodlight of the supreme *atman* all objects disappear.

Q: *That is the transcendental state.*

A: No. Transcending what, and by whom? You alone exist.[6]

Q: *It is said that the Self is beyond the mind and yet the realisation is with the mind. 'The mind cannot think it. It cannot be thought of by the mind and the mind alone can realise it.' How are these contradictions to be reconciled?*

A: *Atman* is realised with *mruta manas* [dead mind], that is, mind devoid of thoughts and turned inward. Then the mind sees its own source and becomes that [the Self]. It is not as the subject perceiving an object.

When the room is dark a lamp is necessary to illumine and eyes to cognise objects. But when the sun has risen there is no need of a lamp to see objects. To see the sun no lamp is necessary, it is enough that you turn your eyes towards the self-luminous sun.

Similarly with the mind. To see objects the reflected light of the mind is necessary. To see the Heart it is enough that the mind is turned towards it. Then mind loses itself and Heart shines forth.[7]

The essence of mind is only awareness or consciousness. When the ego, however, dominates it, it functions as the reasoning, thinking or sensing faculty. The cosmic mind, being not limited by the ego, has nothing separate from itself and is therefore only aware. This is what the Bible means by 'I am that I am'.[8]

When the mind perishes in the supreme consciousness of one's own Self, know that all the various powers beginning with the power of liking [and including the power of doing and the power of knowing] will entirely disappear, being found to be an unreal imagination appearing in one's own form of consciousness. The impure mind which functions as thinking and forgetting, alone is *samsara*, which is the cycle of birth and death. The real 'I' in which the activity of thinking and forgetting has perished, alone is the pure liberation. It is devoid of *pramada* [forgetfulness of Self] which is the cause of birth and death.[9]

Q: *How is the ego to be destroyed?*

A: Hold the ego first and then ask how it is to be destroyed. Who asks the question? It is the ego. This question is a sure way to cherish the ego and not to kill it. If you seek the ego you will find that it does not exist. That is the way to destroy it.[10]

Q: *How is realisation made possible?*

A: There is an absolute Self from which a spark proceeds as from a fire. The spark is called the ego. In the case of an ignorant man it identifies itself with an object simultaneously with its rise. It cannot remain independent of such association with objects. The association is *ajnana* or ignorance and its destruction is the object of our efforts. If its objectifying tendency is killed it remains pure, and also merges into the source. The wrong identification with the body is *dehatma buddhi* ['I am the body' idea]. This must go before good results follow.

The 'I' in its purity is experienced in intervals between the two states or two thoughts. Ego is like that caterpillar which leaves its hold only after catching another. Its true nature can be found when it is out of contact with objects or thoughts.[11]

This ghostly ego which is devoid of form comes into existence by grasping a form; grasping a form it endures; feeding upon forms which it grasps it waxes more; leaving one form it grasps another form, but when sought for it takes to flight.

Only if that first person, the ego, in the form 'I am the body', exists will the second and third persons [you, he, they, etc.] exist. If by one's scrutinising the truth of the first person the first person is destroyed, the second and third persons will cease to exist and one's own nature which will then shine as one will truly be the state of Self.[12]

The thought 'I am this body of flesh and blood' is the one thread on which are strung the various other thoughts. Therefore, if we turn inwards enquiring 'Where is this I?' all thoughts (including the 'I'-thought) will come to an end and Self-knowledge will then spontaneously shine forth.[13]

Q: *When I read Sri Bhagavan's works I find that investigation is said to be the one method for realisation.*

A: Yes, that is *vichara* [self-enquiry].

Q: *How is that to be done?*

A: The questioner must admit the existence of his Self. 'I am' is the realisation. To pursue the clue till realisation is *vichara*. *Vichara* and realisation are the same.

Q: *It is elusive. What shall I meditate upon?*

A: Meditation requires an object to meditate upon, whereas there is only the subject without the object in *vichara*. Meditation differs from *vichara* in this way.

Q: *Is not* dhyana *[meditation] one of the efficient processes for realisation?*

A: *Dhyana* is concentration on an object. It fulfils the purpose of keeping away diverse thoughts and fixing the mind on a single thought, which must also disappear before realisation. But realisation is nothing new to be acquired. It is already there, but obstructed by a screen of thoughts. All our attempts are directed to lifting this screen and then realisation is revealed.

If seekers are advised to meditate, many may go away satisfied with the advice. But someone among them may turn round and ask, 'Who am I to meditate on an object?' Such a one must be told to find the Self. That is the finality. That is *vichara*.

Q: *Will* vichara *alone do in the absence of meditation?*

A: *Vichara* is the process and the goal also. 'I am' is the goal and the final reality. To hold to it with effort is *vichara*. When spontaneous and natural it is realisation.[14] If one leaves aside *vichara*, the most efficacious *sadhana*, there are no other adequate means whatsoever to make the mind subside. If made to subside by other means, it will remain as if subsided but will rise again.[15] Self-enquiry is the one infallible means, the only direct one, to realise the unconditioned, absolute being that you really are.

Q: *Why should self-enquiry alone be considered the direct means to* jnana?

A: Because every kind of *sadhana* except that of *atma-vichara* [self-enquiry] presupposes the retention of the mind as the instrument for carrying on the *sadhana*, and without the mind it cannot be practised. The ego may take different and subtler forms at the different stages of one's practice, but is itself never destroyed.

When Janaka exclaimed, 'Now I have discovered the thief who has been ruining me all along. He shall be dealt with summarily', the king was really referring to the ego or the mind.

Q: *But the thief may well be apprehended by the other* sadhanas *as well.*

A: The attempt to destroy the ego or the mind through *sadhanas* other than *atma-vichara* is just like the thief pretending to be a policeman to catch the thief, that is, himself. *Atma-vichara* alone can reveal the truth that neither the ego nor the mind really exists, and enable one to realise the pure, undifferentiated being of the Self or the absolute.

Having realised the Self, nothing remains to be known, because it is perfect bliss, it is the all.[16]

Q: *Why is self-enquiry more direct than other methods?*

A: Attention to one's own Self, which is ever shining as 'I', the one undivided and pure reality, is the only raft with which the individual, who is deluded by thinking 'I am the body', can cross the ocean of unending births.[17]

Reality is simply the loss of ego. Destroy the ego by seeking its identity. Because the ego is no entity it will automatically vanish and reality will shine forth by itself. This is the direct method, whereas all other methods are done only by retaining the ego. In those paths there arise so many doubts and the eternal question 'Who am I?' remains to be tackled finally. But in this method the final question is the only one and it is raised from the beginning. No *sadhanas* are necessary for engaging in this quest.

There is no greater mystery than this – that being the reality we seek to gain reality. We think that there is something hiding our reality and that it must be destroyed before the reality is gained. It is ridiculous. A day will dawn when you will yourself laugh at your past efforts. That which will be on the day you laugh is also here and now.[18]

CHAPTER 5
Self-enquiry – practice

Beginners in self-enquiry were advised by Sri Ramana to put their attention on the inner feeling of 'I' and to hold that feeling as long as possible. They would be told that if their attention was distracted by other thoughts they should revert to awareness of the 'I'-thought whenever they became aware that their attention had wandered. He suggested various aids to assist this process – one could ask oneself 'Who am I?' or 'Where does this I come from?' – but the ultimate aim was to be continuously aware of the 'I' which assumes that it is responsible for all the activities of the body and the mind.

In the early stages of practice attention to the feeling 'I' is a mental activity which takes the form of a thought or a perception. As the practice develops the thought 'I' gives way to a subjectively experienced feeling of 'I', and when this feeling ceases to connect and identify with thoughts and objects it completely vanishes. What remains is an experience of being in which the sense of individuality has temporarily ceased to operate. The experience may be intermittent at first but with repeated practice it becomes easier and easier to reach and maintain. When self-enquiry reaches this level there is an effortless awareness of being in which individual effort is no longer possible since the 'I' who makes the effort has temporarily ceased to exist. It is not Self-realisation since the 'I'-thought periodically reasserts itself but it is the highest level of practice. Repeated experience of this state of being weakens and destroys the *vasanas* (mental tendencies) which cause the 'I'-thought to rise, and, when their hold has been sufficiently weakened, the power of the Self destroys the residual tendencies so completely that the 'I'-thought never rises again. This is the final and irreversible state of Self-realisation.

This practice of self-attention or awareness of the 'I'-thought is a gentle technique which bypasses the usual repressive methods of controlling the mind. It is not an exercise in concentration, nor does it aim at suppressing thoughts; it merely invokes awareness of the source from which the mind springs. The method and goal of self-enquiry is to abide in the source of the mind and to be aware of what one really is by withdrawing attention and interest from what one is not. In the early stages effort in the form of transferring attention from the thoughts to the thinker is essential, but once awareness of the 'I'-feeling has been firmly established, further effort is counter-productive. From then on it is more a process of being than doing, of effortless being rather than an effort to be.

Being what one already is is effortless since beingness is always present and always experienced. On the other hand, pretending to be what one is not (i.e. the body and the mind) requires continuous mental effort, even though the effort is nearly always at a subconscious level. It therefore follows that in the higher stages of self-enquiry effort takes attention away from the experience of being while the cessation of mental effort reveals it. Ultimately, the Self is not discovered as a result of doing anything, but only by being. As Sri Ramana himself once remarked:

'Do not meditate – be!
Do not think that you are – be!
Don't think about being – you are!'[1]

Self-enquiry should not be regarded as a meditation practice that takes place at certain hours and in certain positions; it should continue throughout one's waking hours, irrespective of what one is doing. Sri Ramana saw no conflict between working and self-enquiry and he maintained that with a little practice it could be done under any circumstances. He did sometimes say that regular periods of formal practice were good for beginners, but he never advocated long periods of sitting meditation and he always showed his disapproval when any of his devotees expressed a desire to give up their mundane activities in favour of a meditative life.

Q: *You say one can realise the Self by a search for it. What is the character of this search?*

A: You are the mind or think that you are the mind. The mind is nothing but thoughts. Now behind every particular thought there is a general thought which is the 'I', that is yourself. Let us call this 'I' the first thought. Stick to this 'I'-thought and question it to find out what it is. When this question takes strong hold on you, you cannot think of other thoughts.

Q: *When I do this and cling to my self, that is, the 'I'-thought, other thoughts come and go, but I say to myself 'Who am I?' and there is no answer forthcoming. To be in this condition is the practice. Is it so?*

A: This is a mistake that people often make. What happens when you make a serious quest for the Self is that the 'I'-thought disappears and something else from the depths takes hold of you and that is not the 'I' which commenced the quest.

Q: *What is this something else?*

A: That is the real Self, the import of 'I'. It is not the ego. It is the supreme being itself.

Q: *But you have often said that one must reject other thoughts when one begins the quest but the thoughts are endless. If one thought is rejected, another comes and there seems to be no end at all.*

A: I do not say that you must go on rejecting thoughts. Cling to yourself, that is, to the 'I'-thought. When your interest keeps you to that single idea, other thoughts will automatically get rejected and they will vanish.

Q: *And so rejection of thoughts is not necessary?*

A: No. It may be necessary for a time or for some. You fancy that there is no end if one goes on rejecting every thought when it rises. It is not true, there is an end. If you are vigilant and make a stern effort to reject every thought when it rises you will soon find that you are going deeper and deeper into your own inner self. At that level it is not necessary to make an effort to reject thoughts.

Q: *Then it is possible to be without effort, without strain.*

A: Not only that, it is impossible for you to make an effort beyond a certain extent.

Q: *I want to be further enlightened. Should I try to make no effort at all?*

A: Here it is impossible for you to be without effort. When you go deeper, it is impossible for you to make any effort.[2]

If the mind becomes introverted through enquiry into the source of *aham-vritti*, the *vasanas* become extinct. The light of the Self falls on the *vasanas* and produces the phenomenon of reflection we call the mind. Thus, when the *vasanas* become extinct the mind also disappears, being absorbed into the light of the one reality, the Heart.

This is the sum and substance of all that an aspirant needs to know. What is imperatively required of him is an earnest and one-pointed enquiry into the source of the *aham-vritti*.[3]

Q: *How should a beginner start this practice?*

A: The mind will subside only by means of the enquiry 'Who am I?' The thought 'Who am I?', destroying all other thoughts, will itself finally be destroyed like the stick used for stirring the funeral pyre. If other thoughts rise one should, without attempting to complete them, enquire 'To whom did they rise?' What does it matter however many thoughts rise? At the very moment that each thought rises, if one vigilantly enquires 'To whom did this rise?', it will be known 'To me'. If one then enquires 'Who am I?', the mind will turn back to its source [the Self] and the thought which had risen will also subside. By repeatedly practising thus, the power of the mind to abide in its source increases.

Although tendencies towards sense-objects [*vishaya vasanas*], which have been recurring down the ages, rise in countless numbers like the waves of the ocean, they will all perish as meditation on one's nature becomes more and more intense. Without giving room even to the doubting thought, 'Is it possible to destroy all these tendencies [*vasanas*] and to remain as Self alone?', one should persistently cling fast to self-attention.

As long as there are tendencies towards sense-objects in the mind, the enquiry 'Who am I?' is necessary. As and when thoughts rise, one should annihilate all of them through enquiry then and there in their very place of origin. Not attending to what-is-other [*anya*] is non-attachment [*vairagya*] or desirelessness [*nirasa*]. Not leaving Self is knowledge [*jnana*]. In truth, these two [desireless-ness and knowledge] are one and the same. Just as a pearl-diver, tying a stone to his waist, dives into the sea and takes the pearl lying at the bottom, so everyone, diving deep within himself with non-attachment, can attain the pearl of Self. If one resorts uninterruptedly to remembrance of one's real nature [*swarupa-smarana*] until one attains Self, that alone will be sufficient.

Enquiring 'Who am I that is in bondage?' and knowing one's real nature [*swarupa*] alone is liberation. Always keeping the mind fixed in Self alone is called 'self-enquiry', whereas meditation [*dhyana*] is thinking oneself to be the absolute [*Brahman*], which is existence-consciousness-bliss [*sat-chit-ananda*].[4]

Q: *The yogis say that one must renounce this world and go off into secluded jungles if one wishes to find the truth.*

A: The life of action need not be renounced. If you meditate for an hour or two every day you can then carry on with your duties. If you meditate in the right manner then the current of mind induced will continue to flow even in the midst of your work. It is as though there were two ways of expressing the same idea; the same line which you take in meditation will be expressed in your activities.

Q: *What will be the result of doing that?*

A: As you go on you will find that your attitude towards people, events and objects gradually changes. Your actions will tend to follow your meditations of their own accord.

Q: *Then you do not agree with the yogis?*

A: A man should surrender the personal selfishness which binds him to this world. Giving up the false self is the true renunciation.

Q: *How is it possible to become selfless while leading a life of worldly activity?*

A: There is no conflict between work and wisdom.

Q: *Do you mean that one can continue all the old activities in one's profession, for instance, and at the same time get enlightenment?*

A: Why not? But in that case one will not think that it is the old personality which is doing the work, because one's consciousness will gradually become transferred until it is centred in that which is beyond the little self.

Q: *If a person is engaged in work, there will be little time left for him to meditate.*

A: Setting apart time for meditation is only for the merest spiritual novices. A man who is advancing will begin to enjoy the deeper beatitude whether he is at work or not. While his hands are in society, he keeps his head cool in solitude.

Q: *Then you do not teach the way of yoga?*

A: The yogi tries to drive his mind to the goal, as a cowherd drives a bull with a stick, but on this path the seeker coaxes the bull by holding out a handful of grass.

Q: *How is that done?*

A: You have to ask yourself the question 'Who am I?' This investigation will lead in the end to the discovery of something within you which is behind the mind. Solve that great problem and you will solve all other problems.[5]

Q: *Seeking the 'I' there is nothing to be seen.*

A: Because you are accustomed to identify yourself with the body and sight with the eyes, therefore you say you do not see anything. What is there to be seen? Who is to see? How to see? There is only one consciousness which, manifesting as 'I'-thought, identifies itself with the body, projects itself through the eyes and sees the objects around. The individual is limited in the waking state and expects to see something different. The evidence of his senses will be the seal of authority. But he will not admit that the seer, the seen and the seeing are all manifestations of the same consciousness – namely, 'I, I'. Contemplation helps one to overcome the illusion that the Self must be visual. In truth, there is nothing visual. How do you feel the 'I' now? Do you hold a mirror before you to know your own being? The awareness is the 'I'. Realise it and that is the truth.

Q: *On enquiry into the origin of thoughts there is a perception of 'I'. But it does not satisfy me.*

A: Quite right. The perception of 'I' is associated with a form, maybe the body. There should be nothing associated with the pure Self. The Self is the unassociated, pure reality, in whose light the body and the ego shine. On stilling all thoughts the pure consciousness remains.

Just on waking from sleep and before becoming aware of the world there is that pure 'I, I'. Hold on to it without sleeping or without allowing thoughts to possess you. If that is held firm it does not matter even if the world is seen. The seer remains unaffected by the phenomena.[6]

What is the ego? Enquire. The body is insentient and cannot say 'I'. The Self is pure consciousness and non-dual. It cannot say 'I'. No one says 'I' in sleep. What is the ego then? It is something intermediate between the inert body and the Self. It has no *locus standi*. If sought for it vanishes like a ghost. At night a man may imagine that there is a ghost by his side because of the play of shadows. If he looks closely he discovers that the ghost is not really there, and what he imagined to be a ghost was merely a tree or a post. If he does not look closely the ghost may terrify him. All that is required is to look closely and the ghost vanishes. The ghost was never there. So also with the ego. It is an intangible link between the body and pure consciousness. It is not real. So long as one does not look closely at it, it continues to give trouble. But when one looks for it, it is found not to exist.

There is another story which illustrates this. In Hindu marriage

functions the feasts often continue for five or six days. On one of
these occasions a stranger was mistaken for the best man by the
bride's party and they therefore treated him with special regard.
Seeing him treated with special regard by the bride's party, the
bridegroom's party considered him to be some man of importance
related to the bride's party and therefore they too showed him
special respect. The stranger had altogether a happy time of it. He
was also all along aware of the real situation. On one occasion the
groom's party wanted to refer to him on some point and so they
asked the bride's party about him. Immediately he scented trouble
and made himself scarce. So it is with the ego. If looked for, it
disappears. If not, it continues to give trouble.[7]

Q: *If I try to make the 'Who am I?' enquiry, I fall into sleep.
What should I do?*

A: Persist in the enquiry throughout your waking hours. That
would be quite enough. If you keep on making the enquiry till you
fall asleep, the enquiry will go on during sleep also. Take up the
enquiry again as soon as you wake up.[8]

Q: *How can I get peace? I do not seem to obtain it through*
vichara.

A: Peace is your natural state. It is the mind that obstructs the
natural state. If you do not experience peace it means that your
vichara has been made only in the mind. Investigate what the
mind is, and it will disappear. There is no such thing as mind
apart from thought. Nevertheless, because of the emergence of
thought, you surmise something from which it starts and term that
the mind. When you probe to see what it is, you find there is really
no such thing as mind. When the mind has thus vanished, you
realise eternal peace.[9]

Q: *When I am engaged in enquiry as to the source from which
the 'I' springs, I arrive at a stage of stillness of mind beyond which
I find myself unable to proceed further. I have no thought of any
kind and there is an emptiness, a blankness. A mild light pervades
and I feel that it is myself bodiless. I have neither cognition nor
vision of body and form. The experience lasts nearly half an hour
and is pleasing. Would I be correct in concluding that all that was
necessary to secure eternal happiness, that is freedom or salvation
or whatever one calls it, was to continue the practice till this
experience could be maintained for hours, days and months
together?*

A: This does not mean salvation. Such a condition is termed

manolaya or temporary stillness of thought. *Manolaya* means concentration, temporarily arresting the movement of thoughts. As soon as this concentration ceases, thoughts, old and new, rush in as usual; and even if this temporary lulling of mind should last a thousand years, it will never lead to total destruction of thought, which is what is called liberation from birth and death. The practitioner must therefore be ever on the alert and enquire within as to who has this experience, who realises its pleasantness. Without this enquiry he will go into a long trance or deep sleep [*yoga nidra*]. Due to the absence of a proper guide at this stage of spiritual practice, many have been deluded and fallen a prey to a false sense of liberation and only a few have managed to reach the goal safely.

The following story illustrates the point very well. A yogi was doing penance [*tapas*] for a number of years on the banks of the Ganges. When he had attained a high degree of concentration, he believed that continuance in that stage for prolonged periods constituted liberation and practised it. One day, before going into deep concentration, he felt thirsty and called to his disciple to bring a little drinking water from the Ganges. But before the disciple arrived with the water, he had gone into *yoga nidra* and remained in that state for countless years, during which time much water flowed under the bridge. When he woke up from this experience he immediately called 'Water! Water!'; but there was neither his disciple nor the Ganges in sight.

The first thing which he asked for was water because, before going into deep concentration, the topmost layer of thought in his mind was water and by concentration, however deep and prolonged it might have been, he had only been able temporarily to lull his thoughts. When he regained consciousness this topmost thought flew up with all the speed and force of a flood breaking through the dykes. If this is the case with regard to a thought which took shape immediately before he sat for meditation, there is no doubt that thoughts which took root earlier would also remain unannihilated. If annihilation of thoughts is liberation can he be said to have attained salvation?

Sadhakas [seekers] rarely understand the difference between this temporary stilling of the mind [*manolaya*] and permanent destruction of thoughts [*manonasa*]. In *manolaya* there is temporary subsidence of thought-waves, and though this temporary period may even last for a thousand years, thoughts, which are thus temporarily stilled, rise up as soon as the *manolaya* ceases. One must therefore watch one's spiritual progress carefully. One must not allow oneself to be overtaken by such spells of stillness of thought. The moment one experiences this, one must revive consciousness and enquire within as to who it is who experiences this stillness. While not allowing any thoughts to intrude, one must not, at the same time, be overtaken by this deep sleep [*yoga nidra*] or self-hypnotism. Though this is a sign of progress towards the goal, yet it is also the point where the divergence between the road to liberation and *yoga nidra* takes place. The easy way, the direct way, the shortest cut to salvation is the enquiry method. By such enquiry, you will drive the thought force deeper till it reaches its source and merges therein. It is then that you will have the response from within and find that you rest there, destroying all thoughts, once and for all.[10]

Q: *This 'I'-thought rises from me. But I do not know the Self.*

A: All these are only mental concepts. You are now identifying yourself with a wrong 'I', which is the 'I'-thought. This 'I'-thought rises and sinks, whereas the true significance of 'I' is beyond both. There cannot be a break in your being. You who slept are also now awake. There is no unhappiness in your deep sleep whereas it exists now. What is it that has happened now so that this difference is experienced? There was no 'I'-thought in your sleep, whereas it is present now. The true 'I' is not apparent and the false 'I' is parading itself. This false 'I' is the obstacle to your right knowledge. Find out from where this false 'I' arises. Then it will disappear. You will then be only what you are, that is, absolute being.

Q: *How to do it? I have not succeeded so far.*

A: Search for the source of the 'I'-thought. That is all that one has to do. The universe exists on account of the 'I'-thought. If that ends there is an end to misery also. The false 'I' will end only when its source is sought.[11]

Again people often ask how the mind is controlled. I say to them, 'Show me the mind and then you will know what to do.' The fact is that the mind is only a bundle of thoughts. How can you extinguish it by the thought of doing so or by a desire? Your thoughts and desires are part and parcel of the mind. The mind is simply fattened by new thoughts rising up. Therefore it is foolish to attempt to kill the mind by means of the mind. The only way of doing it is to find its source and hold on to it. The mind will then fade away of its own accord. Yoga teaches *chitta vritti nirodha* [control of the activities of the mind]. But I say *atma vichara* [self-investigation]. This is the practical way. *Chitta vritti nirodha* is brought about in sleep, swoon, or by starvation. As soon as the cause is withdrawn there is a recrudescence of thoughts. Of what use is it then? In the state of stupor there is peace and no misery. But misery recurs when the stupor is removed. So *nirodha* [control] is useless and cannot be of lasting benefit.

How then can the benefit be made lasting? It is by finding the cause of misery. Misery is due to the perception of objects. If they are not there, there will be no contingent thoughts and so misery is wiped off. 'How will objects cease to be?' is the next question. The *srutis* [scriptures] and the sages say that the objects are only mental creations. They have no substantive being. Investigate the matter and ascertain the truth of the statement. The result will be the conclusion that the objective world is in the subjective consciousness. The Self is thus the only reality which permeates and also envelops the world. Since there is no duality, no thoughts will arise to disturb your peace. This is realisation of the Self. The Self is eternal and so also is realisation.

Abhyasa [spiritual practice] consists in withdrawal within the Self every time you are disturbed by thought. It is not concentration or destruction of the mind but withdrawal into the Self.[12]

Q: *Why is concentration ineffective?*

A: To ask the mind to kill the mind is like making the thief the policeman. He will go with you and pretend to catch the thief, but nothing will be gained. So you must turn inward and see from where the mind rises and then it will cease to exist.

Q: *In turning the mind inwards, are we not still employing the mind?*

A: Of course we are employing the mind. It is well known and admitted that only with the help of the mind can the mind be killed. But instead of setting about saying there is a mind, and I want to kill it, you begin to seek the source of the mind, and you find the mind does not exist at all. The mind, turned outwards, results in thoughts and objects. Turned inwards, it becomes itself the Self.[13]

Q: *Even so, I do not understand. 'I', you say, is the wrong 'I' now. How to eliminate the wrong 'I'?*

A: You need not eliminate the wrong 'I'. How can 'I' eliminate itself? All that you need do is to find out its origin and abide there. Your efforts can extend only thus far. Then the beyond will take care of itself. You are helpless there. No effort can reach it.

Q: *If 'I' am always, here and now, why do I not feel so?*

A: That is it. Who says it is not felt? Does the real 'I' say it or the false 'I'? Examine it. You will find it is the wrong 'I'. The wrong 'I' is the obstruction. It has to be removed in order that the true 'I' may not be hidden. The feeling that I have not realised is the obstruction to realisation. In fact it is already realised and there is nothing more to be realised. Otherwise, the realisation will be new. If it has not existed so far, it must take place hereafter. What is born will also die. If realisation is not eternal it is not worth having. Therefore what we seek is not that which must happen afresh. It is only that which is eternal but not now known due to obstructions. It is that which we seek. All that we need do is remove the obstruction. That which is eternal is not known to be so because of ignorance. Ignorance is the obstruction. Get over the ignorance and all will be well.

The ignorance is identical with the 'I'-thought. Find its source and it will vanish.

The 'I'-thought is like a spirit which, although not palpable, rises up simultaneously with the body, flourishes and disappears with it. The body-consciousness is the wrong 'I'. Give up this body-consciousness. It is done by seeking the source of the 'I'. The body does not say 'I am'. It is you who say, 'I am the body'. Find out who this 'I' is. Seeking its source it will vanish.[14]

Q: *How long can the mind stay or be kept in the Heart?*

A: The period extends by practice.

Q: *What happens at the end of the period?*

A: The mind returns to the present normal state. Unity in the Heart is replaced by a variety of perceived phenomena. This is called the outgoing mind. The Heart-going mind is called the resting mind.[15]

When one daily practises more and more in this manner, the mind will become extremely pure due to the removal of its defects and the practice will become so easy that the purified mind will plunge into the Heart as soon as the enquiry is commenced.[16]

Q: *Is it possible for a person who once has had the experience of* sat-chit-ananda *in meditation to identify himself with the body when out of meditation?*

A: Yes, it is possible, but he gradually loses the identification in the course of his practice. In the floodlight of the Self the darkness of illusion dissipates for ever.[17]

Experience gained without rooting out all the *vasanas* cannot remain steady. Efforts must be made to eradicate the *vasanas*; knowledge can only remain unshaken after all the *vasanas* are rooted out.[18]

We have to contend against age-long mental tendencies. They will all go. Only they go comparatively soon in the case of those who have made *sadhana* in the past and later in the case of others.

Q: *Do these tendencies go gradually or will they suddenly all disappear one day? I ask this because although I have remained here for a long time I do not perceive any gradual change in me.*

A: When the sun rises, does the darkness go gradually or all at once?[19]

Q: *How can I tell if I am making progress with my enquiry?*

A: The degree of the absence of thoughts is the measure of your progress towards Self-realisation. But Self-realisation itself does not admit of progress, it is ever the same. The Self remains always in realisation. The obstacles are thoughts. Progress is measured by the degree of removal of the obstacles to understanding that the Self is always realised. So thoughts must be checked by seeking to whom they arise. So you go to their source, where they do not arise.

Q: *Doubts are always arising. Hence my question.*

A: A doubt arises and is cleared. Another arises and that is cleared, making way for yet another; and so it goes on. So there is no possibility of clearing away all doubts. See to whom the doubts arise. Go to their source and abide in it. Then they cease to arise. That is how doubts are to be cleared.[20]

Q: *Should I go on asking 'Who am I?' without answering? Who asks whom? Which* bhavana *[attitude] should be in the mind at the time of enquiry? What is 'I', the Self or the ego?*

A: In the enquiry 'Who am I?', 'I' is the ego. The question really means, what is the source or origin of this ego? You need not have any *bhavana* [attitude] in the mind. All that is required is that you must give up the *bhavana* that you are the body, of such and such a description, with such and such a name, etc. There is no need to have a *bhavana* about your real nature. It exists as it always does. It is real and no *bhavana*.[21]

Q: *But is it not funny that the 'I' should be searching for the 'I'? Does not the enquiry 'Who am I?' turn out in the end to be an*

*empty formula? Or, am I to put the question to myself endlessly,
repeating it like some* mantra?

A: Self-enquiry is certainly not an empty formula and it is
more than the repetition of any *mantra.* If the enquiry 'Who am
I?' were a mere mental questioning, it would not be of much
value. The very purpose of self-enquiry is to focus the entire mind
at its source. It is not, therefore, a case of one 'I' searching for
another 'I'. Much less is self-enquiry an empty formula, for it
involves an intense activity of the entire mind to keep it steadily
poised in pure Self-awareness.[22]

Q: *Is it enough if I spend some time in the mornings and some
time in the evenings for this* atma-vichara? *Or should I do it
always, even when I am writing or walking?*

A: What is your real nature? Is it writing, walking or being?
The one unalterable reality is being. Until you realise that state of
pure being you should pursue the enquiry. If once you are
established in it there will be no further worry.

No one will enquire into the source of thoughts unless thoughts
arise. So long as you think 'I am walking' or 'I am writing',
enquire who does it.[23]

Q: *If I go on rejecting thoughts can I call it* vichara?

A: It may be a stepping stone. But really *vichara* begins when
you cling to your Self and are already off the mental movement,
the thought waves.

Q: *Then* vichara *is not intellectual?*

A: No, it is *antara vichara*, inner quest.[24]

Holding the mind and investigating it is advised for a beginner.
But what is mind after all? It is a projection of the Self. See for
whom it appears and from where it rises. The 'I'-thought will be
found to be the root-cause. Go deeper. The 'I'-thought disappears
and there is an infinitely expanded 'I'-consciousness.[25]

Q: *I asked Mother in Sri Aurobindo Ashram the following
question: 'I keep my mind blank without thoughts arising so that
God might show himself in his true being. But I do not perceive
anything.' The reply was to this effect: 'The attitude is right. The
power will come down from above. It is a direct experience.'
Should I do anything further?*

A: Be what you are. There is nothing to come down or become
manifest. All that is necessary is to lose the ego. That which is is
always there. Even now you are that. You are not apart from it.
The blank is seen by you. You are there to see the blank. What do

you wait for? The thought, 'I have not seen', the expectation to
see and the desire of getting something, are all the workings of the
ego. You have fallen into snares of the ego. The ego says all these
and not you. Be yourself and nothing more!

Once born you reach something. If you reach it you return also.
Therefore leave off all this verbiage. Be as you are. See who you
are and remain as the Self, free from birth, going, coming and
returning.[26]

Q: *How is one to know the Self?*

A: Knowing the Self means being the Self. Can you say that
you do not know the Self? Though you cannot see your own eyes
and though not provided with a mirror to look in, do you deny
the existence of your eyes? Similarly, you are aware of the Self
even though the Self is not objectified. Or, do you deny your Self
because it is not objectified? When you say 'I cannot know the
Self', it means absence in terms of relative knowledge, because you
have been so accustomed to relative knowledge that you identify
yourself with it. Such wrong identity has forged the difficulty of
not knowing the obvious Self because it cannot be objectified. And
then you ask 'how is one to know the Self?'

Q: *You talk of being. Being what?*

A: Your duty is to be and not to be this or that. 'I am that I
am' sums up the whole truth. The method is summed up in the
words 'Be still'. What does stillness mean? It means destroy
yourself. Because any form or shape is the cause of trouble. Give
up the notion that 'I am so and so'.[27] All that is required to realise
the Self is to be still. What can be easier than that? Hence *atmavidya* [Self-knowledge] is the easiest to attain.[28]

The truth of oneself alone is worthy to be scrutinised and
known. Taking it as the target of one's attention, one should
keenly know it in the Heart. This knowledge of oneself will be
revealed only to the consciousness which is silent, clear and free
from the activity of the agitated and suffering mind. Know that
the consciousness which always shines in the Heart as the
formless Self, 'I', and which is known by one's being still without
thinking about anything as existent or non-existent, alone is the
perfect reality.[29]

CHAPTER 6
Self-enquiry – misconceptions

Sri Ramana's philosophical pronouncements were very similar to those upheld by the followers of *advaita vedanta*, an Indian philosophical school which has flourished for well over a thousand years. Sri Ramana and the *advaitins* agree on most theoretical matters but their attitudes to practice are radically different. While Sri Ramana advocated self-enquiry, most *advaitic* teachers recommended a system of meditation which mentally affirmed that the Self was the only reality. These affirmations such as 'I am *Brahman*' or 'I am he', are usually used as *mantras*, or, more rarely, one meditates on their meaning and tries to experience the implications of the statement.

Because self-enquiry often starts with the question 'Who am I?', many of the traditional followers of *advaita* assumed that the answer to the question was 'I am *Brahman*' and they occupied their minds with repetitions of this mental solution. Sri Ramana criticised this approach by saying that while the mind was constantly engaged in finding or repeating solutions to the question it would never sink into its source and disappear. He was equally critical, for the same reason, of those who tried to use 'Who am I?' as a *mantra*, saying that both approaches missed the point of self-enquiry. The question 'Who am I?', he said, is not an invitation to analyse the mind and to come to conclusions about its nature, nor is it a *mantric* formula, it is simply a tool which facilitates redirecting attention from the objects of thought and perception to the thinker and perceiver of them. In Sri Ramana's opinion, the solution to the question 'Who am I?' is not to be found in or by the mind since the only real answer is the experience of the absence of mind.

Another widespread misunderstanding arose from the Hindu belief that the Self could be discovered by mentally rejecting all the objects of thought and perception as not-Self. Traditionally this is called the *neti-neti* approach (not this, not this). The practitioner of this system verbally rejects all the objects that the 'I' identifies with – 'I am not the mind', 'I am not the body', etc. – in the expectation that the real 'I' will eventually be experienced in its pure uncontaminated form. Hinduism calls this practice 'self-enquiry' and, because of the identity of names, it was often confused with Sri Ramana's method. Sri Ramana's attitude to this traditional system of self-analysis was wholly negative and he discouraged his own followers from practising it by telling them that it was an intellectual activity which could not take them beyond the mind. In his standard reply to questions about the effectiveness of this practice he would say that the 'I'-thought is sustained by such acts of discrimination and that the 'I' which eliminates the body and the mind as 'not I' can never eliminate itself.

The followers of the 'I am *Brahman*' and '*neti-neti*' schools share a common belief that the Self can be discovered by the mind, either through affirmation or negation. This belief that the mind can, by its own activities, reach the Self is the root of most of the misconceptions about the practice of self-enquiry. A classic example of this is the belief that self-enquiry involves concentrating on a particular centre in the body called the Heart-centre. This widely-held view results from a misinterpretation of some of Sri Ramana's statements on the Heart, and to understand how this belief has come about it will be necessary to take a closer look at some of his ideas on the subject.

In describing the origin of the 'I'-thought he sometimes said that it rose to the brain through a channel which started from a centre in the right-hand side of the chest. He called this centre the Heart-centre and said that when the 'I'-thought subsided into the Self it went back into the centre and disappeared. He also said that when the Self is consciously experienced, there is a tangible awareness that this centre is the source of both the mind and the world. However, these statements are not strictly true and Sri Ramana sometimes qualified them by saying that they were only schematic representations which were given to those people who persisted in identifying with their bodies. He said that the Heart is not really located in the body and that from the highest standpoint it is equally untrue to say that the 'I'-thought arises and subsides into this centre on the right of the chest.

Because Sri Ramana often said 'Find the place where the "I" arises' or 'Find the source of the mind', many people interpreted these statements to mean that they should concentrate on this

particular centre while doing self-enquiry. Sri Ramana rejected
this interpretation many times by saying that the source of the
mind or the 'I' could only be discovered through attention to the
'I'-thought and not through concentration on a particular part of
the body. He did sometimes say that putting attention on this
centre is a good concentration practice, but he never associated it
with self-enquiry. He also occasionally said that meditation on the
Heart was an effective way of reaching the Self, but again, he
never said that this should be done by concentrating on the Heart-
centre. Instead he said that one should meditate on the Heart 'as it
is'.[1] The Heart 'as it is' is not a location, it is the immanent Self
and one can only be aware of its real nature by being it. It cannot
be reached by concentration.

Although there are several potentially ambiguous comments of
this kind about the Heart and the Heart-centre, in all his writings
and recorded conversations there is not a single statement to
support the contention that self-enquiry is to be practised by
concentrating on this centre. In fact, by closely examining his
statements on the subject one can only conclude that while the
experience of the Self contains an awareness of this centre,
concentration on this centre will not result in the experience of the
Self.

Q: *I begin to ask myself 'Who am I?', eliminate the body as not
'I', the breath as not 'I', and I am not able to proceed further.*

A: Well, that is as far as the intellect can go. Your process is
only intellectual. Indeed, all the scriptures mention the process
only to guide the seeker to know the truth. The truth cannot be
directly pointed out. Hence this intellectual process.

You see, the one who eliminates all the 'not I' cannot eliminate
the 'I'. To say 'I am not this' or 'I am that' there must be the 'I'.
This 'I' is only the ego or the 'I'-thought. After the rising up of this
'I'-thought, all other thoughts arise. The 'I'-thought is therefore
the root-thought. If the root is pulled out all others are at the same
time uprooted. Therefore seek the root 'I', question yourself 'Who
am I?'. Find out its source, and then all these other ideas will
vanish and the pure Self will remain.

Q: *How to do it?*

A: The 'I' is always there – in deep sleep, in dream and in
wakefulness. The one in sleep is the same as that who now speaks.

There is always the feeling of 'I'. Otherwise do you deny your existence? You do not. You say 'I am'. Find out who is.[2]

Q: *I meditate* neti-neti *[not this – not this].*

A: No – that is not meditation. Find the source. You must reach the source without fail. The false 'I' will disappear and the real 'I' will be realised. The former cannot exist apart from the latter.[3]

There is now wrong identification of the Self with the body, senses, etc. You proceed to discard these, and this is *neti*. This can be done only by holding to the one which cannot be discarded. That is *iti* [that which is].[4]

Q: *When I think 'Who am I?', the answer comes 'I am not this mortal body but I am* chaitanya, atma *[consciousness, the Self].' And suddenly another question arises, 'Why has* atma *come into* maya *[illusion]?' or in other words, 'Why has God created this world?'*

A: To enquire 'Who am I?' really means trying to find out the source of the ego or the 'I'-thought. You are not to think of other thoughts, such as 'I am not this body'. Seeking the source of 'I' serves as a means of getting rid of all other thoughts. We should not give scope to other thoughts, such as you mention, but must keep the attention fixed on finding out the source of the 'I'-thought by asking, as each thought arises, to whom the thought arises. If the answer is 'I get the thought' continue the enquiry by asking 'Who is this "I" and what is its source?'[5]

Q: *Am I to keep on repeating 'Who am I?' so as to make a* mantra *of it?*

A: No. 'Who am I?' is not a *mantra*. It means that you must find out where in you arises the 'I'-thought which is the source of all other thoughts.[6]

Q: *Shall I meditate on 'I am* Brahman' *[aham Brahmasmi]?*

A: The text is not meant for thinking 'I am *Brahman*'. *Aham* ['I'] is known to every one. *Brahman* abides as *aham* in every one. Find out the 'I'. The 'I' is already *Brahman*. You need not think so. Simply find out the 'I'.

Q: *Is not discarding of the sheaths* [neti-neti] *mentioned in the* sastras?

A: After the rise of the 'I'-thought there is the false identification of the 'I' with the body, the senses, the mind, etc. 'I' is wrongly associated with them and the true 'I' is lost sight of. In order to sift the pure 'I' from the contaminated 'I', this discarding is mentioned. But it does not mean exactly discarding of the non-Self, it means the finding of the real Self. The real Self is the infinite 'I'. That 'I' is perfection. It is eternal. It has no origin and no end. The other 'I' is born and also dies. It is impermanent. See to whom the changing thoughts belong. They will be found to arise after the 'I'-thought. Hold the 'I'-thought and they subside. Trace back the source of the 'I'-thought. The Self alone will remain.

Q: *It is difficult to follow. I understand the theory. But what is the practice?*

A: The other methods are meant for those who cannot take to the investigation of the Self. Even to repeat *aham Brahmasmi* or think of it, a doer is necessary. Who is it? It is 'I'. Be that 'I'. It is the direct method. The other methods also will ultimately lead everyone to this method of the investigation of the Self.

Q: *I am aware of the 'I'. Yet my troubles are not ended.*

A: This 'I'-thought is not pure. It is contaminated with the association of the body and senses. See to whom the trouble is. It is to the 'I'-thought. Hold it. Then the other thoughts vanish.

Q: *Yes. How to do it? That is the whole trouble.*

A: Think 'I, I', and hold to that one thought to the exclusion of all others.[7]

Q: *Is not affirmation of God more effective than the quest, 'Who am I?' Affirmation is positive, whereas the other is negation. Moreover, it indicates separateness.*

A: So long as you seek to know how to realise, this advice is given to find your Self. Your seeking the method denotes your separateness.

Q: *Is it not better to say 'I am the supreme being' than ask 'Who am I?'*

A: Who affirms? There must be one to do it. Find that one.

Q: *Is not meditation better than investigation?*

A: Meditation implies mental imagery, whereas investigation is for the reality. The former is objective, whereas the latter is subjective.

Q: *There must be a scientific approach to this subject.*

A: To eschew unreality and seek the reality is scientific.

Q: *I mean there must be a gradual elimination, first of the mind, then of the intellect, then of the ego.*

A: The Self alone is real. All others are unreal. The mind and intellect do not remain apart from you.

The Bible says, 'Be still and know that I am God.' Stillness is the sole requisite for the realisation of the Self as God.[8]

Q: *Is* soham *[the affirmation 'I am he'] the same as 'Who am I?'*

A: *Aham* ['I'] alone is common to them. One is *soham*. The other is *koham* (Who am I?). They are different. Why should we go on saying *soham*? One must find out the real 'I'. In the question 'Who am I?', 'I' refers to the ego. Trying to trace it and find its source, we see it has no separate existence but merges in the real 'I'.[9]

You see the difficulty. *Vichara* is different in method from the meditation *sivoham* or *soham* ['I am Siva' or 'I am he']. I rather lay stress upon Self-knowledge, for you are first concerned with yourself before you proceed to know the world and its Lord. The *soham* meditation or 'I am *Brahman*' meditation is more or less a mental thought. But the quest for the Self I speak of is a direct method, indeed superior to the other meditation. The moment you start looking for the self and go deeper and deeper, the real Self is waiting there to take you in. Then whatever is done is done by something else and you have no hand in it. In this process, all doubts and discussions are automatically given up just as one who sleeps forgets, for the time being, all his cares.

Q: *What certainty is there that something else waits there to welcome me?*

A: When one is a sufficiently developed soul [*pakvi*] one becomes naturally convinced.

Q: *How is this development possible?*

A: Various answers are given. But whatever the previous development, *vichara* quickens the development.

Q: *That is arguing in a circle. I am developed and so I am suitable for the quest but the quest itself causes me to develop.*

A: The mind has always this sort of difficulty. It wants a certain theory to satisfy itself. Really, no theory is necessary for the man who seriously desires to approach God or to realise his own true being.[10]

Q: *No doubt the method taught by Bhagavan is direct. But it is so difficult. We do not know how to begin it. If we go on asking, 'Who am I?', 'Who am I?' like a* japa *[repetition of the name of God] or a mantra, it becomes dull. In other methods there is something preliminary and positive with which one can begin and then go step by step. But in Bhagavan's method, there is no such thing, and to seek the Self at once, though direct, is difficult.*

A: You yourself concede it is the direct method. It is the direct and easy method. When going after other things that are alien to us is so easy, how can it be difficult for one to go to one's own Self? You talk of 'Where to begin?' There is no beginning and no end. You are yourself in the beginning and the end. If you are here and the Self somewhere else, and you have to reach that Self, you may be told how to start, how to travel and then how to reach. Suppose you who are now in Ramanasramam ask, 'I want to go to Ramanasramam. How shall I start and how to reach it?', what is one to say? A man's search for the Self is like that. He is always the Self and nothing else. You say 'Who am I?' becomes a *japa*. It is not meant that you should go on asking 'Who am I?' In that case, thought will not so easily die. In the direct method, as you call it, in asking yourself 'Who am I?', you are told to concentrate within yourself where the 'I'-thought, the root of all other thoughts, arises. As the Self is not outside but inside you, you are asked to dive within, instead of going without. What can be more easy than going to yourself? But the fact remains that to some this method will seem difficult and will not appeal. That is why so many different methods have been taught. Each of them will appeal to some as the best and easiest. That is according to their *pakva* or fitness. But to some, nothing except the *vichara marga* [the path of enquiry] will appeal. They will ask, 'You want me to know or to see this or that. But who is the knower, the seer?' Whatever other method may be chosen, there will be always a doer. That cannot be escaped. One must find out who the doer is. Till then, the *sadhana* cannot be ended. So eventually, all must come to find out 'Who am I?' You complain that there is nothing preliminary or positive to start with. You have the 'I' to start with. You know you exist always, whereas the body does not exist always, for example in sleep. Sleep reveals that you exist even without a body. We identify the 'I' with a body, we regard the Self as having a body, and as having limits, and hence all our trouble. All that we have to do is to give up identifying the Self with the body, with forms and limits, and then we shall know ourselves as the Self that we always are.[11]

Q: *Am I to think 'Who am I?'*

A: You have known that the 'I'-thought springs forth. Hold the 'I'-thought and find its source.

Q: *May I know the way?*

A: Do as you have now been told and see.

Q: *I do not understand what I should do.*

A: If it is anything objective the way can be shown objectively. This is subjective.

Q: *But I do not understand.*

A: What! Do you not understand that you are?

Q: *Please tell me the way.*

A: Is it necessary to show the way in the interior of your own home? This is within you.[12]

Q: *You have said that the Heart is the centre of the Self.*

A: Yes, it is the one supreme centre of the Self. You need have no doubt about it. The real Self is there in the Heart behind the *jiva* or ego-self.

Q: *Now be pleased to tell me where it is in the body.*

A: You cannot know it with your mind. You cannot realise it by imagination, when I tell you here is the centre [pointing to the right side of the chest]. The only direct way to realise it is to cease to fantasise and try to be yourself. When you realise, you automatically feel that the centre is there.

This is the centre, the Heart, spoken of in the scriptures as *hritguha* [cavity of the heart], *arul* [grace], *ullam* [the Heart].

Q: *In no book have I found it stated that it is there.*

A: Long after I came here I chanced upon a verse in the Malayalam version of *Ashtangahridayam*, the standard work on *ayurveda* [Hindu medicine], wherein the *ojas sthana* [source of bodily vitality or place of light] is mentioned as being located in the right side of the chest and called the seat of consciousness [*samvit*]. But I know of no other work which refers to it as being located there.

Q: *Can I be sure that the ancients meant this centre by the term 'Heart'?*

A: Yes, that is so. But you should try to have rather than to locate the experience. A man need not find out where his eyes are situated when he wants to see. The Heart is there ever open to you if you care to enter it, ever supporting all your movements even when you are unaware. It is perhaps more proper to say that the Self is the Heart itself than to say that it is in the Heart. Really, the Self is the centre itself. It is everywhere, aware of itself as 'Heart', the Self-awareness.[13]

Q: *In that case, how can it be localised in any part of the body? Fixing a place for the Heart would imply setting physiological limitations to that which is beyond space and time.*

A: That is right. But the person who puts the question about the position of the Heart considers himself as existing with or in the body. While putting the question now, would you say that your body alone is here but you are speaking from somewhere else? No, you accept your bodily existence. It is from this point of view that any reference to a physical body comes to be made.

Truly speaking, pure consciousness is indivisible, it is without parts. It has no form and shape, no 'within' and 'without'. There is no 'right' or 'left' for it. Pure consciousness, which is the Heart, includes all, and nothing is outside or apart from it. That is the ultimate truth.

From this absolute standpoint, the Heart, Self or consciousness can have no particular place assigned to it in the physical body. What is the reason? The body is itself a mere projection of the mind, and the mind is but a poor reflection of the radiant Heart. How can that, in which everything is contained, be itself confined as a tiny part within the physical body which is but an infinitesimal, phenomenal manifestation of the one reality?

But people do not understand this. They cannot help thinking in terms of the physical body and the world. For instance, you say, 'I have come to this ashram all the way from my country beyond the Himalayas.' But that is not the truth. Where is 'coming' or 'going' or any movement whatever, for the one, all-pervading spirit which you really are? You are where you have always been. It is your body that moved or was conveyed from place to place till it reached this ashram. This is the simple truth, but to a person who considers himself a subject living in an objective world, it appears as something altogether visionary!

It is by coming down to the level of ordinary understanding that a place is assigned to the Heart in the physical body.

Q: *How then shall I understand Sri Bhagavan's statement that the experience of the Heart-centre is at the particular place in the chest?*

A: Once you accept that from the true and absolute standpoint, the Heart as pure consciousness is beyond space and time, it will be easy for you to understand the rest in its correct perspective.[14]

Q: *The Heart is said to be on the right, on the left, or in the centre. With such differences of opinion how are we to meditate on it?*

A: You are and it is a fact. *Dhyana* [meditation] is by you, of you, and in you. It must go on where you are. It cannot be outside you. So you are the centre of *dhyana* and that is the Heart.

Doubts arise only when you identify it with something tangible and physical. Heart is no conception, no object for meditation. But it is the seat of meditation. The Self remains all alone. You see the body in the Heart, the world is also in it. There is nothing separate from it. So all kinds of effort are located there only.[15]

Q: *You say the 'I'-thought rises from the Heart-centre. Should we seek its source there?*

A: I ask you to see where the 'I' arises in your body, but it is really not quite correct to say that the 'I' rises from and merges in the Heart in the right side of the chest. The Heart is another name for the reality and it is neither inside nor outside the body. There can be no in or out for it, since it alone is.[16]

Q: *Should I meditate on the right chest in order to meditate on the Heart?*

A: The Heart is not physical. Meditation should not be on the right or the left. Meditation should be on the Self. Everyone knows 'I am'. Who is the 'I'? It will be neither within nor without, neither on the right nor on the left. 'I am' – that is all.[17] Leave alone the idea of right and left. They pertain to the body. The Heart is the Self. Realise it and then you will see for yourself.[18] There is no need to know where and what the Heart is. It will do its work if you engage in the quest for the Self.[19]

Q: *What is the Heart referred to in the verse of* Upadesa Saram *where it is said, 'Abiding in the Heart is the best* karma, yoga, bhakti *and* jnana?'

A: That which is the source of all, that in which all live, and that into which all finally merge, is the Heart referred to.

Q: *How can we conceive of such a Heart?*

A: Why should you conceive of anything? You have only to see from where the 'I' springs.[20] That from which all thoughts of embodied beings issue forth is called the Heart. All descriptions of it are only mental concepts.[21]

Q: *There are said to be six organs of different colours in the chest, of which the Heart is said to be two finger-breadths to the right of the middle line.[22] But the Heart is also formless. Should we then imagine it to have a shape and meditate on it?*

A: No. Only the quest 'Who am I?' is necessary. What remains all through deep sleep and waking is the same. But in waking there is unhappiness and the effort to remove it. Asked who wakes up from sleep you say 'I'. Now you are told to hold fast to this 'I'. If it is done the eternal being will reveal itself. Investigation of 'I' is the point and not meditation on the Heart-centre. There is nothing like within or without. Both mean either the same thing or nothing.

Of course there is also the practice of meditation on the Heart-centre. It is only a practice and not investigation. Only the one who meditates on the Heart can remain aware when the mind ceases to be active and remains still, whereas those who meditate on other centres cannot be so aware but infer that the mind was still only after it becomes again active.[23]

In whatever place in the the body one thinks Self to be residing, due to the power of that thinking it will appear to the one who thinks thus as if Self is residing in that place. However, the beloved Heart alone is the refuge for the rising and subsiding of that 'I'. Know that though it is said that the Heart exists both inside and outside, in absolute truth it does not exist both inside and outside, because the body, which appears as the base of the differences 'inside' and 'outside', is an imagination of the thinking mind. Heart, the source, is the beginning, the middle and the end of all. Heart, the supreme space, is never a form. It is the light of truth.[24]

CHAPTER 7
Surrender

Many of the world's religious traditions advocate surrender to God as a means of transcending the individual self. Sri Ramana accepted the validity of such an approach and often said that this method was as effective as self-enquiry. Traditionally the path of surrender is associated with dualistic devotional practices, but such activities were only of secondary importance to Sri Ramana. Instead he stressed that true surrender transcended worshipping God in a subject – object relationship since it could only be successfully accomplished when the one who imagined that he was separate from God had ceased to exist. To achieve this goal he recommended two distinct practices:

1   Holding on to the 'I'-thought until the one who imagines that he is separate from God disappears.
2   Completely surrendering all responsibility for one's life to God or the Self. For such self-surrender to be effective one must have no will or desire of one' own and one must be completely free of the idea that there is an individual person who is capable of acting independently of God.

The first method is clearly self-enquiry masquerading under a different name. Sri Ramana often equated the practices of surrender and enquiry either by saying that they were different names for the same process or that they were the only two effective means by which Self-realisation could be achieved. This is quite consistent with his view that any practice which involved awareness of the 'I'-thought was a valid and direct route to the Self, whereas all practices which didn't were not.

This insistence on the subjective awareness of 'I' as the only means of reaching the Self coloured his attitude towards practices of devotion (*bhakti*) and worship which are usually associated with surrender to God. He never discouraged his devotees from following such practices, but he pointed out that any relationship with God (devotee, worshipper, servant, etc.) was an illusory one since God alone exists. True devotion, he said, is to remain as one really is, in the state of being in which all ideas about relationships with God have ceased to exist.

The second method, of surrendering responsibility for one's life to God, is also related to self-enquiry since it aims to eliminate the 'I'-thought by separating it from the objects and actions that it constantly identifies with. In following this practice there should be a constant awareness that there is no individual 'I' who acts or desires, that only the Self exists and that there is nothing apart from the Self that is capable of acting independently of it. When following this practice, whenever one becomes aware that one is assuming responsibility for thoughts and actions – for example, 'I want' or 'I am doing this' – one should try to withdraw the mind from its external contacts and fix it in the Self. This is analogous to the transfer of attention which takes place in self-enquiry when one realises that self-attention has been lost. In both cases the aim is to isolate the 'I'-thought and make it disappear in its source.

Sri Ramana himself admitted that spontaneous and complete surrender of the 'I' by this method was an impossible goal for many people and so he sometimes advised his followers to undertake preliminary exercises which would cultivate their devotion and control their minds. Most of these practices involved thinking of or meditating on God or the Guru either by constantly repeating his name (*japa*) or by visualising his form. He told his devotees that if this was done regularly with love and devotion then the mind would become effortlessly absorbed in the object of meditation.

Once this has been achieved complete surrender becomes much easier. The constant awareness of God prevents the mind from identifying with other objects and enhances the conviction that God alone exists. It also produces a reciprocal flow of power or grace from the Self which weakens the hold of the 'I'-thought and destroys the *vasanas* which perpetuate and reinforce its existence. Eventually the 'I'-thought is reduced to manageable proportions and with a little self-attention it can be made to sink temporarily into the Heart.

As with self-enquiry, final realisation is brought about automatically by the power of the Self. When all the outgoing tendencies of the mind have been dissolved in the repeated experiences of being, the Self destroys the vestigial 'I'-thought so

completely that it never rises again. This final destruction of the 'I'
takes place only if the self-surrender has been completely
motiveless. If it is done with a desire for grace or Self-realisation it
can never be more than partial surrender, a business transaction in
which the 'I'-thought makes an effort in the expectation of
receiving a reward.

Q: *What is unconditional surrender?*
A: If one surrenders oneself there will be no one to ask
questions or to be thought of. Either the thoughts are eliminated
by holding on to the root-thought 'I', or one surrenders oneself
unconditionally to the higher power. These are the only two ways
for realisation.[1]
Q: *Does not total or complete surrender require that one
should not have left even the desire for liberation or God?*
A: Complete surrender does require that you have no desire of
your own. You must be satisfied with whatever God gives you and
that means having no desires of your own.
Q: *Now that I am satisfied on that point, I want to know what
the steps are by which I could achieve surrender.*
A: There are two ways. One is looking into the source of 'I'
and merging into that source. The other is feeling 'I am helpless by
myself, God alone is all-powerful and except by throwing myself
completely on him, there is no other means of safety for me.' By
this method one gradually develops the conviction that God alone
exists and that the ego does not count. Both methods lead to the
same goal. Complete surrender is another name for *jnana* or
liberation.[2]
Q: *I find surrender is easier. I want to adopt that path.*
A: By whatever path you go, you will have to lose yourself in
the one. Surrender is complete only when you reach the stage
'Thou art all' and 'Thy will be done'.
The state is not different from *jnana*. In *soham* [the affirmation
of 'I am he'] there is *dvaita* [dualism]. In surrender there is *advaita*
[non-dualism]. In the reality there is neither *dvaita* nor *advaita*,
but that which is. Surrender appears easy because people imagine
that, once they say with their lips 'I surrender' and put their
burdens on their Lord, they can be free and do what they like. But
the fact is that you can have no likes or dislikes after your
surrender; your will should become completely non-existent, the

Lord's will taking its place. The death of the ego in this way brings about a state which is not different from *jnana*. So by whatever path you may go, you must come to *jnana* or oneness.[3]

Q: *What is the best way of killing the ego?*

A: To each person that way is the best which appears easiest or appeals most. All the ways are equally good, as they lead to the same goal, which is the merging of the ego in the Self. What the *bhakta* [devotee] calls surrender, the man who does *vichara* calls *jnana*. Both are trying only to take the ego back to the source from which it sprang and make it merge there.[4]

Q: *Cannot grace hasten such competence in a seeker?*

A: Leave it to God. Surrender unreservedly. One of two things must be done. Either surrender because you admit your inability and require a higher power to help you, or investigate the cause of misery by going to the source and merging into the Self. Either way you will be free from misery. God never forsakes one who has surrendered.

Q: *What is the drift of the mind after surrender?*

A: Is the surrendered mind raising the question?[5]

Q: *By constantly desiring to surrender I hope that increasing grace is experienced.*

A: Surrender once for all and be done with the desire. So long as the sense of doership is retained there is the desire. That is also personality. If this goes the Self is found to shine forth pure. The sense of doership is the bondage and not the actions themselves. 'Be still and know that I am God.' Here stillness is total surrender without a vestige of individuality. Stillness will prevail and there will be no agitation of mind. Agitation of mind is the cause of desire, the sense of doership and personality. If that is stopped there is quiet. There 'knowing' means 'being'. It is not the relative knowledge involving the triads, knowledge, knowing and known.

Q: *Is the thought 'I am God' or 'I am the supreme being' helpful?*

A: 'I am that I am.' 'I am' is God, not thinking 'I am God.' Realise 'I am' and do not think 'I am.' 'Know I am God,' it is said, and not 'Think I am God.'[6]

All talk of surrender is like pinching brown sugar from a brown sugar image of Lord Ganesa and offering it as *naivedya* [food offering] to the same Lord Ganesa. You say you offer your body, soul and all possessions to God. Were they yours that you could

offer them? At best, you can only say, 'I falsely imagined till now
that all these which are yours were mine. Now I realise they are
yours. I shall no more act as if they are mine.' This knowledge
that there is nothing but God or Self, that I and mine don't exist
and that only the Self exists, is *jnana*. Thus there is no difference
between *bhakti* and *jnana*. *Bhakti* is *jnana mata* or the mother of
jnana.[7]

Q: *Men of the world that we are, we have some kind of grief
or another and do not know how to get over it. We pray to God
and still are not satisfied. What can we do?*

A: Trust God.

Q: *We surrender; but still there is no help.*

A: Yes. If you have surrendered, you must be able to abide by
the will of God and not make a grievance of what may not please
you. Things may turn out differently from the way they look
apparently. Distress often leads men to faith in God.

Q: *But we are worldly. There is the wife, there are the
children, friends and relatives. We cannot ignore their existence
and resign ourselves to divine will, without retaining some little of
the personality in us.*

A: That means you have not surrendered as professed by you.
You must only trust God.[8]

Surrender to him and abide by his will whether he appears or
vanishes. Await his pleasure. If you ask him to do as you please, it
is not surrender but command to him. You cannot have him obey
you and yet think that you have surrendered. He knows what is
best and when and how to do it. Leave everything entirely to him.
His is the burden, you have no longer any cares. All your cares are
his. Such is surrender. This is *bhakti*.

Or, enquire to whom these questions arise. Dive deep in the
Heart and remain as the Self. One of these two ways is open to the
aspirant.[9]

Q: *Surrender is impossible.*

A: Yes. Complete surrender is impossible in the beginning.
Partial surrender is certainly possible for all. In course of time that
will lead to complete surrender. Well, if surrender is impossible,
what can be done? There is no peace of mind. You are helpless to
bring it about. It can be done only by surrender.[10]

Q: *Is surrender, by itself, sufficient to reach the Self?*

A: It is enough that one surrenders oneself. Surrender is to give
oneself up to the original cause of one's being. Do not delude

yourself by imagining such a source to be some God outside you. Your source is within yourself. Give yourself up to it. That means that you should seek the source and merge in it.[11]

Q: *[Given to Sri Ramana in the form of a written note.] They say that one can obtain everything if one takes refuge in God wholly and solely, and without thought of anything else. Does it mean sitting still in one place and contemplating God entirely at all times, discarding all thoughts, including even thoughts about food, which is essential for the sustenance of the body? Does it mean that when one gets ill, one should not think of medicine and treatment, but entrust one's health or sickness exclusively to providence?*

In the Bhagavad Gita *it says: 'The man who sheds all longing and moves without concern, free from the sense of "I" and "mine", he attains peace' (2:71). It means the discarding of all desires. Therefore should we devote ourselves exclusively to the contemplation of God, and accept food and water only if they are available by God's grace, without asking for them? Or does it mean that we should make a little effort? Bhagavan, please explain the secret of this* saranagati *[surrender].*

A: [After reading the note Sri Ramana addressed everyone in the room.] *Ananya saranagati* [complete surrender] means to be without any attachment to thoughts, no doubt, but does it mean to discard even thoughts of food and water which are essential for the sustenance of the physical body? He asks, 'Should I eat only if I get anything by God's direction, and without my asking for it? Or should I make a little effort?' All right. Let us take it that what we have to eat comes of its own accord. But even then, who is to eat? Suppose somebody puts it in our mouth, should we not swallow it at least? Is that not an effort? He asks, 'If I become sick, should I take medicine or should I keep quiet leaving my health and sickness in the hands of God?' In the book *Sadhana Panchakam* written by Sankara, it is stated that for treatment of the disease called hunger one should eat food received as alms. But then one must at least go out and beg for it. If all people close their eyes and sit still saying if the food comes we eat, how is the world to get on? Hence one must take things as they come in accordance with one's traditions, but one must be free from the feeling that one is doing them oneself. The feeling that I am doing it is the bondage. It is therefore necessary to consider and find out the method whereby such a feeling can be overcome, instead of

doubting as to whether medicine should be administered if one is
sick or whether food should be taken if one is hungry. Such
doubts will continue to come up and will never end. Even such
doubts as 'May I groan if there is pain? May I inhale air after
exhaling?' also occur. Call it *Iswara* [God] or call it *karma*
[destiny]; some *karta* [higher power] will carry on everything in
this world according to the development of the mind of each
individual. If the responsibility is thrown on the higher power
things will go on of their own accord. We walk on this ground.
While doing so, do we consider at every step whether we should
raise one leg after the other or stop at some stage? Isn't the
walking done automatically? The same is the case with inhaling
and exhaling. No special effort is made to inhale or exhale. The
same is the case with this life also. Can we give up anything if we
want to, or do anything as we please? Quite a number of things
are done automatically without our being conscious of it.
Complete surrender to God means giving up all thoughts and
concentrating the mind on him. If we can concentrate on him,
other thoughts disappear. If the actions of the mind, speech and
body are merged with God, all the burdens of our life will be on
him.[12]

Q: *But is God really the doer of all the actions I perform?*

A: The present difficulty is that man thinks he is the doer. But
it is a mistake. It is the higher power which does everything and
man is only a tool. If he accepts that position he is free from
troubles, otherwise he courts them. Take, for instance, the
sculpted figure at the base of a *gopuram* [temple tower], which is
made to appear as if it is bearing the burden of the tower on its
shoulder. Its posture and look are a picture of great strain which
gives the impression that it is bearing the weight of the tower. But
think. The tower is built on the earth and it rests on its
foundations. The figure is a part of the tower, but it is made to
look as if it is bearing the weight of the tower. Is it not funny? So
also is the man who takes on himself the sense of doing.[13]

Q: *Swami, it is good to love God, is it not? Then why not
follow the path of love?*

A: Who said you couldn't follow it? You can do so. But when
you talk of love, there is duality, is there not – the person who
loves and the entity called God who is loved? The individual is not
separate from God. Hence love means one has love towards one's
own Self.

Q: *That is why I am asking you whether God could be worshipped through the path of love.*

A: That is exactly what I have been saying. Love itself is the actual form of God. If by saying, 'I do not love this, I do not love that', you reject all things, that which remains is *swarupa*, that is the real form of the Self. That is pure bliss. Call it pure bliss, God, *atma*, or what you will. That is devotion, that is realisation and that is everything.

If you thus reject everything, what remains is the Self alone. That is real love. One who knows the secret of that love finds the world itself full of universal love.[14]

The experience of not forgetting consciousness alone is the state of devotion [*bhakti*] which is the relationship of unfading real love, because the real knowledge of Self, which shines as the undivided supreme bliss itself, surges up as the nature of love.

Only if one knows the truth of love, which is the real nature of Self, will the strong entangled knot of life be untied. Only if one attains the height of love will liberation be attained. Such is the heart of all religions. The experience of Self is only love, which is seeing only love, hearing only love, feeling only love, tasting only love and smelling only love, which is bliss.[15]

Q: *I long for* bhakti. *I want more of this longing. Even realisation does not matter for me. Let me be strong in my longing.*

A: If the longing is there, realisation will be forced on you even if you do not want it.[16] Long for it intensely so that the mind melts in devotion. After camphor burns away no residue is left. The mind is the camphor. When it has resolved itself into the Self without leaving even the slightest trace behind, it is realisation of the Self.[17]

Q: *I have faith in* murti dhyana [*worship of form*]. *Will it not help me to gain* jnana?

A: Surely it will. *Upasana* [meditation] helps concentration of mind. Then the mind is free from other thoughts and is full of the meditated form. The mind then becomes one with the object of meditation, and this makes it quite pure. Then think who is the worshipper. The answer is 'I', that is, the Self. In this way the Self is ultimately gained.[18]

Worshipping the formless reality by unthought thought is the best kind of worship. But when one is not fit for such formless worship of God, worship of form alone is suitable. Formless worship is possible only for people who are devoid of the ego-form. Know that all the worship done by people who possess the ego-form is only worship of form.

The pure state of being attached to grace [Self], which is devoid of any attachment, alone is one's own state of silence, which is devoid of any other thing. Know that one's ever abiding as that silence, having experienced it as it is, alone is true mental worship [*manasika-puja*]. Know that the performance of the unceasing, true and natural worship in which the mind is submissively established as the one Self, having installed the Lord on the Heart-throne, is silence, the best of all forms of worship. Silence, which is devoid of the assertive ego, alone is liberation. The evil forgetfulness of Self which causes one to slip down from that silence, alone is non-devotion [*vibhakti*]. Know that abiding as that silence with the mind subsided as non-different from Self, is the truth of Siva *bhakti* [devotion to God].

When one has completely surrendered oneself at the feet of Siva, thereby becoming of the nature of the Self, the resulting abundant peace, in which there is not even the least room within the Heart for one to make any complaint about one's defects and deficiencies, alone is the nature of supreme devotion. One's thus becoming a slave to the Lord and one's remaining quiet and silent, devoid even of the egotistical thought 'I am his slave', is Self-abidance, and this is the supreme knowledge.[19]

Q: *Can spiritual seekers attain this goal in life if they go about the world absorbed in singing songs in praise of God? Or should they stay at one place only?*

A: It is good to keep the mind concentrated on one thing only wherever the person wanders. What is the use of keeping the body at one place if the mind is allowed to wander?

Q: *Is* ahetuka bhakti *[devotion without a motive] possible?*

A: Yes it is possible.[20] Worshipping God for the sake of a desired object is worshipping that desired object alone. The complete cessation of any thought of a desired object is the first prerequisite in a mind which wishes to attain the state of Siva.[21]

Q: Sri Bhagavatam *outlines a way to find Krishna in the Heart by prostrating to all and looking on all as the Lord himself. Is this the right path leading to Self-realisation? Is it not easier to adore Bhagavan in whatever meets the mind, than to seek the supramental through the mental enquiry 'Who am I?'*

A: Yes, when you see God in all, do you think of God or do

you not? You must certainly think of God if you want to see God all round you. Keeping God in your mind in this way becomes *dhyana* [meditation] and *dhyana* is the stage before realisation. Realisation can only be in and of the Self. It can never be apart from the Self. *Dhyana* must precede realisation, but whether you make *dhyana* on God or on the Self is immaterial, for the goal is the same. You cannot, by any means, escape the Self. You want to see God in all, but not in yourself? If everything is God, are you not included in that everything? Being God yourself, is it a wonder that all is God? This is the method advised in *Sri Bhagavatam*, and elsewhere by others. But even for this practice there must be the seer or thinker. Who is he?

Q: *How to see God who is all-pervasive?*

A: To see God is to be God. There is no all apart from God for him to pervade. He alone is.[22]

Q: *The* bhakta *requires a God to whom he can do* bhakti. *Is he to be taught that there is only the Self, not a worshipper and the worshipped?*

A: Of course, God is required for *sadhana*. But the end of the *sadhana*, even in *bhakti marga* [the path of devotion], is attained only after complete surrender. What does it mean, except that effacement of the ego results in Self remaining as it always has been? Whatever path one may choose, the 'I' is inescapable, the 'I' that does the *nishkama karma* [motiveless acts], the 'I' that pines for joining the Lord from whom it feels it has been separated, the 'I' that feels it has slipped from its real nature, and so on. The source of this 'I' must be found out. Then all questions will be solved.[23]

Q: *If 'I' also is an illusion, who then casts off the illusion?*

A: The 'I' casts off the illusion of 'I' and yet remains as 'I'. Such is the paradox of Self-realisation. The realised do not see any contradiction in it. Take the case of *bhakti*. I approach *Iswara* and pray to be absorbed in him. I then surrender myself with faith and concentrate on him. What remains afterwards? In place of the original 'I', perfect self-surrender leaves a residuum of God in which the 'I' is lost. This is the highest form of devotion [*parabhakti*] and surrender and the height of *vairagya* [non-attachment].

You give up this and that of 'my' possessions. If you give up 'I' and 'mine' instead, all are given up at a stroke. The very seed of possession is lost. Thus the evil is nipped in the bud or crushed in the germ itself. Dispassion [*vairagya*] must be very strong to do this. Eagerness to do it must be equal to that of a man kept under water trying to rise up to the surface for his life.[24]

PART THREE

The Guru

God and Guru are in truth not different. Just as the prey that has fallen into the jaws of a tiger cannot escape, so those who have come under the glance of the Guru's grace will surely be saved and will never be forsaken; yet one should follow without fail the path shown by the Guru.[1]

From Bhagavan's point of view there are no disciples but from the point of view of the disciple the grace of the Guru is like an ocean. If he comes with a cup he will only get a cupful. It is no use complaining of the niggardliness of the ocean; the bigger the vessel the more he will be able to carry. It is entirely up to him.[2]

One method of securing the temporary cessation of mental activities is association with sages. They are adepts in *samadhi* and it has become easy, natural and perpetual with them. Those moving with them closely, and in sympathetic contact, gradually absorb the *samadhi* habit from them.[3]

CHAPTER 8
The Guru

The term Guru is often loosely used to describe anyone who gives out spiritual advice, but in Sri Ramana's vocabulary the word has a much more restricted definition. For him, a true Guru is someone who has realised the Self and who is able to use his power to assist others towards the goal of Self-realisation.

Sri Ramana often said that God, Guru and the Self are identical; the Guru is God in human form and, simultaneously, he is also the Self in the Heart of each devotee. Because he is both inside and outside, his power works in two different ways. The outer Guru gives instructions and by his power enables the devotee to keep his attention on the Self; the inner Guru pulls the devotee's mind back to its source, absorbs it in the Self and finally destroys it.

It is a basic tenet of Sri Ramana's teaching that a Guru is necessary for almost everyone who is striving towards a permanent awareness of the Self. The catalytic role of the Guru in spiritual development is therefore crucial; except in rare instances, ignorance of the Self is so deeply rooted that individual seekers are unable to escape from it by their own efforts.

Although Sri Ramana taught that a Guru is indispensable for those seeking Self-realisation, he also pointed out that the Guru has no power to bring about realisation in those who are not energetically seeking it. If the individual seeker makes a serious attempt to discover the Self, then the grace and power of the Guru will automatically start to flow. If no such attempt is made, the Guru is helpless.

The conversations in this chapter summarise Sri Ramana's views on the nature of the Guru and the role he plays in bringing about realisation of the Self. The distinctive way in which Sri Ramana utilised his own power will be explored in greater detail in chapter nine.

Q: *What is Guru's grace? How does it lead to Self-realisation?*

A: Guru is the Self. Sometimes in his life a man becomes dissatisfied and, not content with what he has, he seeks the satisfaction of his desires through prayer to God. His mind is gradually purified until he longs to know God, more to obtain his grace than to satisfy his worldly desires. Then, God's grace begins to manifest. God takes the form of a Guru and appears to the devotee, teaches him the truth and, moreover, purifies his mind by association. The devotee's mind gains strength and is then able to turn inward. By meditation it is further purified and it remains still without the least ripple. That calm expanse is the Self.

The Guru is both external and internal. From the exterior he gives a push to the mind to turn it inwards. From the interior he pulls the mind towards the Self and helps in the quietening of the mind. That is Guru's grace. There is no difference between God, Guru and the Self.

Q: *In the Theosophical Society they meditate in order to seek masters to guide them.*

A: The master is within; meditation is meant to remove the ignorant idea that he is only outside. If he is a stranger whom you await, he is bound to disappear also. What is the use of a transient being like that? But so long as you think you are separate or that you are the body, an external master is also necessary and he will appear to have a body. When the wrong identification of oneself with the body ceases, the master will be found to be none other than the Self.

Q: *Will the Guru help us to know the Self through initiation?*

A: Does the Guru hold you by the hand and whisper in the ear? You may imagine him to be what you are yourself. Because you think you are with a body, you think he also has a body and that he will do something tangible to you. His work lies within, in the spiritual realm.

Q: *How is the Guru found?*

A: God, who is immanent, in his grace takes pity on the loving devotee and manifests himself according to the devotee's development. The devotee thinks that he is a man and expects a relationship between two physical bodies. But the Guru who is God or the Self incarnate works from within, helps the man to see the error of his ways and guides him on the right path until he realises the Self within.[1]

Q: *What are the marks of a real teacher* [sadguru]?

A: Steady abidance in the Self, looking at all with an equal eye unshakeable courage at all times, in all places and circumstances.[2]

Q: *There are a number of spiritual teachers teaching various paths. Whom should one take for one's Guru?*

A: Choose that one where you find you get *shanti* [peace].[3]

Q: *Should we not also consider his teachings?*

A: He who instructs an ardent seeker to do this or that is not a true master. The seeker is already afflicted by his activities and wants peace and rest. In other words he wants cessation of his activities. If a teacher tells him to do something in addition to, or in place of, his other activities, can that be a help to the seeker?

Activity is creation. Activity is the destruction of one's inherent happiness. If activity is advocated the adviser is not a master but a killer. In such circumstances either the creator [Brahma] or death [Yama] may be said to have come in the guise of a master. Such a person cannot liberate the aspirant, he can only strengthen his fetters.[4]

Q: *How can I find my own Guru?*

A: By intense meditation.[5]

Q: *If it is true that the Guru is one's own Self, what is the principle underlying the doctrine which says that, however learned a disciple may be or whatever occult powers he may possess, he cannot attain Self-realisation without the grace of the Guru?*

A: Although in absolute truth the state of the Guru is that of oneself [the Self], it is very hard for the self which has become the individual [*jiva*] through ignorance to realise its true state or nature without the grace of the Guru.

Q: *What are the marks of the Guru's grace?*

A: It is beyond words or thoughts.

Q: *If that is so, how is it that it is said that the disciple realises his true state by the Guru's grace?*

A: It is like the elephant which wakes up on seeing a lion in its dream. Even as the elephant wakes up at the mere sight of the lion, so too is it certain that the disciple wakes up from the sleep of ignorance into the wakefulness of true knowledge through the Guru's benevolent look of grace.

Q: *What is the significance of the saying that the nature of the real Guru is that of the supreme Lord [sarvesvara]?*

A: First, the individual soul which desires to attain the state of Godhood, or the state of true knowledge, practises incessant devotion. When the individual's devotion has reached a mature stage, the Lord, who is the witness of that individual soul and identical with it, manifests. He appears in human form with the help of *sat-chit-ananda*, his three natural features, and form and name which he also graciously assumes. In the guise of blessing the disciple he absorbs him in himself. According to this doctrine the Guru can truly be called the Lord.

Q: *How then did some great persons attain knowledge without a Guru?*

A: To a few mature persons the Lord shines as the formless light of knowledge and imparts awareness of the truth.[6]

Q: *How is one to decide upon a proper Guru? What is the* swarupa *[nature or real form] of a Guru?*

A: He is the proper Guru to whom your mind is attuned. If you ask, 'How to decide who is the Guru and what is his *swarupa*?', he should be endowed with tranquillity, patience, forgiveness and other virtues; he should be capable of attracting others even with his eyes just as a magnet attracts iron; he should have a feeling of equality towards all. He who has these virtues is the true Guru, but if one wants to know the *swarupa* of the Guru, one must know one's own *swarupa* first. How can one know the real nature of the Guru if one does not know one's own real nature first? If you want to perceive the real nature or form of the Guru you must first learn to look upon the whole universe as *Guru rupam* [the form of the Guru]. One must see the Guru in all living beings. It is the same with God. You must look upon all objects as God's *rupa* [form]. How can he who does not know his own Self perceive the real form of God or the real form of the Guru? How can he determine them? Therefore, first of all know your own real form and nature.

Q: *Isn't a Guru necessary to know even that?*

A: That is true. The world contains many great men. Look upon him as your Guru with whom your mind gets attuned. The one in whom you have faith is your Guru.[7]

Q: *What is the significance of Guru's grace in the attainment of liberation?*

A: Liberation is not anywhere outside you. It is only within. If a man is anxious for deliverance, the internal Guru pulls him in and the external Guru pushes him into the Self. This is the grace of the Guru.[8]

Q: *Some people reported you to have said that there was no need for a Guru. Others gave the opposite report. What does Maharshi say?*

A: I have never said that there is no need for a Guru.

Q: *Sri Aurobindo and others refer to you as having had no Guru.*

A: It all depends on what you call a Guru. He need not be in a human form. Dattatreya had twenty-four Gurus including the five elements — earth, water, etc. Every object in this world was his Guru.

The Guru is absolutely necessary. The *Upanishads* say that none but a Guru can take a man out of the jungle of intellect and sense-perceptions. So there must be a Guru.

Q: *I mean a human Guru — Maharshi did not have one.*

A: I might have had one at one time or other. But did I not sing hymns to Arunachala?[9] What is a Guru? Guru is God or the Self. First a man prays to God to fulfil his desires. A time comes when he will no more pray for the fulfilment of material desires but for God himself. God then appears to him in some form or other, human or non-human, to guide him to himself in answer to his prayer and according to his needs.[10]

Q: *When loyal to one Master can you respect others?*

A: Guru is only one. He is not physical. So long as there is weakness the support of strength is needed.

Q: *J. Krishnamurti says, 'No Guru is necessary.'*

A: How did he know it? One can say so after realising but not before.[11]

Q: *Can Sri Bhagavan help us to realise the truth?*

A: Help is always there.

Q: *Then there is no need to ask questions. I do not feel the ever-present help.*

A: Surrender and you will find it.

Q: *I am always at your feet. Will Bhagavan give us some upadesa [teaching] to follow? Otherwise how can I get help living 600 miles away?*

A: The *sadguru* [the Guru who is one with being] is within.

Q: Sadguru *is necessary to guide me to understand it.*

A: The *sadguru* is within.

Q: *I want a visible Guru.*

A: That visible Guru says that he is within.[12]

Q: *Is success not dependent on the Guru's grace?*

A: Yes, it is. Is not your practice itself due to such grace? The fruits are the result of the practice and follow it automatically. There is a stanza in *Kaivalya* which says, 'O Guru! You have been always with me, watching me through several reincarnations, and ordaining my course until I was liberated.' The Self manifests externally as the Guru when the occasion arises, otherwise he is always within, doing what is necessary.[13]

Q: *Some disciples of Shirdi Sai Baba worship a picture of him and say that it is their Guru. How could that be? They can worship it as God, but what benefit could they get by worshipping it as their Guru?*

A: They secure concentration by that.

Q: *That is all very well, I agree. It may be to some extent an exercise in concentration. But isn't a Guru required for that concentration?*

A: Certainly, but after all, Guru only means *guri*, concentration.

Q: *How can a lifeless picture help in developing deep concentration? It requires a living Guru who could show it in practice. It is possible perhaps for Bhagavan to attain perfection without a living Guru, but is it possible for people like myself?*

A: That is true. Even so, by worshipping a lifeless portrait, the mind gets concentrated to a certain extent. That concentration will not remain constant unless one knows one's own Self by enquiring. For that enquiry, a Guru's help is necessary.[14]

Q: *It is said that the Guru can make his disciple realise the Self by transmitting some of his own power to him? Is it true?*

A: Yes. The Guru does not bring about Self-realisation. He simply removes the obstacles to it. The Self is always realised.

Q: *Is it absolutely necessary to have a Guru if one is seeking Self-realisation?*

A: So long as you seek Self-realisation the Guru is necessary. Guru is the Self. Take Guru to be the real Self and your self as the individual self. The disappearance of this sense of duality is the removal of ignorance. So long as duality persists in you the Guru is necessary. Because you identify yourself with the body you think that the Guru is also a body. You are not the body, nor is the Guru. You are the Self and so is the Guru. This knowledge is gained by what you call Self-realisation.

Q: *How can one know whether a particular individual is competent to be a Guru?*

A: By the peace of mind found in his presence and by the sense of respect you feel for him.

Q: *If the Guru happens to turn out incompetent, what will be the fate of the disciple who has implicit faith in him?*

A: Each one according to his merits.[15]

Q: *May I have Guru's grace?*

A: Grace is always there.

Q: *But I do not feel it.*

A: Surrender will make one understand the grace.

Q: *I have surrendered heart and soul. I am the best judge of my heart. Still I do not feel the grace.*

A: If you had surrendered the questions would not arise.

Q: *I have surrendered. Still the questions arise.*

A: Grace is constant. Your judgment is the variable. Where else should the fault lie?[16]

Q: *May one have more than one spiritual master?*

A: Who is a master? He is the Self after all. According to the stages of development of the mind the Self manifests as the master externally. The famous ancient saint Dattatreya said that he had more than twenty-four masters. The master is one from whom one learns anything. The Guru may be sometimes inanimate also, as in the case of Dattatreya. God, Guru and the Self are identical.

A spiritually-minded man thinks that God is all-pervading and takes God for his Guru. Later, God brings him in contact with a personal Guru and the man recognises him as all in all. Lastly the same man is made by the grace of the master to feel that his Self is the reality and nothing else. Thus he finds that the Self is the master.[17]

Q: *It is said in* Srimad Bhagavad Gita: *'Realise the Self with pure intellect and also by service to the Guru and by enquiry.' How are they to be reconciled?*

A: *'Iswaro Gururatmeti'* – Iswara, Guru and Self are identical. So long as the sense of duality persists in you, you seek a Guru, thinking that he is different from you. However, he teaches you the truth and you gain the insight.[18]

He who bestows the supreme knowledge of Self upon the soul by making it face towards Self, alone is the supreme Guru who is praised by sages as the form of God, who is Self. Cling to him. By approaching the Guru and serving him faithfully one should learn through his grace the cause of one's birth and one's suffering. Knowing then that these are due to one's straying from Self, it is best to abide firmly as Self.

Although those who have embraced and are steadfastly

following the path to salvation may at times happen to swerve from the Vedic path either due to forgetfulness or due to some other reasons, know that they should not at any time go against the words of the Guru. The words of sages assure that if one does a wrong to God, it can be rectified by the Guru, but that a wrong done to a Guru cannot be rectified even by God.

For one who, due to rare, intense and abundant love, has complete faith in the glance of grace bestowed by the Guru, there will be no suffering and he will live in this world like Puruhuta [a name of Indra, the king of the gods].

Peace, the one thing which is desired by everyone, cannot be attained in any way, by anyone, at any time or in any place, unless stillness of mind is obtained through the grace of the *sadguru*. Therefore always seek that grace with a one-pointed mind.[19]

Q: *There are disciples of Bhagavan who have had his grace and realised without any considerable difficulty. I too wish to have that grace. Being a woman and living at a long distance I cannot avail myself of Maharshi's holy company as much as I would wish and as often as I would. Possibly I may not be able to return. I request Bhagavan's grace. When I am back in my place, I want to remember Bhavagan. May Bhagavan be pleased to grant my prayer.*

A: Where are you going? You are not going anywhere. Even supposing you are the body, has your body come from Lucknow to Tiruvannamalai? You simply sat in the car and one conveyance or another moved. And finally you say that you have come here. The fact is that you are not the body. The Self does not move, the world moves in it. You are only what you are. There is no change in you. So then, even after what looks like departure from here, you are here and there and everywhere. These scenes shift.

As for grace, grace is within you. If it is external it is useless. Grace is the Self. You are never out of its operation. Grace is always there.

Q: *I mean that when I remember your form, my mind should be strengthened and a response should come from your side too. I should not be left to my individual efforts which are after all only weak.*

A: Grace is the Self. I have already said, if you remember Bhagavan, you are prompted to do so by the Self. Is not grace already there? Is there a moment when grace is not operating in you? Your remembrance is the forerunner of grace. That is the response, that is the stimulus, that is the Self and that is grace. There is no cause for anxiety.[20]

Q: *Can I dispense with outside help and by my own effort get to the deeper truth by myself?*

A: The very fact that you are possessed of the quest for the Self is a manifestation of the divine grace. It is effulgent in the Heart, the inner being, the real Self. It draws you from within. You have to attempt to get in from outside. Your attempt is the earnest quest, the deep inner movement is grace. That is why I say there is no real quest without grace, nor is there grace active for him who does not seek the Self. Both are necessary.[21]

Q: *How long is a Guru necessary for Self-realisation?*

A: Guru is necessary so long as there is ignorance. Ignorance is due to the self-imposed but wrong limitation of the Self. God, on being worshipped, bestows steadiness in devotion which leads to surrender. On the devotee surrendering, God shows his mercy by manifesting as the Guru. The Guru, otherwise God, guides the devotee, saying that God is within and that he is not different from the Self. This leads to introversion of mind and finally to realisation.

Q: *If grace is so important, what is the role of individual effort?*

A: Effort is necessary up to the state of realisation. Even then the Self should spontaneously become evident, otherwise happiness will not be complete. Up to that state of spontaneity there must be effort in some form or another.[22]

There is a state beyond our efforts or effortlessness. Until it is realised effort is necessary. After tasting such bliss, even once, one will repeatedly try to regain it. Having once experienced the bliss of peace no one wants to be out of it or to engage in any other activity.[23]

Q: *Is divine grace necessary for attaining realisation, or can an individual's honest efforts by themselves lead to the state from which there is no return to life and death?*

A: Divine grace is essential for realisation. It leads one to God realisation. But such grace is vouchsafed only to him who is a true devotee or a yogi. It is given only to those who have striven hard and ceaselessly on the path towards freedom.[24]

Q: *Does distance have any effect upon grace?*

A: Time and space are within us. You are always in your Self. How do time and space affect it?

Q: *On the radio those who are nearer hear sooner. You are Hindu, we are American. Does it make any difference?*

A: No.

Q: *Even thoughts are read by others.*

A: That shows that all are one.[25]

Q: *Does Bhagavan feel for us and show grace?*

A: You are neck-deep in water and yet cry for water. It is as good as saying that one neck-deep in water feels thirsty, or that a fish in water feels thirsty, or that water feels thirsty.[26]

Grace is always there. 'Dispassion cannot be acquired, nor realisation of the truth, nor inherence in the Self, in the absence of Guru's grace'.

But practice is also necessary. Staying in the Self by one's efforts is like training a roguish bull confined to his stall by tempting him with luscious grass and preventing him from straying.[27]

Q: *I have recently come across a Tamil song in which the author laments he is not like the tenacious young monkey that can hold on to its mother tightly, but rather like a puling kitten that must be carried by the neck in its mother's jaws. The author therefore prays to God to take care of him. My case is exactly the same. You must take pity on me Bhagavan. Hold me by the neck and see that I don't fall and get injured.*

A: That is impossible. It is necessary both for you to strive and for the Guru to help.[28]

Q: *How long will it take for one to get the grace of the Guru?*

A: Why do you desire to know?

Q: *To give me hope.*

A: Even such a desire is an obstacle. The Self is ever there, there is nothing without it. Be the Self and the desires and doubts will disappear.[29]

Grace is the beginning, middle and end. Grace is the Self. Because of the false identification of the Self with the body the Guru is considered to be a body. But from the Guru's outlook the Guru is only the Self. The Self is one only and the Guru tells you that the Self alone is. Is not then the Self your Guru? Where else will grace come from? It is from the Self alone. Manifestation of the Self is a manifestation of grace and vice versa. All these doubts arise because of the wrong outlook and consequent expectation of things external to oneself. Nothing is external to the Self.[30]

CHAPTER 9
Silence and sat-sanga

Although Sri Ramana was happy to give his verbal teachings to anyone who asked for them, he frequently pointed out that his 'silent teachings' were more direct and more powerful. These 'silent teachings' consisted of a spiritual force which seemed to emanate from his form, a force so powerful that he considered it to be the most direct and important aspect of his teachings. Instead of giving out verbal instructions on how to control the mind, he effortlessly emitted a silent power which automatically quietened the minds of everyone in his vicinity. The people who were attuned to this force report that they experienced it as a state of inner peace and well-being; in some advanced devotees it even precipitated a direct experience of the Self.

This method of teaching has a long tradition in India, its most famous exponent being Dakshinamurti, a manifestation of Siva who brought four learned sages to an experience of the Self through the power of his silence. Sri Ramana frequently spoke of Dakshinamurti with great approval and his name crops up in many of the conversations in this chapter.

This flow of power from the Guru can be received by anyone whose attention is focused on the Self or on the form of the Guru; distance is no impediment to its efficacy. This attention is often called *sat-sanga*, which literally means 'association with being'. Sri Ramana wholeheartedly encouraged this practice and frequently said that it was the most efficient way of bringing about a direct experience of the Self. Traditionally it involves being in the physical presence of one who has realised the Self, but Sri Ramana gave it a much wider definition. He said that the most important element in *sat-sanga* was the mental connection with the Guru; *sat-sanga* takes place not only in his presence but whenever and wherever one thinks of him.

The following quotation gives an indication of the power of *sat-sanga*. It consists of five stray Sanskrit verses which Sri Ramana came across at various times. He was so impressed by their contents that he translated them into Tamil and incorporated them in *Ulladu Narpadu Anubandham*, one of his own written works which deals with the nature of reality.

1   By *sat-sanga* the association with the objects of the world will be removed. When that worldly association is removed the attachment or tendencies of the mind will be destroyed. Those who are devoid of mental attachment will perish in that which is motionless. Thus they attain *jivan mukti* [liberation]. Cherish their association.

2   The supreme state which is praised and which is attained here in this life by clear *vichara*, which arises in the Heart when association with a *sadhu* [a noble person, or one who has realised the Self] is gained, is impossible to attain by listening to preachers, by studying and learning the meaning of the scriptures, by virtuous deeds or by any other means.

3   If one gains association with *sadhus*, of what use are all the religious observances [*niyamas*]? When the excellent cool southern breeze itself is blowing, what is the use of holding a hand-fan?

4   Heat will be removed by the cool moon, poverty by the celestial wish-fulfilling tree and sin by the Ganges. But know that all these, beginning with heat, will be removed merely by having the *darshan* [sight] of incomparable *sadhus*.

5   Sacred bathing places, which are composed of water, and images of deities, which are made of stone and earth, cannot be comparable to those great souls [*mahatmas*]. Ah, what a wonder! The bathing places and deities bestow purity of mind after countless days, whereas such purity is instantly bestowed upon people as soon as *sadhus* see them with their eyes.[1]

Q: *Why does not Bhagavan go about and preach the truth to the people at large?*
A: How do you know I am not doing it? Does preaching consist in mounting a platform and haranguing the people around? Preaching is simple communication of knowledge; it can really be done in silence only. What do you think of a man who

listens to a sermon for an hour and goes away without having been impressed by it so as to change his life? Compare him with another, who sits in a holy presence and goes away after some time with his outlook on life totally changed. Which is the better, to preach loudly without effect or to sit silently sending out inner force?

Again, how does speech arise? First there is abstract knowledge. Out of this arises the ego, which in turn gives rise to thought, and thought to the spoken word. So the word is the great-grandson of the original source. If the word can produce an effect, judge for yourself, how much more powerful must be the preaching through silence.[2]

Q: *How can silence be so powerful?*

A: A realised one sends out waves of spiritual influence which draw many people towards him. Yet he may sit in a cave and maintain complete silence. We may listen to lectures upon truth and come away with hardly any grasp of the subject, but to come into contact with a realised one, though he speaks nothing, will give much more grasp of the subject. He never needs to go out among the public. If necessary he can use others as instruments.[3]

The Guru is the bestower of silence who reveals the light of Self-knowledge which shines as the residual reality. Spoken words are of no use whatsoever if the eyes of the Guru meet the eyes of the disciple.[4]

Q: *Does Bhagavan give* diksha *[initiation]?*

A: *Mouna* [silence] is the best and the most potent *diksha*. That was practised by Sri Dakshinamurti. Initiation by touch, look, etc., are all of a lower order. Silent initiation changes the hearts of all.[5]

Dakshinamurti observed silence when the disciples approached him. That is the highest form of initiation. It includes the other forms. There must be subject–object relationship established in the other *dikshas*. First the subject must emanate and then the object. Unless these two are there how is the one to look at the other or touch him? *Mouna diksha* is the most perfect; it comprises looking, touching and teaching. It will purify the individual in every way and establish him in the reality.[6]

Q: *Swami Vivekananda says that a spiritual Guru can transfer spirituality substantially to the disciple.*

A: Is there a substance to be transferred? Transfer means eradication of the sense of being the disciple. The master does it.

Not that the man was something at one time and metamorphosed later into another.

Q: *Is not grace the gift of the Guru?*

A: God, grace and Guru are all synonymous and also eternal and immanent. Is not the Self already within? Is it for the Guru to bestow it by his look? If a Guru thinks so, he does not deserve the name.

The books say that there are so many kinds of *diksha*, initiation by hand, by touch, by eye, etc. They also say that the Guru makes some rites with fire, water, *japa* or *mantras* and calls such fantastic performances *dikshas*, as if the disciple becomes ripe only after such processes are gone through by the Guru.

If the individual is sought he is nowhere to be found. Such is the Guru. Such is Dakshinamurti. What did he do? He was silent when the disciples appeared before him. He maintained silence and the doubts of the disciples were dispelled, which means that they lost their individual identities. That is *jnana* and not all the verbiage usually associated with it.

Silence is the most potent form of work. However vast and emphatic the *sastras* may be they fail in their effect. The Guru is quiet and peace prevails in all. His silence is more vast and more emphatic than all the *sastras* put together. These questions arise because of the feeling that, having been here so long, heard so much, exerted so hard, one has not gained anything. The work proceeding within is not apparent. In fact the Guru is always within you.[7]

Q: *Can the Guru's silence really bring about advanced states of spiritual awareness?*

A: There is an old story which demonstrates the power of the Guru's silence. Tattvaraya composed a *bharani*, a kind of poetic composition in Tamil, in honour of his Guru Swarupananda, and convened an assembly of learned pandits to hear the work and assess its value. The pandits raised the objection that a *bharani* was only composed in honour of great heroes capable of killing a thousand elephants in battle and that it was not in order to compose such a work in honour of an ascetic. Thereupon the author said, 'Let us all go to my Guru and we shall have this matter settled there.' They went to the Guru and, after they had all taken their seats, the author told his Guru the purpose of their visit. The Guru sat silent and all the others also remained in *mouna*. The whole day passed, the night came, and some more days and nights, and yet all sat there silently, no thought at all occurring to any of them and nobody thinking or asking why they had come there. After three or four days like this, the Guru moved his mind a bit, and the people assembled immediately regained their thought activity. They then declared, 'Conquering a thousand elephants is nothing beside this Guru's power to conquer the rutting elephants of all our egos put together. So certainly he deserves the *bharani* in his honour!'[8]

Q: *How does this silent power work?*

A: Language is only a medium for communicating one's thoughts to another. It is called in only after thoughts arise. Other thoughts arise after the 'I'-thought rises and so the 'I'-thought is the root of all conversation. When one remains without thinking one understands another by means of the universal language of silence.

Silence is ever-speaking. It is a perennial flow of language which is interrupted by speaking. These words I am speaking obstruct that mute language. For example, there is electricity flowing in a wire. With resistance to its passage, it glows as a lamp or revolves as a fan. In the wire it remains as electric energy. Similarly also, silence is the eternal flow of language, obstructed by words.

What one fails to know by conversation extending to several years can be known instantly in silence, or in front of silence – Dakshinamurti and his four disciples are a good example of this. This is the highest and most effective language.[9]

Q: *Bhagavan says, 'The influence of the* jnani *steals into the devotee in silence.' Bhagavan also says, 'Contact with great men* [mahatmas] *is one efficacious means of realising one's true being.'*

A: Yes. What is the contradiction? *Jnani*, great men, *mahatmas* – do you differentiate between them?

Q: *No.*

A: Contact with them is good. They will work through silence. By speaking their power is reduced. Silence is most powerful. Speech is always less powerful than silence, so mental contact is the best.

Q: *Does this hold good even after the dissolution of the physical body of the* jnani *or is it true only so long as he is in flesh and blood?*

A: Guru is not the physical form. So the contact will remain even after the physical form of the Guru vanishes. One can go to

another Guru after one's Guru passes away, but all Gurus are one
and none of them is the form you see. Always mental contact is
the best.[10]

Q: *Is the operation of grace the mind of the Guru acting on
the mind of the disciple or is it a different process?*

A: The highest form of grace is silence. It is also the highest
upadesa [teaching].

Q: *Vivekananda has also said that silence is the loudest form
of prayer.*

A: It is so for the seeker's silence. The Guru's silence is the
loudest *upadesa*. It is also grace in its highest form. All other
dikshas [initiations] are derived from *mouna*, and are therefore
secondary. *Mouna* is the primary form. If the Guru is silent the
seeker's mind gets purified by itself.[11]

Q: *Sri Bhagavan's silence is itself a powerful force. It brings
about a certain peace of mind in us.*

A: Silence is never-ending speech. Vocal speech obstructs the
other speech of silence. In silence one is in intimate contact with
the surroundings. The silence of Dakshinamurti removed the
doubts of the four sages. *Mouna vyakhya prakatita tattvam* means
the truth expounded by silence. Silence is said to be exposition.
Silence is so potent.

For vocal speech, organs of speech are necessary and they
precede speech. But the other speech lies even beyond thought. It
is in short transcendent speech or unspoken words [*para vak*].[12]

Q: *Can everyone benefit from this silence?*

A: Silence is the true *upadesa*. It is the perfect *upadesa*. It is
suited only for the most advanced seeker. The others are unable to
draw full inspiration from it. Therefore they require words to
explain the truth. But truth is beyond words. It does not admit of
explanation. All that it is possible to do is to indicate it.[13]

Q: *It is said that one look of a* mahatma *is enough, that idols,
pilgrimages, etc., are not so effective. I have been here for three
months, but I do not know how I have been benefited by the look
of Maharshi.*

A: The look has a purifying effect. Purification cannot be
visualised. Just as a piece of coal takes a long time to be ignited, a
piece of charcoal takes a shorter time, and a mass of gunpowder is
instantaneously ignited, so it is with grades of men coming into
contact with *mahatmas*.[14] The fire of wisdom consumes all
actions. Wisdom is acquired by association with the wise [*sat-*

sanga] or rather its mental atmosphere.[15]

Q: *Can the Guru's silence bring about realisation if the disciple makes no effort?*

A: In the proximity of a great master, the *vasanas* cease to be active, the mind becomes still and *samadhi* results. Thus the disciple gains true knowledge and right experience in the presence of the master. To remain unshaken in it further efforts are necessary. Eventually the disciple will know it to be his real being and will thus be liberated even while alive.[16]

Q: *If the search has to be made within, is it necessary to be in the physical proximity of the Master?*

A: It is necessary to be so until all doubts are at an end.[17]

Q: *I am not able to concentrate by myself. I am in search of a force to help me.*

A: Yes, that is called grace. Individually we are incapable because the mind is weak. Grace is necessary. *Sadhu seva* [serving a *sadhu*] will bring it about. There is however nothing new to get. Just as a weak man comes under the control of a stronger one, the weak mind of a man comes under control easily in the presence of strong-minded *sadhus*. That which is is only grace; there is nothing else.[18]

Q: *Is it necessary to serve the Guru physically?*

A: The *sastras* say that one must serve a Guru for twelve years in order to attain Self-realisation. What does the Guru do? Does he hand it over to the disciple? Is not the Self always realised? What does the common belief mean then? Man is always the Self and yet he does not know it. Instead he confounds it with the non-Self, the body, etc. Such confusion is due to ignorance. If ignorance is wiped out the confusion will cease to exist and the true knowledge will be unfolded. By remaining in contact with realised sages the man gradually loses the ignorance until its removal is complete. The eternal Self is thus revealed.[19]

Q: *You say that association with the wise [sat-sanga] and service of them is required of the disciple.*

A: Yes, the first really means association with the unmanifest *sat* or absolute existence, but as very few can do that, they have to take second best which is association with the manifest *sat*, that is, the Guru. Association with sages should be made because thoughts are so persistent. The sage has already overcome the mind and remains in peace. Being in his proximity helps to bring about this condition in others, otherwise there is no meaning in

seeking his company. The Guru provides the needed strength for
this, unseen by others. Service is primarily to abide in the Self, but
it also includes making the Guru's body comfortable and looking
after his place of abode. Contact with the Guru is also necessary,
but this means spiritual contact. If the disciple finds the Guru
internally, then it does not matter where he goes. Staying here or
elsewhere must be understood to be the same and to have the
same effect.[20]

Q: *My profession requires me to stay near my place of work. I
cannot remain in the vicinity of* sadhus. *Can I have realisation
even in the absence of* sat-sanga?

A: *Sat* is *aham pratyaya saram*, the Self of selves. The *sadhu* is
that Self of selves. He is immanent in all. Can anyone remain
without the Self? No. So no one is away from *sat-sanga*.[21]

Q: *Is proximity to the Guru helpful?*

A: Do you mean physical proximity? What is the good of it?
The mind alone matters. The mind must be contacted.[22] *Sat-sanga*
will make the mind sink into the Heart.

Such association is both mental and physical. The extremely
visible being of the Guru pushes the mind inward. He is also in the
Heart of the seeker and so he draws the latter's inward-bent mind
into the Heart.[23]

Q: *All that I want to know is whether* sat-sanga *is necessary
and whether my coming here will help me or not.*

A: First you must decide what is *sat-sanga*. It means
association with *sat* or reality. One who knows or has realised *sat*
is also regarded as *sat*. Such association with *sat* or with one who
knows *sat* is absolutely necessary for all. Sankara has said that in
all the three worlds there is no boat like *sat-sanga* to carry one
safely across the ocean of births and deaths.[24]

Sat-sanga means *sanga* [association] with *sat*. *Sat* is only the
Self. Since the Self is not now understood to be *sat*, the company
of the sage who has thus understood it is sought. That is *sat-
sanga*. Introversion results. Then *sat* is revealed.[25]

PART FOUR

Meditation and yoga

The best meditation is that which continues in all the three states. It must be so intense that it does not give room even to the thought 'I am meditating'.[1]

Having made the liking to see through the deceitful senses subside, and having thereby ended the objective knowing of the mind, the jumping ego, to know the lightless light and the soundless sound in the Heart is the true power of yoga [*yoga-sakti*].[2]

CHAPTER 10
Meditation and concentration

Sri Ramana's insistence that awareness of the 'I'-thought was a prerequisite for Self-realisation led him to the conclusion that all spiritual practices which did not incorporate this feature were indirect and inefficient:

> This path [attention to the 'I'] is the direct path; all others are indirect ways. The first leads to the Self, the others elsewhere. And even if the latter do arrive at the Self it is only because they lead at the end to the first path which ultimately carries them to the goal. So, in the end, the aspirants must adopt the first path. Why not do so now? Why waste time?[1]

That is to say, other techniques may sometimes bring one to an inner state of stillness in which self-attention or self-awareness inadvertently takes place, but it is a very roundabout way of reaching the Self. Sri Ramana maintained that other techniques could only take one to the place where self-enquiry starts and so he never endorsed them unless he felt that particular questioners were unable or unwilling to adopt self-enquiry. This is illustrated by a conversation in *Sri Ramana Gita* (an early collection of his questions and answers) in which Sri Ramana explained in detail why self-enquiry was the only way to realise the Self. After listening carefully to Sri Ramana's explanation the questioner was still unwilling to accept that self-enquiry was the only route to the Self and so he asked if there were any other methods by which the Self could be realised. Sri Ramana replied:

> The goal is the same for the one who meditates [on an object] and the one who practises self-enquiry. One attains stillness through meditation, the other through knowledge. One strives to attain something; the other seeks the one who strives to attain. The former takes a longer time, but in the end attains the Self.[2]

Not wanting to shake the faith of a man who had a known predilection for subject-object meditation and, having already ascertained that he was unwilling to take up self-enquiry, Sri Ramana encouraged him to follow his own chosen method by telling him that it would enable him to reach the Self. In Sri Ramana's view any method is better than no method since there is always the possibility that it will lead to self-enquiry.

He gave many other similar replies to other people for similar reasons. These replies, which indicate that methods other than self-enquiry or surrender could result in Self-realisation, should not be taken at face value since they were only given to people who were not attracted to self-enquiry and who wanted to follow their own methods. When he spoke to other devotees who were not attached to what he called 'indirect methods', he would usually reaffirm that self-attention was ultimately indispensable.

Although Sri Ramana vigorously defended his views on self-enquiry he never insisted that anyone change their beliefs or practices and, if he was unable to convince his followers to take up self-enquiry, he would happily give advice on other methods. In the conversations in this chapter he is mostly answering questions from devotees who wanted advice on conventional forms of meditation (*dhyana*). In giving this advice he usually defined meditation as concentration on one thought to the exclusion of all others, but he sometimes gave it a higher definition by saying that keeping the mind fixed in the Self was true meditation. This latter practice is really another name for self-enquiry, for, as he explained in one of his early written works, 'Always keeping the mind fixed in Self alone is called self-enquiry, whereas meditation is thinking oneself to be *Brahman*.'[3]

Q: *What is the difference between meditation* [dhyana] *and investigation* [vichara]?

A: Both amount to the same. Those unfit for investigation must practise meditation. In meditation the aspirant forgetting himself meditates 'I am *Brahman*' or 'I am Siva' and by this method holds on to *Brahman* or Siva. This will ultimately end with the residual awareness of *Brahman* or Siva as being. He will then realise that this is pure being, that is, the Self.

He who engages in investigation starts by holding on to

himself, and by asking himself 'Who am I?' the Self becomes clear to him.[4]

Mentally imagining oneself to be the supreme reality, which shines as existence-consciousness-bliss, is meditation. Fixing the mind in the Self so that the unreal seed of delusion will die is enquiry.

Whoever meditates upon the Self in whatever *bhava* [mental image] attains it only in that image. Those peaceful ones who remain quiet without any such *bhava* attain the noble and unqualified state of *kaivalya*, the formless state of the Self.[5]

Q: *Meditation is more direct than investigation because the former holds on to the truth whereas the latter sifts the truth from the untruth.*

A: For the beginner meditation on a form is more easy and agreeable. Practice of it leads to self-enquiry which consists in sifting the reality from unreality.

What is the use of holding on to truth when you are filled with antagonistic factors?

Self-enquiry directly leads to realisation by removing the obstacles which make you think that the Self is not already realised.[6]

Meditation differs according to the degree of advancement of the seeker. If one is fit for it one might directly hold on to the thinker, and the thinker will then automatically sink into his source, pure consciousness.

If one cannot directly hold on to the thinker one must meditate on God and in due course the same individual will have become sufficiently pure to hold on to the thinker and to sink into absolute being.[7]

Meditation is possible only if the ego is kept up. There is the ego and the object meditated upon. The method is therefore indirect because the Self is only one. Seeking the ego, that is its source, the ego disappears. What is left over is the Self. This method is the direct one.[8]

Q: *There is no way found to go inward by means of meditation.*

A: Where else are we now? Our very being is that.

Q: *Being so, we are ignorant of it.*

A: Ignorant of what, and whose is the ignorance? If ignorant of the Self are there two selves?

Q: *There are not two selves. The feeling of limitation cannot be denied. Due to limitations. . . .*

A: Limitation is only in the mind. Did you feel it in deep sleep? You exist in sleep. You do not deny your existence then. The same Self is here and now in the wakeful state. You are now saying that there are limitations. What has now happened is that there are these differences between the two states. The differences are due to the mind. There was no mind in sleep whereas it is now active. The Self exists in the absence of the mind also.

Q: *Although it is understood, it is not realised.*

A: It will be by and by, with meditation.

Q: *Meditation is with mind. How can it kill the mind in order to reveal the Self?*

A: Meditation is sticking to one thought. That single thought keeps away other thoughts. Distraction of mind is a sign of its weakness. By constant meditation it gains strength, that is to say, the weakness of fugitive thought gives place to the enduring background free from thought. This expanse devoid of thought is the Self. Mind in purity is the Self.[9]

Q: *What is* dhyana *[meditation]?*

A: It is abiding as one's Self without swerving in any way from one's real nature and without feeling that one is meditating.

Q: *What is the difference between* dhyana *and* samadhi?

A: *Dhyana* is achieved through deliberate mental effort. In *samadhi* there is no such effort.

Q: *What are the factors to be kept in view in* dhyana?

A: It is important for one who is established in his Self [*atmanishtha*] to see that he does not swerve in the least from this absorption. By swerving from his true nature he may see before him bright effulgences, or hear unusual sounds, or regard as real the visions of gods appearing within or outside himself. He should not be deceived by these and forget himself.[10]

Q: *How is meditation to be practised?*

A: Meditation is, truly speaking, *atmanishtha* [to be fixed as the Self]. But when thoughts cross the mind and an effort is made to eliminate them the effort is usually termed meditation. *Atmanishtha* is your real nature. Remain as you are. That is the aim.

Q: *But thoughts come up. Is our effort meant to eliminate thoughts only?*

A: Yes. Meditation being on a single thought, the other thoughts are kept away. Meditation is only negative in effect in as much as thoughts are kept away.

Q: *It is said* 'atma samstham manah krtva' *[fixing the mind in the Self]. But the Self is unthinkable.*

A: Why do you wish to meditate at all? Because you wish to do so you are told 'atma samstham manah krtva'. Why do you not remain as you are without meditating? What is that '*manah*' [mind]? When all thoughts are eliminated it becomes '*atma samstha*' [fixed in the Self].

Q: *If a form is given I can meditate on it and other thoughts are eliminated. But the Self is formless.*

A: Meditation on forms or concrete objects is said to be *dhyana*, whereas the enquiry into the Self is *vichara* [enquiry] or *nididhyasana* [uninterrupted awareness of being].[11]

Q: *There is more pleasure in* dhyana *than in sensual enjoyments. Yet the mind runs after the latter and does not seek the former. Why is it so?*

A: Pleasure or pain are aspects of the mind only. Our essential nature is happiness. But we have forgotten the Self and imagine that the body or the mind is the Self. It is that wrong identity that gives rise to misery. What is to be done? This mental tendency is very ancient and has continued for innumerable past births. Hence it has grown strong. That must go before the essential nature, happiness, asserts itself.[12]

Q: *How is* dhyana *practised – with eyes open or closed?*

A: It may be done either way. The point is that the mind must be introverted and kept active in its pursuit. Sometimes it happens that when the eyes are closed the latent thoughts rush forth with great vigour. It may also be difficult to introvert the mind with the eyes open. It requires strength of mind to do so. The mind is contaminated when it takes in objects. Otherwise, it is pure. The main factor in *dhyana* is to keep the mind active in its own pursuit without taking in external impressions or thinking of other matters.[13]

Q: *Bhagavan, whenever I meditate, I feel great heat in the head and, if I persist, my whole body burns. What is the remedy?*

A: If concentration is made with the brain, sensations of heat and even headache ensue. Concentration has to be made in the Heart, which is cool and refreshing. Relax and your meditation will be easy. Keep your mind steady by gently warding off all intruding thoughts but without strain. Soon you will succeed.[14]

Q: *How do I prevent myself falling asleep in meditation?*

A: If you try to prevent sleep it will mean thinking in meditation, which must be avoided. But if you slip into sleep while meditating, the meditation will continue even during and after sleep. Yet, being a thought, sleep must be got rid of, for the final natural state has to be obtained consciously in *jagrat* [the waking state] without the disturbing thought. Waking and sleeping are mere pictures on the screen of the native, thought-free state. Let them pass unnoticed.[15]

Q: *What is to be meditated upon?*

A: Anything that you prefer.

Q: *Siva, Vishnu and* gayatri *are said to be equally efficacious. Which should I meditate upon?*

A: Any one you like best. They are all equal in their effect. But you should stick to one.

Q: *How do I meditate?*

A: Concentrate on that one whom you like best. If a single thought prevails, all other thoughts are put off and finally eradicated. So long as diversity prevails there are bad thoughts. When the object of love prevails only good thoughts hold the field. Therefore hold on to one thought only. *Dhyana* is the chief practice.

Dhyana means fight. As soon as you begin meditation other thoughts will crowd together, gather force and try to sink the single thought to which you try to hold. The good thought must gradually gain strength by repeated practice. After it has grown strong the other thoughts will be put to flight. This is the battle royal always taking place in meditation.

One wants to rid oneself of misery. It requires peace of mind, which means absence of perturbation owing to all kinds of thoughts. Peace of mind is brought about by *dhyana* alone.[16]

Q: *Since Sri Bhagavan says that the Self may function at any of the centres or* chakras *while its seat is in the Heart, is it not possible that by the practice of intense concentration or* dhyana *between the eyebrows this centre may become the seat of the Self?*

A: Any consideration about the seat of the Self is theoretical if you fix your attention on a place in the body. You consider yourself as the subject, the seer, and the place where you fix your attention becomes the object seen. This is merely *bhavana* [mental imagery]. When, on the contrary, you see the seer himself, you merge in the Self and you become one with it. That is the Heart.

Q: *Is the practice of concentration between the eyebrows advisable?*

A: The final result of the practice of any kind of *dhyana* is that the object on which the seeker fixes his mind ceases to exist as distinct and separate from the subject. They, the subject and object, become the one Self, and that is the Heart.

Q: *Why does not Sri Bhagavan direct us to practise concentration on some particular centre or* chakra?

A: *Yoga Sastra* says that the *sahasrara* [the *chakra* located in the brain] or the brain is the seat of the Self. *Purusha Sukta* declares that the Heart is its seat. To enable the *sadhaka* to steer clear of possible doubt, I tell him to take up the thread or the clue of 'I'-ness or 'I am'-ness and follow it up to its source. Because, firstly, it is impossible for anybody to entertain any doubt about this 'I' notion. Secondly, whatever be the means adopted, the final goal is the realisation of the source of 'I am'-ness which is the primary datum of your experience.

If you therefore practise self-enquiry, you will reach the Heart which is the Self.[17]

Q: *I practise* hatha *yoga and I also meditate 'I am* Brahman'. *After a few moments of this meditation, a blank prevails, the brain gets heated and a fear of death arises. What should I do?*

A: 'I am *Brahman*' is only a thought. Who says it? *Brahman* itself does not say so. What need is there for it to say it? Nor can the real 'I' say so. For 'I' always abides as *Brahman*. To be saying it is only a thought. Whose thought is it? All thoughts are from the unreal 'I', that is the 'I'-thought. Remain without thinking. So long as there is thought there will be fear.

Q: *As I go on thinking of it there is forgetfulness, the brain becomes heated and I am afraid.*

A: Yes, the mind is concentrated in the brain and hence you get a hot sensation there. It is because of the 'I'-thought. When the 'I'-thought arises fear of death arises simultaneously. With regard to forgetfulness, so long as there is thought there will be forgetfulness. First there is the thought 'I am *Brahman*', then forgetfulness supervenes. Forgetfulness and thought are for the 'I'-thought only. Hold on to it and it will disappear like a phantom. What remains over is the real 'I' and that is the Self.

'I am *Brahman*' is an aid to concentration since it keeps off other thoughts. When that one thought alone persists, see whose thought it is. It will be found to be from 'I'. From where is the 'I'-

thought? Probe into it, the 'I'-thought will vanish, and the supreme Self will shine forth of itself. No further effort is needed.

When the one real 'I' remains alone, it will not be saying 'I am *Brahman*'. Does a man go on repeating 'I am a man'? Unless he is challenged, why should he declare himself a man? Does anyone mistake himself for an animal that he should say, 'No, I am not an animal, I am a man'? Similarly, *Brahman* or 'I' being the only existing reality, there is no one there to challenge it and so there is no need to be repeating 'I am *Brahman*'.[18]

Q: *Why should one adopt this self-hypnotism by thinking on the unthinkable point? Why not adopt other methods like gazing into light, holding the breath, hearing music, hearing internal sounds, repetition of the sacred syllable* om *or other* mantras?

A: Light-gazing stupefies the mind and produces catalepsy of the will for the time being, but it secures no permanent benefit. Breath control temporarily benumbs the will but it is not permanent. It is the same with listening to sounds, unless the *mantra* is sacred and secures the help of a higher power to purify and raise the thoughts.[19]

Q: *We are advised to concentrate on the spot in the forehead between the eyebrows. Is this right?*

A: Everyone is aware − 'I am'. Leaving aside that awareness one goes about in search of God. What is the use of fixing one's attention between the eyebrows? It is mere folly to say that God is between the eyebrows. The aim of such advice is to help the mind to concentrate. It is one of the forcible methods to check the mind and prevent its dissipation. It is forcibly directed into one channel. It is a help to concentration.

But the best means of realisation is the enquiry 'Who am I?' The present trouble is to the mind and it must be removed by the mind only.[20]

Q: *I do not always concentrate on the same centre in the body. Sometimes I find it easier to concentrate on one centre and sometimes on another. And sometimes when I concentrate on one centre the thought of its own accord goes and fixes itself in another. Why is that?*

A: It may be because of past practices of yours. But in any case it is immaterial on which centre you concentrate since the real Heart is in every centre and even outside the body. On whatever part of the body you may concentrate or on whatever external object, the Heart is there.

Q: *Can one concentrate at one time on one centre and at another time on another or should one concentrate always consistently on the same centre?*

A: As I have just said, there can be no harm wherever you concentrate, because concentration is only a means of giving up thoughts. Whatever the centre or object on which you concentrate, he who concentrates is always the same.[21]

Q: *Some say that one should practise meditation on gross objects only. It may be disastrous if one constantly seeks to kill the mind.*

A: For whom is it disastrous? Can there be disaster apart from the Self?

Unbroken 'I, I' is the infinite ocean. The ego, the 'I'-thought, remains only a bubble on it and is called *jiva* or individual soul. The bubble too is water for when it bursts it only mixes in the ocean. When it remains a bubble it is still a part of the ocean. Ignorant of this simple truth, innumerable methods under different denominations, such as yoga, *bhakti*, *karma*, each again with many modifications, are being taught with great skill and in intricate detail only to entice the seekers and confuse their minds. So also are the religions and sects and dogmas. What are they all for? Only for knowing the Self. They are aids and practices required for knowing the Self.

Objects perceived by the senses are spoken of as immediate knowledge [*pratyaksha*]. Can anything be as direct as the Self – always experienced without the aid of the senses? Sense-perceptions can only be indirect knowledge, and not direct knowledge. Only one's own awareness is direct knowledge, and that is the common experience of one and all. No aids are needed to know one's own Self.[22]

CHAPTER 11
Mantras *and* japa

A *mantra* is a word or phrase which has been given to a disciple by a Guru, usually as part of an initiation rite. If the Guru has accumulated spiritual power as a result of his realisation or meditation, some of this power is transmitted in the *mantra*. If the disciple repeats the word continuously, the power of the Guru is invoked in such a way that it helps the disciple to progress towards the goal of Self-realisation. Sri Ramana accepted the validity of this approach but he very rarely gave out *mantras* himself and he never used them as part of an initiation ceremony. He did, on the other hand, speak highly of the practice of *nama-japa* (the continuous repetition of God's name) and he often advocated it as a useful aid for those who were following the path of surrender.

In chapter 7 it was pointed out that surrender to God or the Self could be effectively practised by being aware at all times that there is no individual 'I' acting and thinking, only a 'higher power' which is responsible for all the activities of the world. Sri Ramana recommended *japa* as an effective way of cultivating this attitude since it replaces an awareness of the individual and the world with a constant awareness of this higher power.

In its early stages the repetition of the name of God is only an exercise in concentration and meditation, but with continued practice a stage is reached in which the repetition proceeds effortlessly, automatically and continuously. This stage is not reached by concentration alone but only by completely surrendering to the deity whose name is being repeated: 'To use the name of God one must call upon him with yearning and unreservedly surrender oneself to him. Only after such surrender is the name of God constantly with the man.'[1]

When Sri Ramana talked about this advanced stage of *japa* there was an almost mystical dimension to his ideas. He would speak of the identity of the name of God with the Self and sometimes he would even say that when the Self is realised the name of God repeats itself effortlessly and continuously in the Heart.

This ultimate stage is only reached after the practice of *japa* merges into the practice of self-attention. Sri Ramana usually illustrated the necessity of this transition by quoting from the words of Namdev, a fourteenth-century Maharashtra saint: 'The all-pervading nature of the Name can only be understood when one recognises one's own 'I'. When one's own name is not recognised, it is impossible to get the all-pervading Name.'[2] This quotation comes from a short work by Namdev entitled *The Philosophy of the Divine Name* and the full text is given in one of Sri Ramana's answers later in the chapter. He first discovered it in 1937 and for the last thirteen years of his life he kept a copy of it on a small bookshelf by his bed. He frequently read it out when visitors asked him about the nature and usefulness of *japa* and from the number of times he spoke of it with approval it is reasonable to assume that he fully endorsed its contents.

Q: *My practice has been a continuous* japa *of the names of God with the incoming breath and the name of Sai Baba with the outgoing breath. Simultaneously with this I see the form of Baba always. Even in Bhagavan, I see Baba. Now, should I continue this or change the method, as something from within says that if I stick to the name and form I shall never go above name and form? But I can't understand what further to do after giving up name and form. Will Bhagavan enlighten me on this point?*

A: You may continue in your present method. When the *japa* becomes continuous, all other thoughts cease and one is in one's real nature, which is *japa* or *dhyana*. We turn our mind outwards on things of the world and are therefore not aware of our real nature being always *japa*. When by conscious effort of *japa* or *dhyana*, as we call it, we prevent our mind from thinking of other things, then what remains is our real nature, which is *japa*.

So long as you think you are name and form, you can't escape name and form in *japa* also. When you realise you are not name and form, then name and form will drop of themselves. No other effort is necessary. *Japa* or *dhyana* will naturally and as a matter of course lead to it. What is now regarded as the means, *japa*, will then be found to be the goal. Name and God are not different. This is clearly shown in the teachings of Namdev.[3]

1   The Name permeates densely the sky and the lowest regions and the entire universe. Who can tell to what depths in the nether regions and to what height in the heavens it extends. The ignorant undergo the 84 *lakhs* [8.4 million] of species of births, not knowing the essence of things. Namdev says the Name is immortal. Forms are innumerable, but the Name is all that.

2   The Name itself is Form. There is no distinction between Name and Form. God became manifest and assumed Name and Form. Hence the Name the *Vedas* established. Beware there is no *mantra* beyond the Name. Those who say otherwise are ignorant. Namdev says the Name is Keshava [God] Himself. This is known only to the loving devotees of the Lord.

3   The all-pervading nature of the Name can only be understood when one recognises one's own 'I'. When one's own name is not recognised, it is impossible to get the all-pervading Name. When one knows oneself, then one finds the Name everywhere. To see the Name as different from the Named creates illusion. Namdev says, 'Ask the Saints.'

4   No one can realise the Name by practice of knowledge, meditation or austerity. Surrender yourself first at the feet of the Guru and learn to know that 'I' myself is that Name. After finding the source of that 'I' merge your individuality in that oneness which is self-existent and devoid of all duality. That which pervades beyond *dvaita* [duality] and *dvaitatita* [that which is beyond duality], that Name has come into the three worlds. The Name is *Parabrahman* itself where there is no action arising out of duality.[4]

The same idea is also found in the Bible: 'In the beginning was the Word and the Word was with God and the Word was God.'[5]

Q: *So the true name of God will ultimately be revealed by self-enquiry?*

A: Since you yourself are the form of the *japa*, if you know your own nature by enquiring who you are, what a wonder it will be! The *japa* which was previously going on with effort will then continue untiringly and effortlessly in the Heart.[6]

Q: *How long should I do* japa *for? Should I also concentrate on an image of God at the same time?*

A: *Japa* is more important than external form. It must be done until it becomes natural. It starts with effort and is continued until it proceeds of itself. When natural it is called realisation.

Japa may be done even while engaged in other work. That which is, is the one reality. It may be represented by a form, a *japa, mantra, vichara,* or any kind of attempt to reach reality. All of them finally resolve themselves into that one single reality. *Bhakti, vichara* and *japa* are only different forms of our efforts to keep out the unreality. The unreality is an obsession at present but our true nature is reality. We are wrongly persisting in unreality, that is, attachment to thoughts and worldly activities. Cessation of these will reveal the truth. Our attempts are directed towards keeping them out and this is done by thinking of the reality only. Although it is our true nature it looks as if we are thinking of it while doing these practices. What we do really amounts to the removal of obstacles for the revelation of our true being.

Q: *Are our attempts sure to succeed?*

A: Realisation is our nature. It is nothing new to be gained. What is new cannot be eternal. Therefore there is no need for doubting whether one could lose or gain the Self.[7]

Q: *Is it good to do* japa *when we know that enquiry into the Self is the real thing?*

A: All methods are good since they will lead to the enquiry eventually. *Japa* is our real nature. When we realise the Self then *japa* goes on without effort. What is the means at one stage becomes the goal at another. When effortless constant *japa* goes on, it is realisation.[8]

Q: *I am not learned in the scriptures and I find the method of self-enquiry too hard for me. I am a woman with seven children and a lot of household cares and it leaves me little time for meditation. I request Bhagavan to give me some simpler and easier method.*

A: No learning or knowledge of scriptures is necessary to know the Self, as no man requires a mirror to see himself. All knowledge is required only to be given up eventually as not-Self. Nor is household work or cares with children necessarily an obstacle. If you can do nothing more at least continue saying 'I, I' to yourself mentally as advised in *Who am I?* '. . . if one incessantly thinks "I, I", it will lead to that state [the Self].' Continue to repeat it whatever work you may be doing, whether you are sitting, standing or walking. 'I' is the name of God. It is the first and greatest of all *mantras*. Even *om* is second to it.[9]

Q: *For controlling the mind, which of the two is better, performing* japa *of the* ajapa *[unspoken]* mantra *or of* omkar *[the sound of 'om']?*

A: What is your idea of unspoken and involuntary *japa* [*ajapa*]? Will it be *ajapa* if you go on repeating with the mouth '*soham, soham*' ['I am he, I am he']? *Ajapa* really means to know that *japa* which goes on involuntarily without being uttered through the mouth. Without knowing this real meaning people think that it means repeating with the mouth the words '*soham, soham*' hundreds of thousands of times, counting them on the fingers or on a string of beads.

Before beginning a *japa* breath control is prescribed. That means, first do *pranayama* [regulating of breath] and then begin repeating the *mantra*. *Pranayama* means first closing the mouth, doesn't it? If, by stopping the breath, the five elements in the body are bound down and controlled, what remains is the real Self. That Self will by itself be repeating always '*aham, aham*' ['I, I']. That is *ajapa*. Knowing this, how could that which is repeated by mouth be *ajapa*? The vision of the real Self which performs *japa* of its own accord involuntarily and in a never-ending stream, like the flowing down continuously of oil, is *ajapa*, *gayatri* and everything.

If you know who it is that is doing *japa* you will know what *japa* is. If you search and try to find out who it is that is doing *japa*, that *japa* itself becomes the Self.

Q: *Is there no benefit at all in doing* japa *with the mouth?*

A: Who said there is no benefit? Such *japa* will be the means for *chitta suddhi* [purifying the mind]. As the *japa* is done repeatedly the effort ripens and sooner or later leads to the right path. Good or bad, whatever is done never goes to waste. Only the differences and the merits and demerits of each will have to be told, looking to the stage of development of the person concerned.[10]

Q: *Is not mental* japa *better than oral* japa?

A: Oral *japa* consists of sounds. The sounds arise from thoughts, for one must think before one expresses the thoughts in words. The thoughts form the mind. Therefore mental *japa* is better than oral *japa*.

Q: *Should we not contemplate the* japa *and repeat it orally also?*

A: When the *japa* becomes mental, where is the need for the sounds?

Japa, becoming mental, becomes contemplation. *Dhyana*, contemplation and mental *japa* are the same. When thoughts cease to be promiscuous and one thought persists to the exclusion of all others, it is said to be contemplation. The object of *japa* or *dhyana* is the exclusion of several thoughts and confining oneself to one single thought. Then that thought too vanishes into its source – absolute consciousness. The Self, the mind engages in *japa* and then sinks into its own source.

Q: *The mind is said to be from the brain.*

A: Where is the brain? It is in the body. I say that the body itself is a projection of the mind. You speak of the brain when you think of the body. It is the mind which creates the body, the brain in it and also ascertains that the brain is its seat.

Q: *Sri Bhagavan has said that the* japa *must be traced to its source. Is it not the mind that is meant?*

A: All these are only the workings of the mind. *Japa* helps to fix the mind on a single thought. All other thoughts are first subordinated until they disappear. When it becomes mental it is called *dhyana*. *Dhyana* is your true nature. It is however called *dhyana* because it is made with effort. Effort is necessary so long as thoughts are promiscuous. Because you are with other thoughts, you call the continuity of a single thought meditation or *dhyana*. If that *dhyana* becomes effortless it will be found to be your real nature.[11]

Q: *People give some names to God and say that the name is sacred and that repetitions of the name bestow merit on the individual. Can it be true?*

A: Why not? You bear a name to which you answer. But your body was not born with that name written on it, nor did it say to anyone that it bore such and such a name. And yet a name is given to you and you answer to that name, because you have identified yourself with the name. Therefore the name signified something and it is not a mere fiction. Similarly, God's name is effective. Repetition of the name is remembrance of what it signifies. Hence its merit.[12]

Q: *While making* japa *for an hour or more I fall into a state like sleep. On waking up I recollect that my* japa *has been interrupted. So I try again.*

A: 'Like sleep', that is right. It is the natural state. Because you are now associated with the ego, you consider that the natural state is something which interrupts your work. So you must have the experience repeated until you realise that it is your natural state. You will then find that *japa* is extraneous but still it will go on automatically. Your present doubt is due to that false identity, namely of identifying yourself with the mind that does the *japa*. *Japa* means clinging to one thought to the exclusion of all other thoughts. That is its purpose. It leads to *dhyana* which ends in Self-realisation or *jnana*.

Q: *How should I carry on* japa?

A: One should not use the name of God mechanically and superficially without the feeling of devotion.[13]

Q: *So mechanical repetition is unproductive?*

A: Acute diseases will not be cured merely by repeating the name of the medicine but only by drinking the medicine. Similarly, the bonds of birth and death will not cease merely by doing many repetitions of *mahavakyas* such as 'I am Siva'. Instead of wandering about repeating 'I am the supreme', abide as the supreme yourself. The misery of birth and death will not cease by vocally repeating countless times 'I am that', but only by abiding as that.[14]

Q: *Can anyone get any benefit by repeating sacred syllables [mantras] picked up casually?*

A: No. He must be competent and initiated in such *mantras*. This is illustrated by the story of the king and his minister. A king visited his premier in his residence. There he was told that the premier was engaged in repetition of sacred syllables. The king waited for him, and on meeting him, asked what the *mantra* was. The premier said that it was the holiest of all, *gayatri*. The king desired to be initiated by the premier but the premier confessed his inability to initiate him. Therefore the king learned it from someone else, and, meeting the minister later, he repeated the *gayatri* and wanted to know if it was right. The minister said that the *mantra* was correct, but it was not proper for him to say it. When pressed for an explanation, the minister called to a page close by and ordered him to take hold of the king. The order was not obeyed. The order was often repeated, and still not obeyed. The king flew into a rage and ordered the same man to hold the minister, and it was immediately done. The minister laughed and said that the incident was the explanation required by the king. 'How?' asked the king. The minister replied, 'The order was the same and the executor also, but the authority was different. When I ordered, the effect was nil, whereas, when you ordered, there was immediate effect. Similarly with *mantras*.[15]

Q: *I am taught that* mantra japa *is very potent in practice.*

A: The Self is the greatest of all *mantras* – it goes on automatically and eternally. If you are not aware of this internal *mantra*, you should take to it consciously as *japa*, which is attended with effort, to ward off all other thoughts. By constant attention to it, you will eventually become aware of the internal *mantra* which is the state of realisation and is effortless. Firmness in this awareness will keep you continually and effortlessly in the current, however much you may be engaged in other activities.[16]

By repetition of *mantras*, the mind gets controlled. Then the *mantra* becomes one with the mind and also with the *prana* [the energy that sustains the body].

When the syllables of the *mantra* become one with the *prana*, it is termed *dhyana*, and when *dhyana* becomes deep and firm it leads to *sahaja sthiti* [the natural state].[17]

Q: *I have received a* mantra. *People frighten me by saying that it may have unforeseen results if repeated. It is only* pranava *[om]. So I seek advice. May I repeat it? I have considerable faith in it.*

A: Certainly, it should be repeated with faith.

Q: *Will it do by itself, or can you kindly give me any further instructions?*

A: The object of *mantra japa* is to realise that the same *japa* is already going on in oneself even without effort. The oral *japa* becomes mental and the mental *japa* finally reveals itself as being eternal. That *mantra* is the person's real nature. That is also the state of realisation.

Q: *Can the bliss of* samadhi *be gained thus?*

A: The *japa* becomes mental and finally reveals itself as the Self. That is *samadhi*.[18]

CHAPTER 12
Life in the world

There is a well-established Hindu tradition which prescribes four stages of life (*asramas*) for serious spiritual seekers:

1 *Brahmacharya* (celibate study). A long period of scriptural study prior to marriage, usually in an institution which specialises in Vedic scholarship.
2 *Grihastha* (marriage and family). At the conclusion of his studies the aspirant is expected to marry and to discharge his business and household duties conscientiously, but without attachment to them.
3 *Vanaprastha* (forest hermit). When all family obligations have been fulfilled (which usually means when the children are married off), the aspirant may retire to a solitary place, usually a forest, and engage in full-time meditation.
4 *Sannyasa* (wandering monk). In the final stage the seeker drops out of the world completely and becomes a wandering mendicant monk. Having no material, social or financial entanglements the *sannyasi* has theoretically removed all the attachments which previously impeded his progress towards Self-realisation.

This time-honoured structure sustained the common Indian belief that it was necessary to abandon one's family and take to a meditative life of celibate asceticism if one was seriously interested in realising the Self. Sri Ramana was asked about this belief many times but he always refused to endorse it. He consistently refused to give his devotees permission to give up their worldly responsibilities in favour of a meditative life and he always insisted that realisation was equally accessible to everyone, irrespective of their physical circumstances. Instead of advising physical renunciation he told all his devotees that it would be spiritually more productive for them to discharge their normal duties and obligations with an awareness that there was no individual 'I' performing or accepting responsibility for the acts which the body performed. He firmly believed that mental attitude had a greater bearing on spiritual progress than physical circumstances and he persistently discouraged all questioners who felt that a manipulation of their environment, however slight, would be spiritually beneficial.

The only physical changes he ever sanctioned were dietary. He accepted the prevailing Hindu theory of diet which claimed that the type of food consumed affected the quantity and quality of one's thoughts and he recommended a moderate intake of vegetarian food as the most useful aid to spiritual practice.

The Hindu dietary theory which Sri Ramana endorsed classifies different foods according to the mental states that they induce:

1 *Sattva* (purity or harmony) Dairy produce, fruit, vegetables and cereals are deemed to be *sattvic* foods. A diet which consists largely of these products helps spiritual aspirants to maintain a still, quiet mind.
2 *Rajas* (activity) *Rajasic* foods include meat, fish and hot spicy foods such as chillies, onions and garlic. Ingestion of these foods results in an overactive mind.
3 *Tamas* (sluggishness) Foods which are decayed, stale or the product of a fermentation process (e.g. alcohol) are classified as *tamasic*. Consumption of these foods leads to apathetic, torpid states of mind which hamper clear decisive thinking.

Q: *I have a good mind to resign from service and remain constantly with Sri Bhagavan.*
A: Bhagavan is always with you, in you, and you are yourself Bhagavan. To realise this it is neither necessary to resign your job nor run away from home. Renunciation does not imply apparent divesting of costumes, family ties, home, etc., but renunciation of desires, affection and attachment. There is no need to resign your job, only resign yourself to God, the bearer of the burden of all. One who renounces desires actually merges in the world and expands his love to the whole universe. Expansion of love and affection would be a far better term for a true devotee of God than renunciation, for one who renounces the immediate ties actually extends the bonds of affection and love to a wider world

beyond the borders of caste, creed and race. A *sannyasi* who apparently casts away his clothes and leaves his home does not do so out of aversion to his immediate relations but because of the expansion of his love to others around him. When this expansion comes, one does not feel that one is running away from home, instead one drops from it like a ripe fruit from a tree. Till then it would be folly to leave one's home or job.[1]

Q: *How does a* grihastha *[householder] fare in the scheme of* moksha *[liberation]? Should he not necessarily become a mendicant in order to attain liberation?*

A: Why do you think you are a *grihastha*? Similar thoughts that you are a *sannyasi* [wandering monk] will haunt you, even if you go out as a *sannyasi*. Whether you continue in the household or renounce it and go to the forest, your mind haunts you. The ego is the source of thought. It creates the body and the world and it makes you think of being the *grihastha*. If you renounce, it will only substitute the thought of *sannyasa* for that of *grihastha* and the environment of the forest for that of the household. But the mental obstacles are always there for you. They even increase greatly in the new surroundings. It is no help to change the environment. The one obstacle is the mind and it must be overcome whether in the home or in the forest. If you can do it in the forest, why not in the home? Therefore, why change the environment? Your efforts can be made even now, whatever the environment.

Q: *Is it possible to enjoy* samadhi *[awareness of reality] while busy in worldly work?*

A: The feeling 'I work' is the hindrance. Ask yourself 'Who works?' Remember who you are. Then the work will not bind you, it will go on automatically. Make no effort either to work or to renounce; it is your effort which is the bondage. What is destined to happen will happen. If you are destined not to work, work cannot be had even if you hunt for it. If you are destined to work, you will not be able to avoid it and you will be forced to engage yourself in it. So, leave it to the higher power; you cannot renounce or retain as you choose.

Q: *Bhagavan said yesterday that while one is engaged in search of God 'within', 'outer' work would go on automatically. In the life of Sri Chaitanya it is said that during his lectures to students he was really seeking Krishna within and he forgot all about his body and went on talking of Krishna only. This raises a doubt as to whether work can safely be left to itself. Should one keep part of one's attention on the physical work?*

A: The Self is all. Are you apart from the Self? Or can the work go on without the Self? The Self is universal so all actions will go on whether you strain yourself to be engaged in them or not. The work will go on of itself. Thus Krishna told Arjuna that he need not trouble to kill the Kauravas because they were already slain by God. It was not for him to resolve to work and worry himself about it, but to allow his own nature to carry out the will of the higher power.

Q: *But the work may suffer if I do not attend to it.*

A: Attending to the Self means attending to the work. Because you identify yourself with the body, you think that work is done by you. But the body and its activities, including that work, are not apart from the Self. What does it matter whether you attend to the work or not? When you walk from one place to another you do not attend to the steps you take and yet you find yourself after a time at your goal. You see how the business of walking goes on without your attending to it. So also with other kinds of work.[2]

Q: *If one holds the Self in remembrance, will one's actions always be right?*

A: They ought to be. However, such a person is not concerned with the right or wrong of actions. His actions are God's and therefore right.

Q: *How can my mind be still if I have to use it more than other people? I want to go into solitude and renounce my headmaster's work.*

A: No. You may remain where you are and go on with the work. What is the undercurrent which vivifies the mind, enables it to do all this work? It is the Self. So that is the real source of your activity. Simply be aware of it during your work and do not forget it. Contemplate in the background of your mind even whilst working. To do that, do not hurry, take your own time. Keep the remembrance of your real nature alive, even while working, and avoid haste which causes you to forget. Be deliberate. Practise meditation to still the mind and cause it to become aware of its true relationship to the Self which supports it. Do not imagine it is you who are doing the work. Think that it is the underlying current which is doing it. Identify yourself with the current. If you work unhurriedly, recollectedly, your work or service need not be a hindrance.[3]

Q: *In the early stages would it not be a help to a man to seek solitude and give up his outer duties in life?*

A: Renunciation is always in the mind, not in going to forests or solitary places or giving up one's duties. The main thing is to see that the mind does not turn outward but inward. It does not really rest with a man whether he goes to this place or that or whether he gives up his duties or not. All these events happen according to destiny. All the activities that the body is to go through are determined when it first comes into existence. It does not rest with you to accept or reject them. The only freedom you have is to turn your mind inward and renounce activities there.

Q: *But is it not possible for something to be a help, especially to a beginner, like a fence round a young tree? For instance, don't our books say that it is helpful to go on pilgrimages to sacred shrines or to get* sat-sanga?

A: Who said they are not helpful? Only such things do not rest with you, whereas turning your mind inward does. Many people desire the pilgrimage or *sat-sanga* that you mention, but do they all get it?

Q: *Why is it that turning inward alone is left to us and not any outer things?*

A: If you want to go to fundamentals, you must enquire who you are and find out who it is who has freedom or destiny. Who are you and why did you get this body that has these limitations?[4]

Q: *Is solitude necessary for* vichara?

A: There is solitude everywhere. The individual is solitary always. His business is to find it out within, not to seek it outside himself.[5]

Solitude is in the mind of man. One might be in the thick of the world and maintain serenity of mind. Such a one is in solitude. Another may stay in a forest, but still be unable to control his mind. Such a man cannot be said to be in solitude. Solitude is a function of the mind. A man attached to desires cannot get solitude wherever he may be, whereas a detached man is always in solitude.

Q: *So then, one might be engaged in work and be free from desire and keep up solitude. Is it so?*

A: Yes. Work performed with attachment is a shackle, whereas work performed with detachment does not affect the doer. One who works like this is, even while working, in solitude.[6]

Q: *Our everyday life is not compatible with such efforts.*

A: Why do you think you are active? Take the gross example of your arrival here. You left home in a cart, took a train, alighted at the railway station here, got into a cart there and found yourself in this ashram. When asked, you say that you travelled here all the way from your town. Is it true? Is it not a fact that you remained as you were and there were movements of conveyances all along the way? Just as those movements are confounded with your own, so also are the other activities. They are not your own, they are God's activities.[7]

Q: *How can cessation of activity [nivritti] and peace of mind be attained in the midst of household duties which are of the nature of constant activity?*

A: As the activities of the wise man exist only in the eyes of others and not in his own, although he may be accomplishing immense tasks, he really does nothing. Therefore his activities do not stand in the way of inaction and peace of mind. For he knows the truth that all activities take place in his mere presence and that he does nothing. Hence he will remain as the silent witness of all the activities taking place.[8]

Q: *Is it harder for westerners to withdraw inwards?*

A: Yes, they are *rajasic* [mentally overactive] and their energy goes outwards. We must be inwardly quiet, not forgetting the Self, and then externally we can go on with activity. Does a man who is acting on the stage in a female part forget that he is a man? Similarly, we too must play our parts on the stage of life, but we must not identify ourselves with those parts.

Q: *How does one remove the spiritual sloth of others?*

A: Have you removed your own? Turn your enquiries towards the Self. The force set up within you will operate on others also.[9]

Q: *But how can I help another with his problem, his troubles?*

A: What is this talk of another − there is only the one. Try to realise that there is no I, no you, no he, only the one Self which is all. If you believe in the problem of another, you are believing in something outside the Self. You will best help him by realising the oneness of everything rather than by outward activity.[10]

Q: *Do you approve of sexual continence?*

A: A true *brahmachari* [celibate] is one who dwells in *Brahman*. Then there is no question of desires any more.

Q: *At Sri Aurobindo's ashram there is a rigid rule that married couples are permitted to live there on condition that they have no sexual intercourse.*

A: What is the use of that? If it exists in the mind, what use is it to force people to abstain?

Q: *Is marriage a bar to spiritual progress?*

A: The householder's life is not a bar, but the householder must do his utmost to practise self-control. If a man has a strong desire for the higher life then the sex tendency will subside. When the mind is destroyed, the other desires are destroyed also.[11]

Q: *I have committed sexual sin.*

A: Even if you have, it does not matter so long as you do not think afterwards that you have done so. The Self is not aware of any sin and renunciation of sex is internal, not merely of the body alone.

Q: *I am carried away by the sight of the breasts of a young woman neighbour and I am often tempted to commit adultery with her. What should I do?*

A: You are always pure. It is your senses and body which tempt you and which you confuse with your real Self. So first know who is tempted and who is there to tempt. But even if you do commit adultery, do not think about it afterwards, because you are yourself always pure. You are not the sinner.[12]

Q: *How do we root out our sex idea?*

A: By rooting out the false idea of the body being the Self. There is no sex in the Self. Be the Self and then you will have no sex troubles.

Q: *Can fasting cure sexual desire?*

A: Yes, but it is temporary. Mental fast is the real aid. Fasting is not an end in itself. There must be spiritual development side by side. Complete fasting makes the mind too weak. The spiritual quest must be kept up right through a fast if it is to benefit spiritually.[13]

Q: *Can one progress spiritually by fasting?*

A: Fasting should be chiefly mental [abstention from thoughts]. Mere abstinence from food will do no good, it will even upset the mind. Spiritual unfoldment will come rather by regulating eating. But if, during a fast of one month, the spiritual outlook has been maintained, then in about ten days after the breaking of the fast (if it be rightly broken and followed by judicious eating) the mind will become pure and steady, and remain so.[14]

In the early days after my coming here, I had my eyes closed and I was so deeply absorbed in meditation that I hardly knew whether it was day or night. I had no food and no sleep. When there is movement in the body, you need food. If you have food, you need sleep. If there is no movement, you do not need sleep. Very little food is enough to sustain life. That used to be my experience. Somebody or other used to offer me a tumblerful of some liquid diet whenever I opened my eyes. That was all I ever ate. But remember one thing: except when one is absorbed in a state where the mind is motionless, it is not possible to give up sleep or food altogether. When the body and mind are engaged in the ordinary pursuits of life, the body reels if you give up food and sleep.

There are differing theories concerning how much a *sadhaka* should eat and how much he should sleep. Some say that it is healthy to go to bed at 10 p.m. and wake up at 2 a.m. That means that four hours sleep is enough. Some say that four hours sleep is not enough, but that it should be six hours. It amounts to this, that sleep and food should not be taken in excess. If you want to cut off either of them completely, your mind will always be directed towards them. Therefore, the *sadhaka* should do everything in moderation.[15]

There is no harm in eating three to four times a day. But only do not say 'I want this kind of food and not that kind' and so on. Moreover, you take these meals in twelve hours of waking whereas you are not eating in twelve hours of sleep. Does sleep lead you to *mukti*? It is wrong to suppose that simple inactivity leads one to *mukti*.[16]

Q: *What about diet?*

A: Food affects the mind. For the practice of any kind of yoga, vegetarianism is absolutely necessary since it makes the mind more *sattvic* [pure and harmonious].

Q: *Could one receive spiritual illumination while eating flesh foods?*

A: Yes, but abandon them gradually and accustom yourself to *sattvic* foods. However, once you have attained illumination it will make less difference what you eat, as, on a great fire, it is immaterial what fuel is added.[17]

Q: *We Europeans are accustomed to a particular diet and a change of diet affects the health and weakens the mind. Is it not necessary to keep up one's physical health?*

A: Quite necessary. The weaker the body the stronger the mind grows.

Q: *In the absence of our usual diet our health suffers and the mind loses strength.*

A: What do you mean by strength of mind?

Q: *The power to eliminate worldly attachment.*

A: The quality of food influences the mind. The mind feeds on the food consumed.

Q: *Really! Then how can Europeans adjust themselves to sattvic food only?*

A: Habit is only adjustment to the environment. It is the mind that matters. The fact is that the mind has been trained to think certain foods tasty and good. The food material is to be had both in vegetarian and non-vegetarian diet equally well. But the mind desires such food as it is accustomed to and considers tasty.

Q: *Are there restrictions for the realised man with regard to food?*

A: No. He is steady and not influenced by the food he takes.

Q: *Is it not killing life to prepare meat diet?*

A: Ahimsa [non-violence] stands foremost in the code of discipline for the yogis.

Q: *Even plants have life.*

A: So too the slabs you sit on!

Q: *May we gradually get ourselves accustomed to vegetarian food?*

A: Yes. That is the way.[18]

Q: *Is it harmless to continue smoking?*

A: No, for tobacco is a poison. It is better to do without it. It is good that you have given up smoking. Men are enslaved by tobacco and cannot give it up. But tobacco only gives a temporary stimulation to which there must be a reaction with craving for more. It is also not good for meditation practice.

Q: *Do you recommend that meat and alcoholic drinks be given up?*

A: It is advisable to give them up because this abstention is a useful aid for beginners. The difficulty in surrendering them does not arise because they are really necessary, but merely because we have become inured by custom and habit to them.[19]

Q: *Generally speaking, what are the rules of conduct which an aspirant should follow?*

A: Moderation in food, moderation in sleep and moderation in speech.[20]

CHAPTER 13
Yoga

Practitioners of yoga aim for union with the Self (yoga is Sanskrit for union) by undertaking distinctive mental and physical exercises. Most of these exercises can be traced back to the *Yoga Sutras* of Patanjali which were written about 2000 years ago. Patanjali's system, known as *raja* yoga, contains eight distinctive levels and practices.

1 *Yama* Conduct of life in relation to others – avoiding untruth, theft, injury to others, sensuality and greed.
2 *Niyama* Conduct towards oneself – cleanliness, tranquillity, austerity, study and devotion.
3 *Asana* Stretching, bending, balancing and sitting exercises. These exercises are nowadays collectively known as *hatha* yoga.
4 *Pranayama* Breathing exercises which aim to control the mind.
5 *Pratyahara* Withdrawing the attention from the body and the senses.
6 *Dharana* Concentration of the mind.
7 *Dhyana* Meditation.
8 *Samadhi* Uninterrupted contemplation of reality.

Most of these practices can be found in other spiritual systems. The only exceptions are *hatha* yoga and *pranayama* and it is these which give *raja* yoga its distinctive character. When visitors asked Sri Ramana about these practices he would usually criticise *hatha* yoga because of its obsession with the body. It is a fundamental premise of his teachings that spiritual problems can only be solved by controlling the mind, and because of this, he never encouraged the practice of spiritual disciplines which devoted themselves primarily to the well-being of the body. He had a higher opinion of *pranayama* (breath control), saying that it was a useful aid for those who could not otherwise control their mind, but on the whole he tended to regard it as a beginner's practice. His views on the other aspects of *raja* yoga (such as morality, meditation and *samadhi*) have been dealt with in separate chapters.

In addition to *raja* yoga there is another popular system called *kundalini* yoga. The practitioners of this system concentrate on psychic centres (*chakras*) in the body in order to generate a spiritual power they call *kundalini*. The aim of this practice is to force the *kundalini* up a psychic channel (the *sushumna*) which runs from the base of the spine to the brain. The *kundalini* yogi believes that when this power reaches the *sahasrara* (the highest *chakra* located in the brain), Self-realisation will result.

Sri Ramana never advised his devotees to practise *kundalini* yoga since he regarded it as being both potentially dangerous and unnecessary. He accepted the existence of the *kundalini* power and the *chakras* but he said that even if the *kundalini* reached the *sahasrara* it would not result in realisation. For final realisation, he said, the *kundalini* must go beyond the *sahasrara*, down another *nadi* (psychic nerve) he called *amritanadi* (also called the *paranadi* or *jivanadi*) and into the Heart-centre on the right-hand side of the chest. Since he maintained that self-enquiry would automatically send the *kundalini* to the Heart-centre, he taught that separate yoga exercises were unnecessary.

> The Self is reached by the search for the origin of the ego and by diving into the Heart. This is the direct method of Self-realisation. One who adopts it need not worry about *nadis*, the brain centre [*sahasrara*], the *sushumna*, the *paranadi*, the *kundalini*, *pranayama* or the six centres [*chakras*].[1]

In addition to the practices outlined above, Hinduism contains another yoga called *karma* yoga, the yoga of action. Practitioners of this system aim to evolve spiritually by selflessly serving and assisting others. Although it is spoken of highly in the *Bhagavad Gita*, Sri Ramana generally discouraged his devotees from following this path since it presupposes the existence of an 'I' who is going to perform the good deeds and 'other people' who are in need of assistance. He only encouraged it if he felt that particular devotees were incapable of following the paths of *jnana*, *bhakti* or *raja* yoga.

> If an aspirant be unsuited temperamentally for the first two methods [*jnana* and *bhakti*], and circumstantially on account

of age for the third method [yoga], he must try the *karma marga* [the path of *karma* yoga]. His nobler instincts become more evident and he derives impersonal pleasure. The man also becomes duly equipped for one of the three aforesaid paths.[2]

Sri Ramana stressed that to be successful, the *karma* yogi must be free of the notion that he himself is helping others, and that he must also be unattached and indifferent to the consequences of his actions. Although he rarely gave *karma* yoga more than a lukewarm endorsement he did admit that both of these conditions would be met if all actions were performed without the 'I am the doer' idea.

Q: *Yoga means union. I wonder union of what with what?*
A: Exactly. Yoga implies prior division and it means later union of one thing with another. But who is to be united and with whom? You are the seeker, seeking union with something. If you assume this then that something must be apart from you. But your Self is intimate to you and you are always aware of it. Seek it and be it. Then it will expand as the infinite and there will be no question of yoga. Whose is the separation [*viyoga*]?[3]
Q: *I don't know. Is there really separation?*
A: Find out to whom is the *viyoga*. That is yoga. Yoga is common to all paths. Yoga is really nothing but ceasing to think that you are different from the Self or reality. All the yogas — *karma*, *jnana*, *bhakti* and *raja* — are just different paths to suit different natures with different modes of evolution. They are all aimed at getting people out of the long-cherished notion that they are different from the Self. There is no question of union or yoga in the sense of going and joining something that is somewhere away from us or different from us, because you never were or could be separate from the Self.[4]
Q: *What is the difference between yoga and enquiry?*
A: Yoga enjoins *chitta-vritti-nirodha* [repression of thoughts][5] whereas I prescribe *atmanveshana* [quest of oneself]. This latter method is more practicable. The mind is repressed in swoon, or as the effect of fasting. But as soon as the cause is withdrawn the mind revives, that is, the thoughts begin to flow as before. There are just two ways of controlling the mind. Either seek its source,

or surrender it to be struck down by the supreme power. Surrender is the recognition of the existence of a higher overruling power. If the mind refuses to help in seeking the source, let it go and wait for its return; then turn it inwards. No one succeeds without patient perseverance.[6]

Q: *Is it necessary to control one's breath?*

A: Breath control is only an aid for diving deep within oneself. One may as well dive down by controlling the mind. When the mind is controlled, the breath is controlled automatically. One need not attempt breath control, mind control is enough. Breath control is only recommended for those who cannot control their minds straightaway.[7]

Q: *When should one do* pranayama *and why is it effective?*

A: In the absence of enquiry and devotion, the natural sedative *pranayama* [breath regulation] may be tried. This is known as *yoga marga* [the path of yoga]. If life is imperilled the whole interest centres round one point, the saving of life. If the breath is held the mind cannot afford to (and does not) jump at its pets – external objects. Thus there is rest for the mind so long as the breath is held. All attention being turned on breath or its regulation, other interests are lost.[8]

The source of breath is the same as that of the mind. Therefore the subsidence of either leads effortlessly to the subsidence of the other.

Q: *Will concentration on* chakras *quieten the mind?*

A: Fixing their minds on psychic centres such as the *sahasrara* [the thousand-petalled lotus *chakra*], yogis remain any length of time without awareness of their bodies. As long as this state continues they appear to be immersed in some kind of joy. But when the mind which has become tranquil emerges and becomes active again it resumes its worldly thoughts. It is therefore necessary to train it with the help of practices like *dhyana* [meditation] whenever it becomes externalised. It will then attain a state in which there is neither subsidence nor emergence.[9]

Q: *Is the mind control induced by* pranayama *also temporary?*

A: Quiescence lasts only so long as the breath is controlled. So it is transient. The goal is clearly not *pranayama*. It extends on to *pratyahara* [withdrawal], *dharana* [concentration of mind], *dhyana* [meditation] and *samadhi*. Those stages deal with control of the mind. Such mind control becomes easier for a person who has earlier practised *pranayama*. *Pranayama* therefore leads one to the higher stages. Because these higher stages involve controlling the mind, one can say that mind control is the ultimate aim of yoga.

A more advanced man will naturally go direct to control of mind without wasting his time in practising control of breath.[10]

Q: Pranayama *has three phases – exhalation, inhalation and retention. How should they be regulated?*

A: Completely giving up identification with the body alone is exhalation [*rechaka*]; merging within through the enquiry 'Who am I?' along is inhalation [*puraka*]; abiding as the one reality 'I am that' alone is retention [*kumbhaka*]. This is the real *pranayama*.[11]

Q: *I find it said in* Maha Yoga *that in the beginning of meditation one may attend to the breath, that is, its inspiration and expiration, and that after a certain amount of stillness of mind is attained, one can dive into the Heart seeking the source of the mind. I have been badly in want of some such practical hint. Can I follow this method? Is it correct?*

A: The thing is to kill the mind somehow. Those who have not the strength to follow the enquiry method are advised to adopt *pranayama* as a help to control the mind. This *pranayama* is of two kinds, controlling and regulating the breath, or simply watching the breath.[12]

Q: *For controlling the breath, is not the ratio 1:4:2 for inhaling, retaining the breath and exhaling best?*

A: All those proportions, sometimes regulated not by counting but by uttering *mantras*, are aids to controlling the mind. That is all. Watching the breath is also one form of *pranayama*. Inhaling, retaining and exhaling is more violent and may be harmful in some cases, for example when there is no proper Guru to guide the seeker at every step and stage. But merely watching the breath is easy and involves no risk.[13]

Q: *Is the manifestation of* kundalini sakti *[kundalini power] possible only for those who follow the yogic path of acquiring* sakti *[power], or is it possible also for those who follow the path of devotion [bhakti] or love [prema]?*

A: Who does not have *kundalini sakti*? When the real nature of that *sakti* is known, it is called *akhandakara vritti* [unbroken consciousness] or *aham sphurana* [effulgence of 'I']. *Kundalini sakti* is there for all people whatever path they follow. It is only a difference in name.

Q: *It is said that the* sakti *manifests itself in five phases, ten phases, a hundred phases and a thousand phases. Which is true:*

five or ten or a hundred or a thousand?

A: *Sakti* has only one phase. If it is said to manifest itself in several phases, it is only a way of speaking. The *sakti* is only one.

Q: *Can a* jnani *help not only those who follow his path but also others who follow other paths such as yoga?*

A: Undoubtedly. He can help people whatever path they choose to follow. It is something like this. Suppose there is a hill. There will be very many paths to climb it. If he were to ask people to climb by the way he came, some may like it and some may not. If people who do not like it are asked to climb by that path, and by that path only, they will not be able to come up. Hence a *jnani* helps people following any particular path, whatever it may be. People who are midway may not know about the merits and demerits of other paths, but one who has climbed to the summit and sits there observing others coming up is able to see all the paths. He will therefore be able to tell people who are coming up to move a little to this side or that or to avoid a pitfall. The goal is the same for all.[14]

Q: *How can one direct the* prana *or life-force into the* sushumna nadi *[a psychic nerve in the spine] so that the* chit-jada-granthi *[the identification of consciousness with the body] can be severed in the manner stated in* Sri Ramana Gita?

A: By enquiring 'Who am I?' The yogi may be definitely aiming at rousing the *kundalini* and sending it up the *sushumna*. The *jnani* may not be having this as his object. But both achieve the same results, that of sending the life-force up the *sushumna* and severing the *chit-jada-granthi. Kundalini* is only another name for *atma* or Self or *sakti*. We talk of it as being inside the body, because we conceive ourselves as limited by this body. But it is in reality both inside and outside, being not different from Self or the *sakti* of Self.

Q: *How to churn up the* nadis *[psychic nerves] so that the* kundalini *may go up the* sushumna?

A: Though the yogi may have his methods of breath control for this object, the *jnani*'s method is only that of enquiry. When by this method the mind is merged in the Self, the *sakti* or *kundalini*, which is not apart from the Self, rises automatically.[15]

The yogis attach the highest importance to sending the *kundalini* up to the *sahasrara*, the brain centre or the thousand-petalled lotus. They point out the scriptural statement that the life-current enters the body through the fontanelle and argue that, *viyoga* [separation] having come about that way, yoga [union] must also be effected in the reverse way. Therefore, they say, we must by yoga practice gather up the *pranas* and enter the fontanelle for the consummation of yoga. The *jnanis* on the other hand point out that the yogi assumes the existence of the body and its separateness from the Self. Only if this standpoint of separateness is adopted can the yogi advise effort for reunion by the practice of yoga.

In fact the body is in the mind which has the brain for its seat. That the brain functions by light borrowed from another source is admitted by the yogis themselves in their fontanelle theory. The *jnani* further argues: if the light is borrowed it must come from its native source. Go to the source direct and do not depend on borrowed resources. That source is the Heart, the Self.[16]

The Self does not come from anywhere else and enter the body through the crown of the head. It is as it is, ever sparkling, ever steady, unmoving and unchanging. The individual confines himself to the limits of the changeful body or of the mind which derives its existence from the unchanging Self. All that is necessary is to give up this mistaken identity, and that done, the ever-shining Self will be seen to be the single non-dual reality.

If one concentrates on the *sahasrara* there is no doubt that the ecstasy of *samadhi* ensues. The *vasanas*, that is the latent mental tendencies, are not however destroyed. The yogi is therefore bound to wake up from the *samadhi* because release from bondage has not yet been accomplished. He must still try to eradicate the *vasanas* inherent in him so that they cease to disturb the peace of his *samadhi*. So he passes down from the *sahasrara* to the Heart through what is called the *jivanadi*, which is only a continuation of the *sushumna*. The *sushumna* is thus a curve. It starts from the lowest *chakra*, rises through the spinal cord to the brain and from there bends down and ends in the Heart. When the yogi has reached the Heart, the *samadhi* becomes permanent. Thus we see that the Heart is the final centre.[17]

Q: Hatha *yogic practices are said to banish diseases effectively and are therefore advocated as necessary preliminaries to* jnana yoga.

A: Let those who advocate them use them. It has not been the experience here. All diseases will be effectively annihilated by continuous self-enquiry.[18] If you proceed on the notion that health of body is necessary for health of mind, there will never be an end to the care of the body.[19]

Q: *Is not* hatha *yoga necessary for the enquiry into the Self?*

A: Each one finds some one method suitable to himself, because of latent tendencies [*purva samskara*].

Q: *Can* hatha *yoga be accomplished at my age?*

A: Why do you think of all that? Because you think the Self is exterior to yourself you desire it and try for it. But do you not exist all along? Why do you leave yourself and go after something external?

Q: *It is said in* Aparoksha Anubhuti *that* hatha *yoga is a necessary aid for enquiry into the Self.*

A: The *hatha* yogis claim to keep the body fit so that the enquiry may be effected without obstacles. They also say that life must be prolonged so that the enquiry may be carried to a successful end. Furthermore there are those who use some medicines [*kayakalpa*] with that end in view. Their favourite example is that the screen must be perfect before the painting is begun. Yes, but which is the screen and which the painting? According to them the body is the screen and the enquiry into the Self is the painting. But is not the body itself a picture on the screen, the Self?

Q: *But* hatha *yoga is so much spoken of as an aid.*

A: Yes. Even great pandits well versed in the *vedanta* continue the practice of it. Otherwise their minds will not subside. So you may say it is useful for those who cannot otherwise still the mind.[20]

Q: *What are* asanas *[postures or seats]? Are they necessary?*

A: Many *asanas* with their effects are mentioned in the yoga *sastras*. The seats are the tiger-skin, grass, etc. The postures are the 'lotus posture', the 'easy posture' and so on. Why all these only to know oneself? The truth is that from the Self the ego rises up, confuses itself with the body, mistakes the world to be real, and then, covered with egotistic conceit, it thinks wildly and looks for *asanas* [seats]. Such a person does not understand that he himself is the centre of all and thus forms the basis for all.

The *asana* [seat] is meant to make him sit firm. Where and how can he remain firm except in his own real state? This is the real *asana*.[21]

Attaining the steadiness of not swerving from the knowledge that the base [*asana*] upon which the whole universe rests is only Self, which is the space of true knowledge, the illustrious ground, alone is the firm and motionless posture [*asana*] for excellent *samadhi*.[22]

Q: *In what* asana *is Bhagavan usually seated?*

A: In what *asana?* In the *asana* of the Heart. Wherever it is pleasant, there is my *asana.* That is called *sukhasana,* the *asana* of happiness. That *asana* of the Heart is peaceful, and gives happiness. There is no need for any other *asana* for those who are seated in that one.[23]

Q: *The* Gita *seems to emphasise* karma yoga, *for Arjuna is persuaded to fight. Sri Krishna himself set the example by an active life of great exploits.*

A: The *Gita* starts by saying that you are not the body and that you are not therefore the *karta* [the doer].

Q: *What is the significance?*

A: It means that one should act without thinking that oneself is the actor. Actions will go on even in the egoless state. Each person has come into manifestation for a certain purpose and that purpose will be accomplished whether he considers himself to be the actor or not.

Q: *What is* karma yoga? *Is it non-attachment to* karma *[action] or its fruit?*

A: *Karma* yoga is that yoga in which the person does not arrogate to himself the function of being the actor. All actions go on automatically.

Q: *Is it non-attachment to the fruits of actions?*

A: The question arises only if there is the actor. It is said in all the scriptures that you should not consider yourself to be the actor.

Q: *So* karma yoga is 'kartritva buddhi rahita karma' – *action without the sense of doership.*

A: Yes. Quite so.

Q: *The* Gita *teaches that one should have an active life from beginning to end.*

A: Yes, the actorless action.[24]

Q: *If one remains quiet how is action to go on? Where is the place for* karma yoga?

A: Let us first understand what *karma* is, whose *karma* it is and who is the doer. Analysing them and enquiring into their truth, one is obliged to remain as the Self in peace. Nevertheless even in that state the actions will go on.

Q: *How will the actions go on if I do not act?*

A: Who asks this question? Is it the Self or another? Is the Self concerned with actions?

Q: *No, not the Self. It is another, different from the Self.*

A: So it is plain that the Self is not concerned with actions and so the question does not arise.[25]

Q: *I want to do* karma *yoga. How can I help others?*

A: Who is there for you to help? Who is the 'I' that is going to help others? First clear up that point and then everything will settle itself.[26]

Q: *That means 'realise the Self'. Does my realisation help others?*

A: Yes, and it is the best help that you can possibly render to others. But really there are no others to be helped. For the realised being sees only the Self, just as the goldsmith sees only the gold while valuing it in various jewels made of gold. When you identify yourself with the body, name and form are there. But when you transcend the body-consciousness, the others also disappear. The realised one does not see the world as different from himself.

Q: *Would it not be better if saints mixed with other people in order to help them?*

A: There are no others to mix with. The Self is the only reality.[27]

The sage helps the world merely by being the real Self. The best way for one to serve the world is to win the egoless state. If you are anxious to help the world, but think that you cannot do so by attaining the egoless state, then surrender to God all the world's problems, along with your own.[28]

Q: *Should I not try to help the suffering world?*

A: The power that created you has created the world as well. If it can take care of you, it can similarly take care of the world also. If God has created the world it is his business to look after it, not yours.[29]

Q: *Is the desire for* swaraj *[political independence] right?*

A: Such desire no doubt begins with self-interest. Yet practical work for the goal gradually widens the outlook so that the individual becomes merged in the country. Such merging of the individuality is desirable and the related *karma* is *nishkama* [unselfish].

Q: *If* swaraj *is gained after a long struggle and terrible sacrifices, is not the person justified in being pleased with the result and elated by it.*

A: He must have in the course of his work surrendered himself to the higher power whose might must be kept in mind and never lost sight of. How then can he be elated? He should not even care for the result of his actions. Then alone the *karma* becomes unselfish.[30]

PART FIVE

Experience

There are no grades of reality. There are grades of experience for the individual but not of reality. Whatever may be the experiences, the experiencer is one and the same.[1]

The Self is certainly within the direct experience of everyone, but not as one imagines it to be. It is only as it is.[2]

CHAPTER 14
Samadhi

The word *samadhi* is widely used in eastern spiritual literature to denote an advanced stage of meditation in which there is a conscious experience of the Self or an intense undisturbed absorption in the object of meditation. Many gradations and subdivisions of *samadhi* have been described, with different schools and religions each tending to produce their own distinctive categories and terminology.

The classification generally used by Sri Ramana divides the various *samadhis* into the following three-fold division:

1 *Sahaja nirvikalpa samadhi*   This is the state of the *jnani* who has finally and irrevocably eliminated his ego. *Sahaja* means 'natural' and *nirvikalpa* means 'no differences'. A *jnani* in this state is able to function naturally in the world, just as any ordinary person does. Knowing that he is the Self, the *sahaja jnani* sees no difference between himself and others and no difference between himself and the world. For such a person, everything is a manifestation of the indivisible Self.

2 *Kevala nirvikalpa samadhi*   This is the stage below Self-realisation. In this state there is a temporary but effortless Self-awareness, but the ego has not been finally eliminated. It is characterised by an absence of body-consciousness. Although one has a temporary awareness of the Self in this state, one is not able to perceive sensory information or function in the world. When body-consciousness returns, the ego reappears.

3 *Savikalpa samadhi*   In this state Self-awareness is maintained by constant effort. The continuity of the *samadhi* is wholly dependent on the effort put in to maintain it. When Self-attention wavers, Self-awareness is obscured.

The following brief definitions formulated by Sri Ramana should be sufficient to guide the uninitiated through the terminological jungle of *samadhi*:

1 Holding on to reality is *samadhi*.
2 Holding on to reality with effort is *savikalpa samadhi*.
3 Merging in reality and remaining unaware of the world is *nirvikalpa samadhi*.
4 Merging in ignorance and remaining unaware of the world is sleep.
5 Remaining in the primal, pure, natural state without effort is *sahaja nirvikalpa samadhi*.[1]

Q: *What is* samadhi?
A: The state in which the unbroken experience of existence-consciousness is attained by the still mind, alone is *samadhi*. That still mind which is adorned with the attainment of the limitless supreme Self, alone is the reality of God.[2]

When the mind is in communion with the Self in darkness, it is called *nidra* [sleep], that is, the immersion of the mind in ignorance. Immersion in a conscious or wakeful state is called *samadhi*. *Samadhi* is continuous inherence in the Self in a waking state. *Nidra* or sleep is also inherence in the Self but in an unconscious state. In *sahaja samadhi* the communion is continuous.

Q: *What are* kevala nirvikalpa samadhi *and* sahaja nirvikalpa samadhi?
A: The immersion of the mind in the Self, but without its destruction, is *kevala nirvikalpa samadhi*. In this state one is not free from *vasanas* and so one does not therefore attain *mukti*. Only after the *vasanas* have been destroyed can one attain liberation.

Q: *When can one practise* sahaja samadhi?
A: Even from the beginning. Even though one practises *kevala nirvikalpa samadhi* for years together, if one has not rooted out the *vasanas* one will not attain liberation.[3]

Q: *May I have a clear idea of the difference between* savikalpa *and* nirvikalpa?
A: Holding on to the supreme state is *samadhi*. When it is with effort due to mental disturbances, it is *savikalpa*. When these

disturbances are absent, it is *nirvikalpa*. Remaining permanently in the primal state without effort is *sahaja*.[4]

Q: *Is nirvikalpa samadhi absolutely necessary before the attainment of* sahaja?

A: Abiding permanently in any of these *samadhis*, either *savikalpa* or *nirvikalpa*, is *sahaja* [the natural state]. What is body-consciousness? It is the insentient body plus consciousness. Both of these must lie in another consciousness which is absolute and unaffected and which remains as it always is, with or without the body-consciousness. What does it then matter whether the body-consciousness is lost or retained, provided one is holding on to that pure consciousness? Total absence of body-consciousness has the advantage of making the *samadhi* more intense, although it makes no difference to the knowledge of the supreme.[5]

Q: *Is* samadhi *the same as* turiya, *the fourth state?*

A: *Samadhi*, *turiya* and *nirvikalpa* all have the same implication, that is, awareness of the Self. *Turiya* literally means the fourth state, the supreme consciousness, as distinct from the other three states: waking, dreaming and dreamless sleep. The fourth state is eternal and the other three states come and go in it. In *turiya* there is the awareness that the mind has merged in its source, the Heart, and is quiescent there, although some thoughts still impinge on it and the senses are still somewhat active. In *nirvikalpa* the senses are inactive and thoughts are totally absent. Hence the experience of pure consciousness in this state is intense and blissful. *Turiya* is obtainable in *savikalpa samadhi*.[6]

Q: *What is the difference between the bliss enjoyed in sleep and the bliss enjoyed in* turiya?

A: There are not different blisses. There is only one bliss which includes the bliss enjoyed in the waking state, the bliss of all kinds of beings from the lowest animal to the highest Brahma. That bliss is the bliss of the Self. The bliss which is enjoyed unconsciously in sleep is enjoyed consciously in *turiya*, that is the only difference. The bliss enjoyed in the waking state is second-hand, it is an adjunct of the real bliss [*upadhi ananda*].[7]

Q: *Is* samadhi, *the eighth stage of* raja *yoga, the same as the* samadhi *you speak of?*

A: In yoga the term *samadhi* refers to some kind of trance and there are various kinds of *samadhi*. But the *samadhi* I speak of is different. It is *sahaja samadhi*. From here you have *samadhana* [steadiness] and you remain calm and composed even while you are active. You realise that you are moved by the deeper real Self within. You have no worries, no anxieties, no cares, for you come to realise that there is nothing belonging to you. You know that everything is done by something with which you are in conscious union.

Q: *If this* sahaja samadhi *is the most desirable condition, is there no need for* nirvikalpa samadhi?

A: The *nirvikalpa samadhi* of *raja* yoga may have its use. But in *jnana* yoga this *sahaja sthiti* [natural state] or *sahaja nishtha* [abidance in the natural state] itself is the *nirvikalpa* state. In this natural state the mind is free from doubts. It has no need to swing between alternatives of possibilities and probabilities. It sees no *vikalpas* [differences] of any kind. It is sure of the truth because it feels the presence of the real. Even when it is active, it knows it is active in the reality, the Self, the supreme being.[8]

Q: *What is the difference between deep sleep,* laya *[a trance-like state in which the mind is temporarily in abeyance] and* samadhi?

A: In deep sleep the mind is merged and not destroyed. That which merges reappears. It may happen in meditation also. But the mind which is destroyed cannot reappear. The yogi's aim must be to destroy it and not to sink into *laya*. In the peace of meditation, *laya* sometimes ensues but it is not enough. It must be supplemented by other practices for destroying the mind. Some people have gone into yogic *samadhi* with a trifling thought and after a long time awakened in the trail of the same thought. In the meantime generations have passed in the world. Such a yogi has not destroyed his mind. The true destruction of the mind is the non-recognition of it as being apart from the Self. Even now the mind is not. Recognise it. How can you do it if not in everyday activities which go on automatically? Know that the mind promoting them is not real but is only a phantom proceeding from the Self. That is how the mind is destroyed.[9]

Q: *Can the meditator be affected by physical disturbances during* nirvikalpa samadhi? *My friend and I disagree on this point.*

A: Both of you are right. One of you is referring to *kevala* and the other to *sahaja samadhi*. In both cases the mind is immersed in the bliss of the Self. In the former, physical movements may cause disturbance to the meditator, because the mind has not completely died out. It is still alive and can, as after deep sleep, at any moment be active again. It is compared to a bucket, which, although completely submerged under water, can be pulled out by a rope which is still attached to it. In *sahaja*, the mind has sunk completely into the Self, like the bucket which has got drowned in the depths of the well along with its rope. In *sahaja* there is nothing left to be disturbed or pulled back to the world. One's activities then resemble that of the child who sucks its mother's milk in sleep, and is hardly aware of the feeding.[10]

Q: *How can one function in the world in such a state?*

A: One who accustoms himself naturally to meditation and enjoys the bliss of meditation will not lose his *samadhi* state whatever external work he does, whatever thoughts may come to him. That is *sahaja nirvikalpa*.[11] *Sahaja nirvikalpa* is *nasa* [total destruction of the mind] whereas *kevala nirvikalpa* is *laya* [temporary abeyance of the mind]. Those who are in the *laya samadhi* state will have to bring the mind back under control from time to time. If the mind is destroyed, as it is in *sahaja samadhi*, it will never sprout again. Whatever is done by such people is just incidental, they will never slide down from their high state.

Those that are in the *kevala nirvikalpa* state are not realised, they are still seekers. Those who are in the *sahaja nirvikalpa* state are like a light in a windless place, or the ocean without waves; that is, there is no movement in them. They cannot find anything which is different from themselves. For those who do not reach that state, everything appears to be different from themselves.[12]

Q: *Is the experience of* kevala nirvikalpa *the same as that of* sahaja, *although one comes down from it to the relative world?*

A: There is neither coming down nor going up – he who goes up and down is not real. In *kevala nirvikalpa* there is the mental bucket still in existence under the water, and it can be pulled out at any moment. *Sahaja* is like the river that has linked up with the ocean from which there is no return. Why do you ask all these questions? Go on practising till you have the experience yourself.[13]

Q: *What is the use of* samadhi *and does thought subsist then?*

A: *Samadhi* alone can reveal the truth. Thoughts cast a veil over reality, and so it is not realised as such in states other than *samadhi*.

In *samadhi* there is only the feeling 'I am' and no thoughts. The experience of 'I am' is 'being still'.

Q: *How can I repeat the experience of* samadhi *or the stillness that I obtain here in your presence?*

A: Your present experience is due to the influence of the

atmosphere in which you find yourself. Can you have it outside this atmosphere? The experience is spasmodic. Until it becomes permanent, practice is necessary.[14]

Q: *Is samadhi an experience of calmness or peace?*

A: The tranquil clarity, which is devoid of mental turmoil, alone is the *samadhi* which is the firm base for liberation. By earnestly trying to destroy the deceptive mental turmoil, experience that *samadhi* as the peaceful consciousness which is inner clarity.[15]

Q: *What is the difference between internal and external* samadhi?

A: External *samadhi* is holding on to the reality while witnessing the world, without reacting to it from within. There is the stillness of a waveless ocean. The internal *samadhi* involves loss of body-consciousness.

Q: *The mind does not sink into that state even for a second.*

A: A strong conviction is necessary that 'I am the Self, transcending the mind and the phenomena.'

Q: *Nevertheless, the mind proves to be an unyielding obstacle which thwarts any attempts to sink into the Self.*

A: What does it matter if the mind is active? It is so only on the substratum of the Self. Hold the Self even during mental activities.[16]

Q: *I have read in a book by Romain Rolland about Ramakrishna that* nirvikalpa samadhi *is a terrible and terrifying experience. Is* nirvikalpa *so terrible? Are we then undergoing all these tedious processes of meditation, purification and discipline only to end in a state of terror? Are we going to turn into living corpses?*

A: People have all sorts of notions about *nirvikalpa*. Why speak of Romain Rolland? If those who have all the *Upanishads* and *vedantic* tradition at their disposal have fantastic notions about *nirvikalpa*, who can blame a westerner for similar notions? Some yogis by breathing exercises allow themselves to fall into a cataleptic state far deeper than dreamless sleep, in which they are aware of nothing, absolutely nothing, and they glorify it as *nirvikalpa*. Some others think that once you dip into *nirvikalpa* you become an altogether different being. Still others take *nirvikalpa* to be attainable only through a trance in which the world-consciousness is totally obliterated, as in a fainting fit. All this is due to their viewing it intellectually.

Nirvikalpa is *chit* – effortless, formless consciousness. Where does the terror come in, and where is the mystery in being oneself? To some people whose minds have become ripe from a long practice in the past, *nirvikalpa* comes suddenly as a flood, but to others it comes in the course of their spiritual practice, a practice which slowly wears down the obstructing thoughts and reveals the screen of pure awareness 'I'–'I'. Further practice renders the screen permanently exposed. This is Self-realisation, *mukti*, or *sahaja samadhi*, the natural, effortless state.[17] Mere non-perception of the differences [*vikalpas*] outside is not the real nature of firm *nirvikalpa*. Know that the non-rising of differences [*vikalpas*] in the dead mind alone is the true *nirvikalpa*.

Q: *When the mind begins to subside into the Self there is often a sensation of fear.*

A: The fear and the quaking of one's body while one is entering *samadhi* is due to the slight ego-consciousness still remaining. But when this dies completely, without leaving even a trace, one abides as the vast space of mere consciousness where bliss alone prevails, and the quaking stops.[18]

Q: *Is* samadhi *a blissful or ecstatic state?*

A: In *samadhi* itself there is only perfect peace. Ecstasy comes when the mind revives at the end of *samadhi*, with the remembrance of the peace of *samadhi*. In devotion the ecstasy comes first. It is manifested by tears of joy, hair standing on end and vocal stumbling. When the ego finally dies and the *sahaja* is won, these symptoms and the ecstasies cease.[19]

Q: *On realising* samadhi, *does not one obtain* siddhis *[supernatural powers] also?*

A: In order to display *siddhis*, there must be others to recognise them. That means, there is no *jnana* in the one who displays them. Therefore, *siddhis* are not worth a thought. *Jnana* alone is to be aimed at and gained.[20]

Q: *It is stated in the* Mandukyopanishad *that unless samadhi, the eighth and last stage of yoga, is also experienced, there can be no liberation [moksha] however much meditation [dhyana] or physical austerities [tapas] are performed. Is that so?*

A: Rightly understood, they are the same. It makes no difference whether you call it meditation or austerities or absorption, or anything else. That which is steady, continuous like the flow of oil, is austerity, meditation and absorption. To be one's own Self is *samadhi*.

Q: *But it is said in the* Mandukyopanishad *that* samadhi *must necessarily be experienced before attaining liberation.*

A: And who says that it is not so? It is stated not only in the *Mandukyopanishad* but in all the ancient books. But it is true *samadhi* only if you know your Self. What is the use of sitting still for some time like a lifeless object. Suppose you get a boil on your hand and have it operated on under anaesthetic. You don't feel any pain at the time, but does that mean that you were in *samadhi*? It is the same with this too. One has to know what *samadhi* is. And how can you know it without knowing your Self? If the Self is known, *samadhi* will be known automatically.[21]

Samadhi is one's natural state. It is the undercurrent in all the three states of waking, dreaming and sleeping. The Self is not in these states, but these states are in the Self. If we get *samadhi* in our waking state, that will persist in deep sleep also. The distinction between consciousness and unconsciousness belongs to the realm of mind, which is transcended by the state of the real Self.[22]

Q: *So one should always be trying to reach* samadhi?

A: Sages say that the state of equilibrium which is devoid of the ego alone is *mouna-samadhi* [the *samadhi* of silence], the pinnacle of knowledge. Until one attains *mouna-samadhi*, the state in which one is the egoless reality, seek only the annihilation of 'I' as your aim.[23]

CHAPTER 15
Visions and psychic powers

Meditation sometimes brings about spectacular side effects; visions of gods may appear and occasionally supernatural powers such as clairvoyance and telepathy are developed. Both of these effects can be deliberately produced. Concentration on a mental image will sometimes result in visions, particularly if the concentration is done with devotion or if there is a strong desire for the visions to appear. Psychic powers (*siddhis*) may also be attained by special yogic exercises. Patanjali's *Yoga Sutras*, the classic text on yoga, lists several exercises which accelerate the development of eight *siddhis* ranging from invisibility to walking on water.

Sri Ramana discouraged his devotees from deliberately pursuing either visions or *siddhis* by pointing out that they were products of the mind which might impede rather than facilitate Self-realisation. If visions came spontaneously he would sometimes admit that they were a sign of progress but he would usually add that they were only temporary experiences in the mind and that they were 'below the plane of Self-realisation'.[1]

If *siddhis* appeared spontaneously he would outline the dangers of becoming attached to them, explain that such powers were more likely to inflate the ego than eliminate it, and emphasise that the desire for *siddhis* and the desire for Self-realisation were mutually exclusive.

The Self is the most intimate and eternal being whereas the *siddhis* are foreign. *Siddhis* are acquired by effort whereas the Self is not. The powers are sought by the mind which must be kept alert whereas the Self is realised when the mind is destroyed. The powers only manifest when there is the ego. The Self is beyond the ego and is realised only after the ego is eliminated.[2]

Q: *I once before told Sri Bhagavan how I had a vision of Siva about the time of my conversion to Hinduism. A similar experience recurred to me at Courtallam. These visions are momentary but they are blissful. I want to know how they might be made permanent and continuous. Without Siva there is no life in what I see around me. I am so happy to think of him. Please tell me how his vision may be everlasting to me.*

A: You speak of a vision of Siva. Vision is always of an object. That implies the existence of a subject. The value of the vision is the same as that of the seer. That is to say, the nature of the vision is on the same plane as that of the seer. Appearance implies disappearance also. Whatever appears must also disappear. A vision can never be eternal. But Siva is eternal.

The vision implies the seer. The seer cannot deny the existence of the Self. There is no moment when the Self as consciousness does not exist, nor can the seer remain apart from consciousness. This consciousness is the eternal being and the only being. The seer cannot see himself. Does he deny his existence because he cannot see himself with the eyes as in a vision? No. So *pratyaksha* [direct experience] does not mean seeing, but being.

To be is to realise. Hence 'I am that I am'. 'I am' is Siva. Nothing else can be without him. Everything has its being in Siva and because of Siva.

Therefore enquire 'Who am I?' Sink deep within and abide as the Self. That is Siva as being. Do not expect to have visions of him repeated. What is the difference between the objects you see and Siva? He is both the subject and the object. You cannot be without Siva because Siva is always realised here and now. If you think you have not realised him it is wrong. This is the obstacle for realising Siva. Give up that thought also and realisation is there.

Q: *Yes. But how shall I effect it as quickly as possible?*

A: This is the obstacle for realisation. Can there be the individual without Siva? Even now he is you. There is no question of time. If there is a moment of non-realisation, the question of realisation can arise. But as it is, you cannot be without him. He is already realised, ever realised and never non-realised.[3]

Q: *I wish to get* sakshatkara *[direct realisation] of Sri Krishna. What should I do to get it?*

A: What is your idea of Sri Krishna and what do you mean by *sakshatkara?*

Q: *I mean Sri Krishna who lived in Brindavan and I want to see him as the* gopis *[his female devotees] saw him.*

A: You see, you think he is a human being or one with a human form, the son of so and so, whereas he himself has said, 'I am in the Heart of all beings, I am the beginning, the middle and the end of all forms of life.' He must be within you, as he is within all. He is your Self or the Self of your Self. So if you see this entity [the Self] or have *sakshatkara* of it, you will have *sakshatkara* of Krishna. Direct realisation of the Self and direct realisation of Krishna cannot be different. However, to go your own way, surrender completely to Krishna and leave it to him to grant the *sakshatkara* you want.[4]

Q: *Is it possible to speak to* Iswara *[God] as Sri Ramakrishna did?*

A: When we can speak to each other why should we not speak to *Iswara* in the same way?

Q: *Then why does it not happen with us?*

A: It requires purity and strength of mind and practice in meditation.

Q: *Does God become evident if the above conditions exist?*

A: Such manifestations are as real as your own reality. In other words, when you identify yourself with the body, as in the waking state, you see gross objects. When in the subtle body or in the mental plane as in dreams, you see objects equally subtle. In the absence of identification in deep sleep you see nothing. The objects seen bear a relation to the state of the seer. The same applies to visions of God.

By long practice the figure of God, as meditated upon, appears in dreams and may later appear in the waking state also.[5]

Q: *Many visitors here tell me that they get visions or thought-currents from you. I have been here for the last month and a half and still I have not the slightest experience of any kind. Is it because I am unworthy of your grace?*

A: Visions and thought-currents are had according to the state of mind. It depends on the individuals and not upon the universal presence. Moreover, they are immaterial. What matters is peace of mind.[6]

What is realisation? Is it to see God with four hands, bearing a conch, a wheel and a club? Even if God should appear in that form, how is the disciple's ignorance wiped out? The truth must be eternal realisation. The direct perception is ever-present experience. God himself is known when he is directly perceived. It does not mean that he appears before the devotee in some

particular form. Unless the realisation is eternal it cannot serve
any useful purpose. Can the appearance of God with four hands
be eternal realisation? It is phenomenal and illusory. There must
be a seer. The seer alone is real and eternal.

Let God appear as the light of a million suns. Is it *pratyaksha*
[direct experience]? To see a vision of God the eyes and the mind
are necessary. It is indirect knowledge, whereas the seer is direct
experience. The seer alone is *pratyaksha*.[7]

Q: *People talk of Vaikuntha, Kailasa, Indraloka, Chandraloka
[the Hindu heavens]. Do they really exist?*

A: Certainly. You can rest assured that they all exist. There
also a swami like me will be found seated on a couch and disciples
will also be seated around him. They will ask something and he
will say something in reply. Everything will be more or less like
this. What of that? If one sees Chandraloka, one will ask for
Indraloka, and after Indraloka, Vaikuntha and after Vaikuntha,
Kailasa, and so on, and the mind goes on wandering. Where is
shanti [peace]? If *shanti* is required, the only correct method of
securing it is by self-enquiry. Through self-enquiry Self-realisation
is possible. If one realises the Self, one can see all these worlds
within one's Self. The source of everything is one's own Self, and
if one realises the Self, one will not find anything different from
the Self. Then these questions will not arise. There may or may
not be a Vaikuntha or a Kailasa but it is a fact that you are here,
isn't it? How are you here? Where are you? After you know about
these things, you can think of all those worlds.[8]

Q: *Are the* siddhis *mentioned in Patanjali's sutras true or only
his dream?*

A: He who is *Brahman* or the Self will not value those *siddhis*.
Patanjali himself says that they are all exercised with the mind and
that they impede Self-realisation.

Q: *What about the powers of so-called supermen?*

A: Whether powers are high or low, whether of the mind or of
a supermind, they exist only with reference to the one who has the
power. Find out who that is.[9]

Q: *Are* siddhis *to be achieved on the spiritual path or are they
opposed to* mukti *[liberation]?*

A: The highest *siddhi* is realisation of the Self, for once you
realise the truth you cease to be drawn to the path of ignorance.

Q: *Then what use are the* siddhis?

A: There are two kinds of *siddhis* and one kind may well be a stumbling block to realisation. It is said that by *mantra*, by some drug possessing occult virtues, by severe austerities or by *samadhi* of a certain kind, powers can be acquired. But these powers are not a means to Self-knowledge, for even when you acquire them, you may quite well be in ignorance.

Q: *What is the other kind?*

A: They are manifestations of power and knowledge which are quite natural to you when you realise the Self. They are *siddhis* which are the products of the normal and natural *tapas* [spiritual practice] of the man who has reached the Self. They come of their own accord, they are God given. They come according to one's destiny but whether they come or not, the *jnani*, who is settled in the supreme peace, is not disturbed by them. For he knows the Self and that is the unshakeable *siddhi*. But these *siddhis* do not come by trying for them. When you are in the state of realisation, you will know what these powers are.[10]

Q: *Does the sage use occult powers for making others realise the Self, or is the mere fact of his Self-realisation enough for it?*

A: The force of his Self-realisation is far more powerful than the use of all other powers.[11]

Though *siddhis* are said to be many and different, *jnana* alone is the highest of those many different *siddhis*, because those who have attained other *siddhis* will desire *jnana*. Those who have attained *jnana* will not desire other *siddhis*. Therefore aspire only for *jnana*.[12]

Although the powers appear to be wonderful to those who do not possess them, yet they are only transient. It is useless to aspire for that which is transient. All these wonders are contained in the one changeless Self.[13]

Greedily begging for worthless occult powers [*siddhis*] from God, who will readily give himself, who is everything, is like begging for worthless stale gruel from a generous-natured philanthropist who will readily give everything.

In the Heart which catches fire with the blazing flame of supreme devotion, all the occult powers will gather together. However, with a heart that has become a complete prey to the feet of the Lord, the devotee will not have any desire for those *siddhis*. Know that if aspirants who are making efforts on the path to liberation set their heart upon occult powers, their dense bondage will be strengthened more and more, and hence the lustre of their ego will wax more and more.

The attainment [*siddhi*] of Self, which is the perfect whole, the radiance of liberation, alone is the attainment of true knowledge, whereas the other kinds of *siddhi*, beginning with *anima* [the ability to become as small as an atom] belong to the delusion of the power of imagination of the foolish mind.[14]

People see many things which are far more miraculous than the so-called *siddhis*, yet do not wonder at them simply because they occur every day. When a man is born he is no bigger than this electric bulb, but then he grows up and becomes a giant wrestler, or a world-famed artist, orator, politician or sage. People do not view this as a miracle but they are wonderstruck if a corpse is made to speak.[15]

Q: *I have been interesting myself in metaphysics for over twenty years. But I have not gained any novel experience as so many others claim to do. I have no powers of clairvoyance, clairaudience, etc. I feel myself locked up in this body and nothing more.*

A: It is right. Reality is only one and that is the Self. All the rest are mere phenomena in it, of it, and by it. The seer, the objects and the sight all are the Self only. Can anyone see or hear, leaving the Self aside? What difference does it make to see or hear anyone in close proximity or over enormous distance? The organs of sight and hearing are needed in both cases and so the mind is also required. None of them can be dispensed with in either case. There is dependence one way or another. Why then should there be a glamour about clairvoyance or clairaudience?

Moreover, what is acquired will also be lost in due course. They can never be permanent.[16]

Q: *Is it not good to acquire powers such as telepathy?*

A: Telepathy or radio enables one to see and hear from afar. They are all the same, hearing and seeing. Whether one hears from near or far does not make any difference to the one who hears. The fundamental factor is the hearer, the subject. Without the hearer or the seer, there can be no hearing or seeing. The latter are the functions of the mind. The occult powers [*siddhis*] are therefore only in the mind. They are not natural to the Self. That which is not natural, but acquired, cannot be permanent, and is not worth striving for.

These *siddhis* denote extended powers. A man is possessed of limited powers and is miserable. Because of this he wants to expand his powers so that he may be happy. But consider if it will be so. If with limited perceptions one is miserable, with extended perceptions the misery must increase proportionately. Occult powers will not bring happiness to anyone, but will make one all the more miserable.

Moreover what are these powers for? The would-be occultist [*siddha*] desires to display the *siddhis* so that others may appreciate him. He seeks appreciation, and if it is not forthcoming he will not be happy. There must be others to appreciate him. He may even find another possessor of higher powers. That will cause jealousy and breed unhappiness.

Which is the real power? Is it to increase prosperity or bring about peace? That which results in peace is the highest perfection [*siddhi*].[17]

CHAPTER 16
Problems and experiences

Physical pain and discomfort, mental anarchy, emotional fluctuations and occasional interludes of blissful peace are frequently experienced as by-products of spiritual practice. Such manifestations may not be as dramatic as the ones outlined in the previous two chapters but they tend to be of great interest to the people who experience them. They are usually interpreted as either milestones or obstacles on the road to the Self and, depending on which interpretation is favoured, great efforts are expended in trying to prolong or eliminate them.

Sri Ramana tended to play down the importance of most spiritual experiences and if they were reported to him he would usually stress that it was more important to be aware of the experiencer than to indulge in or analyse the experience. He would sometimes digress into explanations about the causes of the experiences and he occasionally evaluated them as being either beneficial or detrimental to Self-awareness, but on the whole he tended to discourage interest in them.

He was more forthcoming when devotees asked his advice about problems they had encountered during meditation. He would listen patiently to their complaints, offer constructive solutions to their problems and, if he felt that it was appropriate, try to show them that from the standpoint of the Self all problems were non-existent.

Q: *One has at times vivid flashes of a consciousness whose centre is outside the normal self, and which seems to be all-inclusive. Without concerning ourselves with philosophical concepts, how would Bhagavan advise me to work towards getting, retaining and extending those rare flashes? Does the* abhyasa *[spiritual practice] necessary for such experiences involve retirement?*

A: You say 'outside': for whom is the inside or outside? These

170

can exist only so long as there are the subject and object. For whom are these two again? On investigation you will find that they resolve into the subject only. See who is the subject and this enquiry will lead you to pure consciousness beyond the subject.

You say 'normal self': the normal self is the mind. The mind is with limitations. But pure consciousness is beyond limitations, and is reached by investigation into the 'I'.

You say 'getting': the Self is always there. You have only to remove the veil obstructing the revelation of the Self.

You say 'retaining': once you realise the Self, it becomes your direct and immediate experience. It is never lost.

You say 'extending': there is no extending of the Self, for it is as it always is, without contraction or expansion.

You say 'retirement': abiding in the Self is solitude, because there is nothing alien to the Self. Retirement must be from one place or state to another. There is neither the one nor the other apart from the Self. All being the Self, retirement is impossible and inconceivable.

You say '*abhyasa*': *abhyasa* is only the prevention of disturbance to the inherent peace. You are always in your natural state whether you make *abhyasa* or not. To remain as you are, without question or doubt, is your natural state.[1]

Q: *There are times when persons and things take on a vague, almost transparent form as in a dream. One ceases to observe them from outside, but one is passively conscious of their existence, while not actively conscious of any kind of selfhood. There is a deep quietness in the mind. Is the mind at such times ready to dive into the Self? Or is this condition unhealthy, the result of self-hypnotism? Should it be encouraged as a means of getting temporary peace?*

A: There is consciousness along with quietness in the mind. This is exactly the state to be aimed at. The fact that the question has been framed on this point, without realising that it is the Self, shows that the state is not steady but casual.

The word 'diving' is only appropriate if one has to turn the mind within in order to avoid being distracted by the outgoing tendencies of the mind. At such times one has to dive below the surface of these external phenomena. But when deep quietness prevails without obstructing the consciousness, where is the need to dive?[2]

Q: *When I meditate I feel a certain bliss at times. On such occasions, should I ask myself 'Who is it that experiences this bliss?'*

A: If it is the real bliss of the Self that is experienced, that is, if the mind has really merged in the Self, such a doubt will not arise at all. The question itself shows real bliss was not reached.

All doubts willl cease only when the doubter and his source have been found. There is no use removing doubts one by one. If we clear one doubt, another doubt will arise and there will be no end of doubts. But if, by seeking the source of the doubter, the doubter is found to be really non-existent, then all doubts will cease.

Q: *Sometimes I hear internal sounds. What should I do when such things happen?*

A: Whatever may happen, keep up the enquiry into the self, asking 'Who hears these sounds?' till the reality is reached.[3]

Q: *Sometimes, while in meditation, I feel blissful and tears come to my eyes. At other times I do not have them. Why is that?*

A: Bliss is a thing which is always there and is not something which comes and goes. That which comes and goes is a creation of the mind and you should not worry about it.

Q: *The bliss causes a physical thrill in the body, but when it disappears I feel dejected and desire to have the experience over again. Why?*

A: You admit that you were there both when the blissful feeling was experienced and when it was not. If you realise that 'you' properly, those experiences will be of no account.

Q: *For realising that bliss, there must be something to catch hold of, mustn't there?*

A: There must be a duality if you are to catch hold of something else, but what is is only the one Self, not a duality. Hence, who is to catch hold of whom? And what is the thing to be caught?[4]

Q: *When I reach the thoughtless stage in my* sadhana *I enjoy a certain pleasure, but sometimes I also experience a vague fear which I cannot properly describe.*

A: You may experience anything, but you should never rest content with that. Whether you feel pleasure or fear, ask yourself who feels the pleasure or the fear and so carry on the *sadhana* until pleasure and fear are both transcended, till all duality ceases and till the reality alone remains.

There is nothing wrong in such things happening or being

experienced, but you must never stop at that. For instance, you must never rest content with the pleasure of *laya* [temporary abeyance of the mind] experienced when thought is quelled, you must press on until all duality ceases.[5]

Q: *How does one get rid of fear?*

A: What is fear? It is only a thought. If there is anything besides the Self there is reason to fear. Who sees things separate from the Self? First the ego arises and sees objects as external. If the ego does not rise, the Self alone exists and there is nothing external. For anything external to oneself implies the existence of the seer within. Seeking it there will eliminate doubt and fear. Not only fear, all other thoughts centred round the ego will disappear along with it.[6]

Q: *How can the terrible fear of death be overcome?*

A: When does that fear seize you? Does it come when you do not see your body, say, in dreamless sleep? It haunts you only when you are fully 'awake' and perceive the world, including your body. If you do not see these and remain your pure Self, as in dreamless sleep, no fear can touch you.

If you trace this fear to the object, the loss of which gives rise to it, you will find that that object is not the body, but the mind which functions in it. Many a man would be only too glad to be rid of his diseased body and all the problems and inconvenience it creates for him if continued awareness were vouchsafed to him. It is the awareness, the consciousness, and not the body, he fears to lose. Men love existence because it is eternal awareness, which is their own Self. Why not then hold on to the pure awareness right now, while in the body, and be free from all fear?[7]

Q: *When I try to be without all thoughts, I pass into sleep. What should I do about it?*

A: Once you go to sleep you can do nothing in that state. But while you are awake, try to keep away all thoughts. Why think about sleep? Even that is a thought, is it not? If you are able to be without any thought while you are awake, that is enough. When you pass into sleep the state which you were in before falling asleep will continue when you wake up. You will continue from where you left off when you fell into slumber. So long as there are thoughts of activity there will also be sleep. Thought and sleep are counterparts of one and the same thing.

We should not sleep too much or go without it altogether, but sleep only moderately. To prevent too much sleep, we must try and have no thoughts or *chalana* [movement of the mind], we must eat only *sattvic* food and that only in moderate measure, and not indulge in too much physical activity. The more we control thought, activity and food the more we shall be able to control sleep. But moderation ought to be the rule, as explained in the *Gita*, for the seeker on the path. Sleep is the first obstacle, as explained in the books, for all *sadhaks*. The second obstacle is said to be *vikshepa* or the sense objects of the world which divert one's attention. The third is said to be *kashaya* or thoughts in the mind about previous experiences with sense objects. The fourth, *ananda* [bliss], is also called an obstacle, because in that state a feeling of separation from the source of *ananda*, enabling the enjoyer to say 'I am enjoying *ananda*', is present. Even this has to be surmounted. The final stage of *samadhi* has to be reached in which one becomes *ananda* or one with reality. In this state the duality of enjoyer and enjoyment ceases in the ocean of *sat-chit-ananda* or the Self.[8]

Q: *So one should not try to perpetuate blissful or ecstatic states?*

A: The final obstacle in meditation is ecstasy; you feel great bliss and happiness and want to stay in that ecstasy. Do not yield to it but pass on to the next stage which is great calm. The calm is higher than ecstasy and it merges into *samadhi*. Successful *samadhi* causes a waking sleep state to supervene. In that state you know that you are always consciousness, for consciousness is your nature. Actually, one is always in *samadhi* but one does not know it. To know it all one has to do is to remove the obstacles.[9]

Q: *Through poetry, music,* japa, bhajans *[devotional songs], the sight of beautiful landscapes, reading the lines of spiritual verses, etc., one experiences sometimes a true sense of the all-pervading unity. Is that feeling of deep blissful quiet in which the personal self has no place the same as the entering into the Heart of which Bhagavan speaks? Will undertaking these activities lead to a deeper* samadhi *and so ultimately to a full vision of the real?*

A: There is happiness when agreeable things are presented to the mind. It is the happiness inherent in the Self, and there is no other happiness. And it is not alien and afar. You are diving into the Self on those occasions which you consider pleasurable and that diving results in self-existent bliss. But the association of ideas is responsible for foisting that bliss on other things or occurrences while, in fact, that bliss is within you. On these occasions you are plunging into the Self, though unconsciously. If you do so consciously, with the conviction that comes of the experience that you are identical with the happiness which is truly the Self, the one reality, you call it realisation. I want you to dive consciously into the Self, that is the Heart.[10]

Q: *I have been making* sadhana *for nearly twenty years and I can see no progress. What should I do? From about five o'clock every morning I concentrate on the thought that the Self alone is real and all else unreal. Although I have been doing this for about twenty years I cannot concentrate for more than two or three minutes without my thoughts wandering.*

A: There is no other way to succeed than to draw the mind back every time it turns outwards and fix it in the Self. There is no need for meditation or *mantra* or *japa* or anything of the sort, because these are our real nature. All that is needed is to give up thinking of objects other than the Self. Meditation is not so much thinking of the Self as giving up thinking of the not-Self. When you give up thinking of outward objects and prevent your mind from going outwards by turning it inwards and fixing it in the Self, the Self alone remains.

Q: *What should I do to overcome the pull of these thoughts and desires? How should I regulate my life so as to attain control over my thoughts?*

A: The more you get fixed in the Self the more other thoughts will drop off of themselves. The mind is nothing but a bundle of thoughts, and the 'I'-thought is the root of all of them. When you see who this 'I' is and find out where it comes from all thoughts get merged in the Self.

Regulation of life, such as getting up at a fixed hour, bathing, doing *mantra*, *japa*, observing ritual, all this is for people who do not feel drawn to self-enquiry or are not capable of it. But for those who can practise this method all rules and discipline are unnecessary.[11]

Q: *Why cannot the mind be turned inward in spite of repeated attempts?*

A: It is done by practice and dispassion and it succeeds only gradually. The mind, having been so long a cow accustomed to graze stealthily on others' estates, is not easily confined to her stall. However much her keeper tempts her with luscious grass and fine fodder, she refuses the first time. Then she takes a bit, but her innate tendency to stray away asserts itself and she slips away.

On being repeatedly tempted by the owner, she accustoms herself to the stall until finally, even if let loose, she does not stray away. Similarly with the mind. If once it finds its inner happiness it will not wander outward.

Q: *Are there not modulations in contemplation according to circumstances?*

A: Yes. There are. At times there is illumination and then contemplation is easy. At other times contemplation is impossible even with repeated attempts. This is due to the working of the three *gunas* [*sattva*, *rajas* and *tamas*].

Q: *Is it influenced by one's activities and circumstances?*

A: Those cannot influence it. It is the sense of doership – *kartritva buddhi* – that forms the impediment.[12]

Q: *My mind remains clear for two or three days and turns dull for the next two or three days; and so it alternates. What is it due to?*

A: It is quite natural. It is the play of purity [*sattva*], activity [*rajas*] and inertia [*tamas*] alternating. Do not regret the *tamas*, but when *sattva* comes into play, hold on to it and make the best of it.[13]

Q: *A man sometimes finds that the physical body does not permit steady meditation. Should he practise yoga for training the body for the purpose?*

A: It is according to one's *samskaras* [predispositions]. One man will practise *hatha* yoga for curing his bodily ills, another man will trust to God to cure them, a third man will use his will-power for it and a fourth man may be totally indifferent to them. But all of them will persist in meditation. The quest for the Self is the essential factor and all the rest are mere accessories.[14]

Q: *My attempts at concentration are frustrated by sudden palpitations of the heart and accompanying hard, short and quick breaths. Then my thoughts also rush out and the mind becomes uncontrollable. Under healthy conditions I am more successful and my breath comes to a standstill with deep concentration. I had long been anxious to get the benefit of Sri Bhagavan's proximity for the successful culmination of my meditation and so came here after considerable effort. I fell ill here. I could not meditate and so I felt depressed. I made a determined effort to concentrate my mind even though I was troubled by short and quick breaths. Though partly successful it does not satisfy me. The time for my leaving the place is drawing near. I feel more and more depressed as I contemplate leaving the place. Here I find people obtaining peace by meditation in the hall whereas I am not blessed with such peace. This itself has a depressing effect on me.*

A: This thought, 'I am not able to concentrate', is itself an obstacle. Why should the thought arise?

Q: *Can one remain without thoughts rising all the twenty-four hours of the day? Should I remain without meditation?*

A: What is 'hours' again? It is a concept. Each question of yours is prompted by a thought.

Whenever a thought arises, do not be carried away by it. You become aware of the body when you forget the Self. But can you forget the Self? Being the Self how can you forget it? There must be two selves for one to forget the other. It is absurd. So the Self is not depressed, nor is it imperfect. It is ever happy. The contrary feeling is a mere thought which has actually no stamina in it. Be rid of thoughts. Why should one attempt meditation? Being the Self one remains always realised. Only be free from thoughts.

You think that your health does not permit your meditation. This depression must be traced to its origin. The origin is the wrong identification of the body with the Self. The disease is not of the Self, it is of the body. But the body does not come and tell you that it is possessed by the disease. It is you who say so. Why? Because you have wrongly identified yourself with the body. The body itself is a thought. Be as you really are. There is no reason to be depressed.[15]

Q: *Suppose there is some disturbance during meditation, such as mosquito bites. Should one persist in meditation and try to bear the bites and ignore the interruption, or drive the mosquitoes away and then continue the meditation?*

A: You must do as you find most convenient. You will not attain *mukti* simply because you drive them away. The thing is to attain one-pointedness and then to attain *mano-nasa* [destruction of the mind]. Whether you do this by putting up with the mosquito bites or driving the mosquitoes away is left to you. If you are completely absorbed in your meditation you will not know that the mosquitoes are biting you. Till you attain that stage why should you not drive them away?[16]

Q: *People practising meditation are said to get new diseases; at any rate, I feel some pain in the back and front of the chest. This is stated to be a test by God. Will Bhagavan explain this and say if it is true?*

A: There is no Bhagavan outside you and no test is therefore instituted. What you believe to be a test or a new disease resulting from spiritual practices is really the strain that is now brought to play upon your nerves and the five senses. The mind which was hitherto operating through the *nadis* [nerves] to sense external objects, maintaining a link between itself and the organs of perception, is now required to withdraw from the link' and this action of withdrawal naturally causes a strain, a sprain or a snap attendant with pain. Some people call this a disease and some call it a test of God. All these pains will go if you continue your meditation, bestowing your thought solely on understanding your Self or on Self-realisation. There is no greater remedy than this continuous yoga or union with God or *atman*. Pain is inevitable as a result of discarding the *vasanas* [mental tendencies] which you have had for so long.[17]

Q: *What is the best way of dealing with desires and* vasanas *with a view to getting rid of them – satisfying them or suppressing them?*

A: If a desire can be got rid of by satisfying it, there will be no harm in satisfying such a desire. But desires generally are not eradicated by satisfaction. Trying to root them out that way is like trying to quench a fire by pouring inflammable spirits on it. At the same time, the proper remedy is not forcible suppression, since such repression is bound to react sooner or later into a forceful surging up of desires with undesirable consequences. The proper way to get rid of a desire is to find out 'Who gets the desire? What is its source?' When this is found, the desire is rooted out and it will never again emerge or grow. Small desires such as the desire to eat, drink, sleep and attend to calls of nature, though these may also be classed among desires, you can safely satisfy. They will not implant *vasanas* in your mind, necessitating further birth. Those activities are just necessary to carry on life and are not likely to develop or leave behind *vasanas* or tendencies. As a general rule, therefore, there is no harm in satisfying a desire where the satisfaction will not lead to further desires by creating *vasanas* in the mind.[18]

Q: *In the practice of meditation are there any signs in the realm of subjective experience which will indicate the aspirant's progress towards Self-realisation?*

A: The degree of freedom from unwanted thoughts and the degree of concentration on a single thought are the measures to gauge the progress.[19]

PART SIX

Theory

All metaphysical discussion is profitless unless it causes us to seek within the Self for the true reality.

All controversies about creation, the nature of the universe, evolution, the purpose of God, etc., are useless. They are not conducive to our true happiness. People try to find out about things which are outside of them before they try to find out 'Who am I?' Only by the latter means can happiness be gained.[1]

CHAPTER 17
Creation theories and the reality of the world

Sri Ramana had little or no interest in the theoretical side of spirituality. His principal concern was to bring people to an awareness of the Self and, to achieve this end, he always insisted that practice was more important than speculation. He discouraged questions of a theoretical nature either by remaining silent when they were asked or by asking the questioner to find the source of the 'I' that was asking the question. Occasionally he would relent and give detailed expositions on various aspects of philosophy, but if his questioners persisted too long with their queries, or if the conversation veered towards sterile intellectualism, he would change the subject and direct the attention of his questioners towards more practical matters.

Many of these philosophical conversations centred around the nature and origin of the physical world since Sri Ramana was known to have views which were totally at variance with the common-sense view of the world. As with most other topics he tailored his statements to conform to the different levels of understanding he encountered in his questioners, but even so, almost all his ideas were radical refutations of the concepts of physical reality that most people cherish.

Sri Ramana adopted three different standpoints when he spoke about the nature of the physical world. He advocated all of them at different times but it is clear from his general comments on the subject that he only considered the first two theories given below to be either true or useful.

1 *Ajata vada* (the theory of non-causality). This is an ancient Hindu doctrine which states that the creation of the world never happened at all. It is a complete denial of all causality in the physical world. Sri Ramana endorsed this view by saying that it is the *jnani*'s experience that nothing ever comes into existence or ceases to be because the Self alone exists as the sole unchanging reality. It is a corollary of

this theory that time, space, cause and effect, essential components of all creation theories, exist only in the minds of *ajnanis* and that the experience of the Self reveals their non-existence.

This theory is not a denial of the reality of the world, only of the creative process which brought it into existence. Speaking from his own experience Sri Ramana said that the *jnani* is aware that the world is real, not as an assemblage of interacting matter and energy, but as an uncaused appearance in the Self. He enlarged on this by saying that because the real nature or substratum of this appearance is identical with the beingness of the Self, it necessarily partakes of its reality. That is to say, the world is not real to the *jnani* simply because it appears, but only because the real nature of the appearance is inseparable from the Self.

The *ajnani*, on the other hand, is totally unaware of the unitary nature and source of the world and, as a consequence, his mind constructs an illusory world of separate interacting objects by persistently misinterpreting the sense-impressions it receives. Sri Ramana pointed out that this view of the world has no more reality than a dream since it superimposes a creation of the mind on the reality of the Self. He summarised the difference between the *jnani*'s and the *ajnani*'s standpoint by saying that the world is unreal if it is perceived by the mind as a collection of discrete objects and real when it is directly experienced as an appearance in the Self.

2   *Drishti-srishti vada* If his questioners found the idea of *ajata* or non-causality impossible to assimilate, he would teach them that the world comes into existence simultaneously with the appearance of the 'I'-thought and that it ceases to exist when the 'I'-thought is absent. This theory is known as *drishti-srishti*, or simultaneous creation, and it says, in effect, that the world which appears to an *ajnani* is a product of the mind that perceives it, and that in the absence of that mind it ceases to exist. The theory is true in so far as the mind does create an imaginary world for itself, but from the standpoint of the Self, an imaginary 'I' creating an imaginary world is no creation at all, and so the doctrine of *ajata* is not subverted. Although Sri Ramana sometimes said that *drishti-srishti* was not the ultimate truth about creation

he encouraged his followers to accept it as a working hypothesis. He justified this approach by saying that if one can consistently regard the world as an unreal creation of the mind then it loses its attraction and it becomes easier to maintain an undistracted awareness of the 'I'-thought.

3   *Srishti-drishti vada* (gradual creation). This is the common-sense view which holds that the world is an objective reality governed by laws of cause and effect which can be traced back to a single act of creation. It includes virtually all western ideas on the subject from the 'big bang' theory to the biblical account in Genesis. Sri Ramana only invoked theories of this nature when he was talking to questioners who were unwilling to accept the implications of the *ajata* and *drishti-srishti* theories. Even then, he would usually point out that such theories should not be taken too seriously as they were only promulgated to satisfy intellectual curiosity.

Literally, *drishti-srishti* means that the world only exists when it is perceived whereas *srishti-drishti* means that the world existed prior to anyone's perception of it. Although the former theory sounds perverse, Sri Ramana insisted that serious seekers should be satisfied with it, partly because it is a close approximation to the truth and partly because it is the most beneficial attitude to adopt if one is seriously interested in realising the Self.

Q: *How has* srishti *[creation] come about? Some say it is predestined. Others say it is the Lord's leela or sport. What is the truth?*

A: Various accounts are given in books. But is there creation? Only if there is creation do we have to explain how it came about. We may not know about all these theories but we certainly know that we exist. Why not know the 'I' and then see if there is a creation?[1]

Q: *In the* vedanta *of Sri Sankaracharya the principle of the creation of the world has been accepted for the sake of beginners, but for the advanced the principle of non-creation is put forward. What is your view on this matter?*

A: 'There is no dissolution or creation, no one in bondage, nor anyone pursuing spiritual practices. There is no one desiring

liberation nor anyone liberated. This is the absolute truth.' This
sloka appears in the second chapter of Gaudapada's *karika*. One
who is established in the Self sees this by his knowledge of reality.[2]

Q: *Is not the Self the cause of this world we see around us?*

A: Self itself appears as the world of diverse names and forms.
However, Self does not act as the efficient cause [*nimitta karana*],
creating, sustaining and destroying it. Do not ask 'Why does the
confusion of Self, not knowing the truth that it itself appears as
the world, arise?' If instead you enquire 'To whom does this
confusion occur?', it will be discovered that no such confusion
ever existed for Self.[3]

Q: *You seem to be an exponent of* ajata *doctrine of* advaita
vedanta.

A: I do not teach only the *ajata* doctrine. I approve of all
schools. The same truth has to be expressed in different ways to
suit the capacity of the hearer. The *ajata* doctrine says, 'Nothing
exists except the one reality. There is no birth or death, no
projection or drawing in, no seeker, no bondage, no liberation.
The one unity alone exists.' To such as find it difficult to grasp this
truth and who ask, 'How can we ignore this solid world we see all
around us?', the dream experience is pointed out and they are
told, 'All that you see depends on the seer. Apart from the seer,
there is no seen.' This is called the *drishti-srishti vada* or the
argument that one first creates out of one's mind and then sees
what one's mind itself has created. Some people cannot grasp even
this and they continue to argue in the following terms: 'The dream
experience is so short, while the world always exists. The dream
experience was limited to me. But the world is felt and seen not
only by me, but by so many others. We cannot call such a world
non-existent.' When people argue in this way they can be given a
srishti-drishti theory, for example, 'God first created such and
such a thing, out of such and such an element, and then something
else was created, and so on.' That alone will satisfy this class.
Their minds are otherwise not satisfied and they ask themselves,
'How can all geography, all maps, all sciences, stars, planets and
the rules governing or relating to them and all knowledge be
totally untrue?' To such it is best to say, 'Yes, God created all this
and so you see it.'

Q: *But all these cannot be true. Only one doctrine can be true.*

A: All these theories are only to suit the capacity of the
learner. The absolute can only be one.[4]

The *vedanta* says that the cosmos springs into view simultaneously with the seer and that there is no detailed process of creation. This is said to be *yugapat-srishti* [instantaneous creation]. It is quite similar to the creations in dream where the experiencer springs up simultaneously with the objects of experience. When this is told, some people are not satisfied for they are deeply rooted in objective knowledge. They seek to find out how there can be sudden creation. They argue that an effect must be preceded by a cause. In short, they desire an explanation for the existence of the world which they see around them. Then the *srutis* [scriptures] try to satisfy their curiosity by theories of creation. This method of dealing with the subject of creation is called *krama-srishti* [gradual creation]. But the true seeker can be content with *yugapat-srishti*, instantaneous creation.[5]

Q: *What is the purpose of creation?*

A: It is to give rise to this question. Investigate the answer to this question, and finally abide in the supreme or rather the primal source of all, the Self. The investigation will resolve itself into a quest for the Self and it will cease only after the non-Self is sifted away and the Self realised in its purity and glory.[6]

There may be any number of theories of creation. All of them extend outwardly. There will be no limit to them because time and space are unlimited. They are however only in the mind. If you see the mind, time and space are transcended and the Self is realised.

Creation is explained scientifically or logically to one's own satisfaction. But is there any finality about it? Such explanations are called *krama-srishti* [gradual creation]. On the other hand, *drishti-srishti* [simultaneous creation] is *yugapat-srishti*. Without the seer there are no objects seen. Find the seer and the creation is comprised in him. Why look outward and go on explaining the phenomena which are endless?[7]

Q: *The Vedas contain conflicting accounts of cosmogony. Ether is said to be the first creation in one place; vital energy [prana] in another place; something else in yet another; water in still another, and so on. How are these to be reconciled? Do not these impair the credibility of the Vedas?*

A: Different seers saw different aspects of truth at different times, each emphasising one view. Why do you worry about their conflicting statements? The essential aim of the *Vedas* is to teach us the nature of the imperishable *atman* and show us that we are that.

Q: *I am satisfied with that portion.*

A: Then treat all the rest as *artha vada* [auxiliary arguments] or expositions for the sake of the ignorant who seek to trace the genesis of things.[8]

Q: *I form part of the creation and so remain dependent. I cannot solve the riddle of creation until I become independent. Yet I ask Sri Bhagavan, should he not answer the question for me?*

A: Yes. It is Bhagavan that says, 'Become independent and solve the riddle yourself. It is for you to do it.' Again, where are you now that you ask this question? Are you in the world, or is the world within you? You must admit that the world is not perceived in your sleep although you cannot deny your existence then. The world appears when you wake up. So where is it? Clearly the world is your thought. Thoughts are your projections. The 'I' is first created and then the world. The world is created by the 'I' which in its turn rises up from the Self. The riddle of the creation of the world is thus solved if you solve the creation of the 'I'. So I say, find your Self.

Again, does the world come and ask you 'Why do "I" exist? How was "I" created?' It is you who ask the question. The questioner must establish the relationship between the world and himself. He must admit that the world is his own imagination. Who imagines it? Let him again find the 'I' and then the Self. Moreover, all the scientific and theological explanations do not harmonise. The diversities in such theories clearly show the uselessness of seeking such explanations. Such explanations are purely mental or intellectual and nothing more. Still, all of them are true according to the standpoint of the individual. There is no creation in the state of realisation. When one sees the world, one does not see oneself. When one sees the Self, the world is not seen. So see the Self and realise that there has been no creation.[9]

Q: *'Brahman is real. The world [jagat] is illusion' is the stock phrase of Sri Sankaracharya. Yet others say, 'The world is reality.' Which is true?*

A: Both statements are true. They refer to different stages of development and are spoken from different points of view. The aspirant [*abhyasi*] starts with the definition, that which is real exists always. Then he eliminates the world as unreal because it is changing. The seeker ultimately reaches the Self and there finds unity as the prevailing note. Then, that which was originally rejected as being unreal is found to be a part of the unity. Being absorbed in the reality, the world also is real. There is only being in Self-realisation, and nothing but being.[10]

Q: *Sri Bhagavan often says that* maya *[illusion] and reality are the same. How can that be?*

A: Sankara was criticised for his views on *maya* without being understood. He said that

(1) *Brahman* is real,
(2) the universe is unreal, and
(3) The universe is *Brahman*.

He did not stop at the second, because the third explains the other two. It signifies that the universe is real if perceived as the Self, and unreal if perceived apart from the Self. Hence *maya* and reality are one and the same.[11]

Q: *So the world is not really illusory?*

A: At the level of the spiritual seeker you have got to say that the world is an illusion. There is no other way. When a man forgets that he is *Brahman*, who is real, permanent and omnipresent, and deludes himself into thinking that he is a body in the universe which is filled with bodies that are transitory, and labours under that delusion, you have got to remind him that the world is unreal and a delusion. Why? Because his vision which has forgotten its own Self is dwelling in the external, material universe. It will not turn inwards into introspection unless you impress on him that all this external, material universe is unreal. When once he realises his own Self he will know that there is nothing other than his own Self and he will come to look upon the whole universe as *Brahman*. There is no universe without the Self. So long as a man does not see the Self which is the origin of all, but looks only at the external world as real and permanent, you have to tell him that all this external universe is an illusion. You cannot help it. Take a paper. We see only the script, and nobody notices the paper on which the script is written. The paper is there whether the script on it is there or not. To those who look upon the script as real, you have to say that it is unreal, an illusion, since it rests upon the paper. The wise man looks upon both the paper and script as one. So also with *Brahman* and the universe.[12]

Q: *So the world is real when it is experienced as the Self and unreal when it is seen as separate names and forms?*

A: Just as fire is obscured by smoke, the shining light of consciousness is obscured by the assemblage of names and forms,

the world. When by compassionate divine grace the mind becomes
clear, the nature of the world will be known to be not the illusory
forms but only the reality.

Only those people whose minds are devoid of the evil power of
maya, having given up the knowledge of the world and being
unattached to it, and having thereby attained the knowledge of the
self-shining supreme reality, can correctly know the meaning of
the statement 'The world is real.' If one's outlook has been
transformed to the nature of real knowledge, the world of the five
elements beginning with ether [*akasa*] will be real, being the
supreme reality, which is the nature of knowledge.

The original state of this empty world, which is bewildering
and crowded with many names and forms, is bliss, which is one,
just as the egg-yolk of a multi-coloured peacock is only one. Know
this truth by abiding in the state of Self.[13]

Q: *I cannot say it is all clear to me. Is the world that is seen,
felt and sensed by us in so many ways something like a dream, an
illusion?*

A: There is no alternative for you but to accept the world as
unreal if you are seeking the truth and the truth alone.

Q: *Why so?*

A: For the simple reason that unless you give up the idea that
the world is real your mind will always be after it. If you take the
appearance to be real you will never know the real itself, although
it is the real alone that exists. This point is illustrated by the
analogy of the snake in the rope. You may be deceived into
believing that a piece of rope is a snake. While you imagine that
the rope is a snake you cannot see the rope as a rope. The non-
existent snake becomes real to you, while the real rope seems
wholly non-existent as such.

Q: *It is easy to accept tentatively that the world is not
ultimately real, but it is hard to have the conviction that it is really
unreal.*

A: Even so is your dream world real while you are dreaming.
So long as the dream lasts everything you see and feel in it is real.

Q: *Is then the world no better than a dream?*

A: What is wrong with the sense of reality you have while you
are dreaming? You may be dreaming of something quite
impossible, for instance, of having a happy chat with a dead
person. Just for a moment, you may doubt in the dream, saying to
yourself, 'Was he not dead?', but somehow your mind reconciles

itself to the dream-vision, and the person is as good as alive for the purposes of the dream. In other words, the dream as a dream does not permit you to doubt its reality. It is the same in the waking state, for you are unable to doubt the reality of the world which you see while you are awake. How can the mind which has itself created the world accept it as unreal? That is the significance of the comparison made between the world of the waking state and the dream world. Both are creations of the mind and, so long as the mind is engrossed in either, it finds itself unable to deny their reality. It cannot deny the reality of the dream world while it is dreaming and it cannot deny the reality of the waking world while it is awake. If, on the contrary, you withdraw your mind completely from the world and turn it within and abide there, that is, if you keep awake always to the Self which is the substratum of all experiences, you will find the world of which you are now aware is just as unreal as the world in which you lived in your dream.

Q: *We see, feel and sense the world in so many ways. These sensations are the reactions to the objects seen and felt. They are not mental creations as in dreams, which differ not only from person to person but also with regard to the same person. Is that not enough to prove the objective reality of the world?*

A: All this talk about inconsistencies in the dream-world arises only now, when you are awake. While you are dreaming, the dream was a perfectly integrated whole. That is to say, if you felt thirsty in a dream, the illusory drinking of illusory water quenched your illusory thirst. But all this was real and not illusory to you so long as you did not know that the dream itself was illusory. Similarly with the waking world. The sensations you now have get co-ordinated to give you the impression that the world is real.

If, on the contrary, the world is a self-existent reality (that is what you evidently mean by its objectivity), what prevents the world from revealing itself to you in sleep? You do not say you did not exist in your sleep.

Q: *Neither do I deny the world's existence while I am asleep. It has been existing all the while. If during my sleep I did not see it, others who were not sleeping saw it.*

A: To say you existed while asleep, was it necessary to call in the evidence of others so as to prove it to you? Why do you seek their evidence now? Those others can tell you of having seen the world during your sleep only when you yourself are awake. With regard to your own existence it is different. On waking up you say you had a sound sleep, and so to that extent you are aware of yourself in the deepest sleep, whereas you have not the slightest notion of the world's existence then. Even now, while you are awake, is it the world that says 'I am real', or is it you?

Q: *Of course I say it, but I say it of the world.*

A: Well then, that world, which you say is real, is really mocking at you for seeking to prove its reality while of your own reality you are ignorant.

You want somehow or other to maintain that the world is real. What is the standard of reality? That alone is real which exists by itself, which reveals itself by itself and which is eternal and unchanging.

Does the world exist by itself? Was it ever seen without the aid of the mind? In sleep there is neither mind nor world. When awake there is the mind and there is the world. What does this invariable concomitance mean? You are familiar with the principles of inductive logic which are considered the very basis of scientific investigation. Why do you not decide this question of the reality of the world in the light of those accepted principles of logic?

Of yourself you can say 'I exist'. That is, your existence is not mere existence, it is existence of which you are conscious. Really, it is existence identical with consciousness.

Q: *The world may not be conscious of itself, yet it exists.*

A: Consciousness is always Self-consciousness. If you are conscious of anything you are essentially conscious of yourself. Unself-conscious existence is a contradiction in terms. It is no existence at all. It is merely attributed existence, whereas true existence, the *sat*, is not an attribute, it is the substance itself. It is the *vastu* [reality]. Reality is therefore known as *sat-chit*, being-consciousness, and never merely the one to the exclusion of the other. The world neither exists by itself, nor is it conscious of its existence. How can you say that such a world is real?

And what is the nature of the world? It is perpetual change, a continuous, interminable flux. A dependent, unself-conscious, ever-changing world cannot be real.[14]

Q: *Are the names and forms of the world real?*

A: You won't find them separate from the substratum [*adhishtana*]. When you try to get at name and form, you will find reality only. Therefore attain the knowledge of that which is real for all time.

Q: *Why does the waking state look so real?*

A: We see so much on the cinema screen, but it is not real. Nothing is real there except the screen. In the same way in the waking state, there is nothing but *adhishtana*. Knowledge of the world is knowledge of the knower of the world [*jagrat-prama* is the *prama* of *jagrat-pramata*]. Both go away in sleep.

Q: *Why do we see such permanency and constancy in the world?*

A: It is seen on account of wrong ideas. When someone says that he took a bath in the same river twice he is wrong, because when he bathed for the second time the river is not the same as it was when he bathed for the first time. On looking twice at the brightness of a flame a man says that he sees the same flame, but this flame is changing every moment. The waking state is like this. The stationary appearance is an error of perception.

Q: *Where is the error?*

A: *Pramata* [the knower].

Q: *How did the knower come?*

A: On account of the error of perception. In fact the knower and his misperceptions appear simultaneously, and when the knowledge of the Self is obtained, they disappear simultaneously.

Q: *From where did the knower and his misperceptions come?*

A: Who is asking the question?

Q: *I am.*

A: Find out that 'I' and all your doubts will be solved. Just as in a dream a false knowledge, knower and known rise up, in the waking state the same process operates. In both states on knowing this 'I' you know everything and nothing remains to be known. In deep sleep, knower, knowledge and known are absent. In the same way, at the time of experiencing the real 'I' they will not exist. Whatever you see happening in the waking state happens only to the knower, and since the knower is unreal, nothing in fact ever happens.[15]

Q: *Is the light which gives the 'I'-sense identity and knowledge of the world ignorance or* chit, *consciousness?*

A: It is only the reflected light of *chit* that makes the 'I' believe itself different from others. This reflected light of *chit* also makes the 'I' create objects, but for this reflection there must be a surface on which the reflection takes place.

Q: *What is that surface?*

A: On realisation of the Self you will find that the reflection and the surface on which it takes place do not actually exist, but that both of them are one and the same *chit*. There is the world, which requires location for its existence and light to make it perceptible. Both rise simultaneously. Therefore physical existence and perception depend upon the light of the mind which is reflected from the Self. Just as cinema pictures can be made visible by a reflected light, and only in darkness, so also the world pictures are perceptible only by the light of the Self reflected in the darkness of *avidya* [ignorance]. The world can be seen neither in the utter darkness of ignorance, as in deep sleep, nor in the utter light of the Self, as in Self-realisation or *samadhi*.[16]

CHAPTER 18
Reincarnation

Most religions have constructed elaborate theories which purport to explain what happens to the individual soul after the death of the body. Some claim that the soul goes to heaven or hell while others claim that it is reincarnated in a new body.

Sri Ramana taught that all such theories are based on the false assumption that the individual self or soul is real; once this illusion is seen through, the whole superstructure of after-life theories collapses. From the standpoint of the Self, there is no birth or death, no heaven or hell, and no reincarnation.

As a concession to those who were unable to assimilate the implications of this truth, Sri Ramana would sometimes admit that reincarnation existed. In replying to such people he would say that if one imagined that the individual self was real, then that imaginary self would persist after death and that eventually it would identify with a new body and a new life. The whole process, he said, is sustained by the tendency of the mind to identify itself with a body. Once the limiting illusion of mind is transcended, identification with the body ceases, and all theories about death and reincarnation are found to be inapplicable.

Q: *Is reincarnation true?*

A: Reincarnation exists only so long as there is ignorance. There is really no reincarnation at all, either now or before. Nor will there be any hereafter. This is the truth.

Q: *Can a yogi know his past lives?*

A: Do you know the present life that you wish to know the past? Find the present, then the rest will follow. Even with our present limited knowledge, you suffer so much. Why should you burden yourself with more knowledge? Is it to suffer more?[1]

When seen through the sight of the supreme space of Self, the illusion of taking birth in this mirage-like false world is found to be nothing but the egotistical ignorance of identifying a body as

'I'. Among those whose minds are possessed with forgetfulness of Self, those who are born will die and those who die will be born again. But know that those whose minds are dead, having known the glorious supreme reality, will remain only there in that elevated state of reality, devoid of both birth and death. Forgetting Self, mistaking the body for Self, taking innumerable births, and at last knowing Self and being Self is just like waking from a dream of wandering all over the world.[2]

Q: *How long does it take a man to be reborn after death? Is it immediately after death or some time after?*

A: You do not know what you were before birth, yet you want to know what you will be after death. Do you know what you are now?

Birth and rebirth pertain to the body. You are identifying the Self with the body. It is a wrong identification. You believe that the body has been born and will die, and confound the phenomena relating to the body with the Self. Know your real being and these questions will not arise.

Birth and rebirth are mentioned only to make you investigate the question and find out that there are neither births nor rebirths. They relate to the body and not to the Self. Know the Self and don't be perturbed by doubts.[3]

Q: *Do not one's actions affect the person in later births?*

A: Are you born now? Why do you think of other births? The fact is that there is neither birth nor death. Let him who is born think of death and palliatives for it.[4]

Q: *What happens to a person after death?*

A: Engage yourself in the living present. The future will take care of itself. Do not worry about the future. The state before creation and the process of creation are dealt with in the scriptures in order that you may know the present. Because you say you are born, therefore they say, yes, and add that God created you.

But do you see God or anything else in your sleep? If God is real, why does he not shine forth in your sleep also? You always are, you are the same now as you were in sleep. You are not different from that one in sleep. But why should there be differences in the feelings or experiences of the two states?

Did you ask, while asleep, questions regarding your birth? Did you then ask 'Where do I go after death?' Why think of all these questions now in the waking state? Let what is born think of its birth and the remedy, its cause and ultimate results.[5]

Q: *What becomes of the* jiva *[individual] after death?*

A: The question is not appropriate for a *jiva* now living. A dead *jiva* may ask me, if he wishes to. In the meantime let the embodied *jiva* solve its present problem and find who he is. Then there will be an end of such doubts.[6]

Q: *Is the Buddhist view, that there is no continuous entity answering to the ideas of the individual soul, correct or not? Is this consistent with the Hindu notion of a reincarnating ego? Is the soul a continuous entity which reincarnates again and again, according to the Hindu doctrine, or is it a mere mass of mental tendencies – samskaras?*

A: The real Self is continuous and unaffected. The reincarnating ego belongs to the lower plane, namely, thought. It is transcended by Self-realisation.

Reincarnations are due to a spurious offshoot. Therefore they are denied by the Buddhists. The present state of ignorance is due to the identification of consciousness [*chit*] with the insentient [*jada*] body.[7]

Q: *Do not we go to heaven [svarga] as the result of our actions?*

A: That is as true as the present existence. But if we enquire who we are and discover the Self, what need is there to think of heaven?

Q: *Should I not try to escape rebirth?*

A: Yes. Find out who is born and who now has the trouble of existence. When you are asleep do you think of rebirths or even the present existence? So find out from where the present problem arises and in that place you will find the solution. You will discover that there is no birth, no present trouble or unhappiness. The Self is all and all is bliss. Even now we are free from rebirth so why fret over the misery of it?[8]

Q: *Is there rebirth?*

A: Do you know what birth is?

Q: *Oh yes, I know that I exist now, but I want to know if I'll exist in the future.*

A: Past! . . . Present! . . . Future! . . .

Q: *Yes, today is the result of yesterday, the past, and tomorrow, the future, will be the result of today, the present. Am I right?*

A: There is neither past nor future. There is only the present. Yesterday was the present to you when you experienced it, and tomorrow will be also the present when you experience it. Therefore, experience takes place only in the present, and beyond experience nothing exists.

Q: *Are then past and future mere imagination?*

A: Yes, even the present is mere imagination, for the sense of time is purely mental. Space is similarly mental. Therefore birth and rebirth, which take place in time and space, cannot be other than imagination.[9]

Q: *What is the cause of* tanha, *the thirst for life and the thirst for rebirth?*

A: Real rebirth is dying from the ego into the spirit. This is the significance of the crucifixion of Jesus. Whenever identification with the body exists, a body is always available, whether this or any other one, till the body-sense disappears by merging into the source – the spirit, or Self. The stone which is projected upwards remains in constant motion till it returns to its source, the earth, and rests. Headache continues to give trouble, till the pre-headache state is regained.

Thirst for life is inherent in the very nature of life, which is absolute existence – *sat*. Although indestructible by nature, by false identification with its destructible instrument, the body, consciousness imbibes a false apprehension of its destructibility. Because of that false identification it tries to perpetuate the body, and that results in a succession of births. But however long these bodies may last, they eventually come to an end and yield to the Self, which alone eternally exists.

Q: *Yes, 'Give up thy life if thou wouldst live', says the* Voice of the Silence *of H.P. Blavatsky.*

A: Give up the false identification and remember, the body cannot exist without the Self, whereas the Self can exist without the body. In fact it is always without it.

Q: *A doubt has just now arisen in a friend of mine's mind. She has just heard that a human being may take an animal birth in some other life, which is contrary to what Theosophy has taught her.*

A: Let him who takes birth ask this question. Find out first who it is that is born, and whether there is actual birth and death. You will find that birth pertains to the ego, which is an illusion of the mind.[10]

Q: *Is it possible for a man to be reborn as a lower animal?*

A: Yes. It is possible, as illustrated by Jada Bharata – the scriptural anecdote of a royal sage having been reborn as a deer.

Q: *Is the individual capable of spiritual progress in an animal body?*

A: Not impossible, though it is exceedingly rare.[11] It is not true that birth as a man is necessarily the highest, and that one must attain realisation only from being a man. Even an animal can attain Self-realisation.[12]

Q: *Theosophy speaks of fifty to 10,000 year intervals between death and rebirth. Why is this so?*

A: There is no relation between the standard of measurements of one state of consciousness and another. All such measurements are hypothetical. It is true that some individuals take more time and some less. But it must be distinctly understood that it is no soul which comes and goes, but only the thinking mind of the individual, which makes it appear to do so. On whatever plane the mind happens to act, it creates a body for itself; in the physical world a physical body and in the dream world a dream body which becomes wet with dream rain and sick with dream disease. After the death of the physical body, the mind remains inactive for some time, as in dreamless sleep when it remains worldless and therefore bodiless. But soon it becomes active again in a new world and a new body – the astral – till it assumes another body in what is called a 'rebirth'. But the *jnani*, the Self-realised man, whose mind has already ceased to act, remains unaffected by death. The mind of the *jnani* has ceased to exist; it has dropped never to rise again to cause births and deaths. The chain of illusions has snapped for ever for him.

It should now be clear that there is neither real birth, nor real death. It is the mind which creates and maintains the illusion of reality in this process, till it is destroyed by Self-realisation.[13]

Q: *Does not death dissolve the individuality of a person, so that there can be no rebirth, just as the rivers discharged into the ocean lose their individualities?*

A: But when the waters evaporate and return as rain on the hills, they once more flow in the form of rivers and fall into the ocean. So also the individualities during sleep lose their separateness and yet return as individuals according to their *samskaras* or past tendencies. It is the same after death – the individuality of the person with *samskaras* is not lost.

Q: *How can that be?*

A: See how a tree whose branches have been cut grows again.

So long as the roots of the tree remain unimpaired, the tree will continue to grow. Similarly, the *samskaras* which have merely sunk in the Heart on death, but have not perished for that reason, occasion rebirth at the right time. That is how *jivas* [individuals] are reborn.

Q: *How could the innumerable* jivas *and the wide universe which they produce sprout up from such subtle* samskaras *sunk in the Heart?*

A: Just as the big banyan tree sprouts from a tiny seed, so do the *jivas* and the whole universe with name and form sprout up from the subtle *samskaras.*[14]

Q: *How does the* jiva *transfer from one body to another?*

A: When one begins to die, hard breathing sets in; that means that one has become unconscious of the dying body. The mind at once takes hold of another body, and it swings to and fro between the two, until attachment is fully transferred to the new body. Meanwhile there are occasional violent breaths, and that means that the mind swings back to the dying body. The transitional state of the mind is somewhat like a dream.[15]

Q: *How long is the interval between one's death and reincarnation?*

A: It may be long or short. But a *jnani* does not undergo any such changes; he merges into the universal being.

Some say that those who after death pass into the path of light are not reborn, whereas those who after death take the path of darkness are reborn after they have enjoyed the fruits of *karma* in their subtle bodies.

Some say that if one's merits and demerits are equal, they are directly reborn here. Merits outweighing demerits, the subtle bodies go to heaven and are then reborn here; demerits out-weighing merits, they go to hells and are afterwards reborn here.

A *Yogabrashta* [one who has slipped from the path of yoga] is said to fare in the same manner. All these are described in the *sastras.* But in fact, there is neither birth nor death. One remains only as what one really is. This is the only truth.[16]

Q: *I find this very confusing. Are both births and rebirths ultimately unreal?*

A: If there is birth there must be not only one rebirth but a whole succession of births. Why and how did you get this birth? For the same reason and in the same manner you must have succeeding births. But if you ask who has the birth and whether birth and death are for you or for somebody distinct from you, then you realise the truth and the truth burns up all *karmas* and frees you from all births. The books graphically describe how all *sanchita karma* [*karma* accumulated from previous births], which would take countless lives to exhaust, is burnt up by one little spark of *jnana*, just as a mountain of gunpowder will be blown up by a single spark of fire. It is the ego that is the cause of all the world and of the countless sciences whose researches are so great as to baffle description, and if the ego is dissolved by enquiry all this immediately crumbles and the reality or Self alone remains.[17]

Q: *Do you mean to say that I was never even born?*

A: Yes, you are now thinking that you are the body and therefore confuse yourself with its birth and death. But you are not the body and you have no birth and death.

Q: *So you do not uphold the theory of rebirth?*

A: No. On the other hand I want to remove your confusion that you will be reborn. It is you who think that you will be reborn.

See for whom the question arises. Unless the questioner is found, such questions can never finally be answered.[18]

CHAPTER 19
The nature of God

At first sight, Sri Ramana's statements on God appear to be riddled with contradictions: on one occasion he might say that God never does anything, on another that nothing happens except by his will. Sometimes he would say that God is just an idea in the mind, while at other times he would say that God is the only existing reality.

These contradictory statements are largely a reflection of the differing levels of understanding he encountered in his questioners. Those who worshipped personal Gods would often be given anthropomorphic explanations. They would be told that God created the world, that he sustains it by his divine power, that he looks after the needs of all its inhabitants and that nothing happens that is contrary to his will. On the other hand, those who were not attracted to such a theory would be told that all such ideas about God and his power were mental creations which only obscured the real experience of God which is inherent in everyone.

At the highest level of his teachings the terms 'God' and 'Self' are synonyms for the immanent reality which is discovered by Self-realisation. Thus realisation of the Self is realisation of God; it is not an experience *of* God, rather it is an understanding that one *is* God. Speaking from this ultimate level, Sri Ramana's statements on God can be summarised in the following way:

1 He is immanent and formless; he is pure being and pure consciousness.
2 Manifestation appears in him and through his power, but he is not its creator. God never acts, he just is. He has neither will nor desire.
3 Individuality is the illusion that we are not identical with God; when the illusion is dispelled, what remains is God.

On a lower level he spoke about *Iswara*, the Hindu name for the supreme personal God. He said that *Iswara* exists as a real entity only so long as one imagines that one is an individual person. When individuality persists there is a God who supervises the activities of the universe; in the absence of individuality *Iswara* is non-existent.

Besides *Iswara*, Hinduism has many deities which resemble the gods and demons of Norse and Greek mythology. Such deities are a central feature of popular Hinduism and their reality is still widely accepted. Sri Ramana surprised many people by saying that such beings were as real as the people who believed in them. He admitted that after realisation they shared the same fate as *Iswara*, but prior to that, he seemed to regard them as senior officials in a cosmological hierarchy which looked after the affairs of the world.

Q: *God is described as manifest and unmanifest. As the former he is said to include the world as a part of his being. If that is so, we as part of that world should have easily known him in the manifested form.*

A: Know yourself before you seek to decide about the nature of God and the world.

Q: *Does knowing myself imply knowing God?*

A: Yes, God is within you.

Q: *Then, what stands in the way of my knowing myself or God?*

A: Your wandering mind and perverted ways.

Q: *Is God personal?*

A: Yes, he is always the first person, the I, ever standing before you. Because you give precedence to worldly things, God appears to have receded to the background. If you give up all else and seek him alone, he alone will remain as the 'I', the Self.[1]

Q: *Is God apart from the Self?*

A: The Self is God. 'I am' is God. This question arises because you are holding on to the ego self. It will not arise if you hold onto the true Self. For the real Self will not and cannot ask anything. If God be apart from the Self he must be a Self-less God, which is absurd.[2] God, who seems to be non-existent, alone truly exists, whereas the individual, who seems to be existing, is ever non-existent. Sages say that the state in which one thus knows one's own non-existence [sunya] alone is the glorious supreme knowledge.[3]

You now think that you are an individual, that there is the

universe and that God is beyond the cosmos. So there is the idea
of separateness. This idea must go. For God is not separate from
you or the cosmos. The *Gita* also says:

> The Self am I, O Lord of Sleep,
> In every creature's heart enshrined.
> The rise and noon of every form,
> I am its final doom as well (*Bhagavad Gita*, X.20).

Thus God is not only in the heart of all, he is the prop of all, he
is the source of all, their abiding place and their end. All proceed
from him, have their stay in him, and finally resolve into him.
Therefore he is not separate.

Q: *How are we to understand this passage in the* Gita: *'This
whole cosmos forms a particle of me'?*

A: It does not mean that a small particle of God separates
from him and forms the universe. His *sakti* [power] is acting. As a
result of one phase of such activity the cosmos has become
manifest. Similarly, the statement in *Purusha Sukta*, 'All the beings
form his one foot', does not mean that *Brahman* is in several
parts.

Q: *I understand that*. Brahman *is certainly not divisible*.

A: So the fact is that *Brahman* is all and remains indivisible. It
is ever realised but man is not aware of this. He must come to
know this. Knowledge means the overcoming of obstacles which
obstruct the revelation of the eternal truth that the Self is the same
as *Brahman*. The obstacles taken together form your idea of
separateness as an individual.[4]

Q: *Is God the same as Self?*

A: The Self is known to everyone, but not clearly. You always
exist. The be-ing is the Self. 'I am' is the name of God. Of all the
definitions of God, none is indeed so well put as the Biblical
statement 'I am that I am' in Exodus 3. There are other
statements, such as *Brahmaivaham* [*Brahman* am I], *aham
Brahmasmi* [I am *Brahman*] and *soham* [I am he]. But none is so
direct as the name Jehovah which means 'I am'. The absolute
being is what is. It is the Self. It is God. Knowing the Self, God is
known. In fact God is none other than the Self.[5]

Q: *God seems to be known by many different names. Are any
of them justified?*

A: Among the many thousands of names of God, no name
suits God, who abides in the Heart, devoid of thought, so truly,

aptly, and beautifully as the name 'I' or 'I am'. Of all the known names of God, the name of God 'I' – 'I' alone will resound triumphantly when the ego is destroyed, rising as the silent supreme word [*mouna-para-vak*] in the Heart-space of those whose attention is Selfward-facing. Even if one unceasingly meditates upon that name 'I-I' with one's attention on the feeling 'I', it will take one and plunge one into the source from which thought rises, destroying the ego, the embryo, which is joined to the body.[6]

Q: *What is the relationship between God and the world? Is he the creator or sustainer of it?*

A: Sentient and insentient beings of all kinds are performing actions only by the mere presence of the sun, which rises in the sky without any volition. Similarly all actions are done by the Lord without any volition or desire on his part. In the mere presence of the sun, the magnifying lens emits fire, the lotus-bud blossoms, the water-lily closes and all the countless creatures perform actions and rest.

The order of the great multitude of worlds is maintained by the mere presence of God in the same manner as the needle moves in front of a magnet, and as the moonstone emits water, the water-lily blossoms and the lotus closes in front of the moon.

In the mere presence of God, who does not have even the least volition, the living beings, who are engaged in innumerable activities, after embarking upon many paths to which they are drawn according to the course determined by their own *karmas*, finally realise the futility of action, turn back to Self and attain liberation.

The actions of living beings certainly do not go and affect God, who transcends the mind, in the same manner as the activities of the world do not affect that sun and as the qualities of the conspicuous four elements [earth, water, fire and air] do not affect the limitless space.[7]

Q: *Why is* samsara – *creation and manifestation as finitised – so full of sorrow and evil?*

A: God's will!

Q: *Why does God will it so?*

A: It is inscrutable. No motive can be attributed to that power – no desire, no end to achieve can be asserted of that one infinite, all-wise and all-powerful being. God is untouched by activities, which take place in his presence. Compare the sun and the world activities. There is no meaning in attributing responsibility and motive to the one before it becomes many.[8]

Q: *Does everything happen by the will of God?*

A: It is not possible for anyone to do anything opposed to the ordinance of God, who has the ability to do everything. Therefore to remain silent at the feet of God, having given up all the anxieties of the wicked, defective and delusive mind, is best.[9]

Q: *Is there a separate being* Iswara *[personal God] who is the rewarder of virtue and punisher of sins? Is there a God?*

A: Yes.

Q: *What is he like?*

A: *Iswara* has individuality in mind and body, which are perishable, but at the same time he has also the transcendental consciousness and liberation inwardly.

Iswara, the personal God, the supreme creator of the universe really does exist. But this is true only from the relative standpoint of those who have not realised the truth, those people who believe in the reality of individual souls. From the absolute standpoint the sage cannot accept any other existence than the impersonal Self, one and formless.

Iswara has a physical body, a form and a name, but it is not so gross as this material body. It can be seen in visions in the form created by the devotee. The forms and names of God are many and various and differ with each religion. His essence is the same as ours, the real Self being only one and without form. Hence forms he assumes are only creations or appearances.

Iswara is immanent in every person and every object throughout the universe. The totality of all things and beings constitutes God. There is a power out of which a small fraction has become all this universe, and the remainder is in reserve. Both this reserve power plus the manifested power as material world together constitute *Iswara*.[10]

Q: *So ultimately* Iswara *is not real?*

A: Existence of *Iswara* follows from our conception of *Iswara*. Let us first know whose concept he is. The concept will be only according to the one who conceives. Find out who you are and the other problems will solve themselves.[11]

Iswara, God, the creator, the personal God, is the last of the unreal forms to go. Only the absolute being is real. Hence, not only the world, not only the ego, but also the personal God are of unreality. We must find the absolute – nothing less.[12]

Q: *You say that even the highest God is still only an idea. Does that mean that there is no God?*

A: No, there is an *Iswara*.[13]

Q: *Does he exist in any particular place or form?*

A: If the individual is a form, even Self, the source, who is the Lord, will also appear to be a form. If one is not a form, since there then cannot be knowledge of other things, will that statement that God has a form be correct? God assumes any form imagined by the devotee through repeated thinking in prolonged meditation. Though he thus assumes endless names, the real formless consciousness alone is God.

With regard to his location, God does not reside in any place other than the Heart. It is due to illusion, caused by the ego, the 'I am the body' idea, that the kingdom of God is conceived to be elsewhere. Be sure that the Heart is the kingdom of God.

Know that you are the perfect, shining light which not only makes the existence of God's kingdom possible, but also allows it to be seen as some wonderful heaven. To know this is alone *jnana*. Therefore, the kingdom of God is within you. The unlimited space of *turiyatita* [beyond the four states, i.e. the Self], which shines suddenly, in all its fullness, within the Heart of a highly mature aspirant during the state of complete absorption of mind, as if a fresh and previously unknown experience, is the rarely-attained and true *Siva-loka* [the kingdom of God], which shines by the light of Self.[14]

Q: *They say that the* jiva *[individual] is subject to the evil effects of illusion such as limited vision and knowledge, whereas* Iswara *has all-pervading vision and knowledge. It is also said that* jiva *and* Iswara *become identical if the individual discards his limited vision and knowledge. Should not* Iswara *also discard his particular characteristics such as all-pervading vision and knowledge? They too are illusions, aren't they?*

A: Is that your doubt? First discard your own limited vision and then there will be time enough to think of *Iswara*'s all-pervading vision and knowledge. First get rid of your own limited knowledge. Why do you worry about *Iswara*? He will look after himself. Has he not got as much capacity as we have? Why should we worry about whether he possesses all-pervading vision and knowledge or not? It is indeed a great thing if we can take care of ourselves.[15]

Q: *But does God know everything?*

A: The *Vedas* declare God to be omniscient only to those who ignorantly think themselves to be people of little knowledge. But if one attains and knows him as he really is, it will be found that God does not know anything, because his nature is the ever-real whole, other than which nothing exists to be known.[16]

Q: *Why do religions speak of Gods, heaven, hell, etc.?*

A: Only to make the people realise that they are on a par with this world and that the Self alone is real. The religions are according to the view-point of the seeker.[17]

Q: *Do Vishnu, Siva, etc., exist?*

A: Individual human souls are not the only beings known.[18]

Q: *And their sacred regions* Kailasa *or* Vaikuntha, *are they real?*

A: As real as you are in this body.

Q: *Do they possess a phenomenal existence, like my body? Or are they fictions like the horn of a hare?*

A: They do exist.

Q: *If so, they must be somewhere. Where are they?*

A: Persons who have seen them say that they exist somewhere. So we must accept their statement.

Q: *Where do they exist?*

A: In you.

Q: *Then it is only an idea which I can create and control?*

A: Everything is like that.

Q: *But I can create pure fictions, for example, a hare's horn, or only part truths, for example a mirage, while there are also facts irrespective of my imagination. Do the Gods* Iswara *or* Vishnu *exist like that?*

A: Yes.

Q: *Is God subject to* pralaya[19] *[cosmic dissolution]?*

A: Why? Man becoming aware of the Self transcends cosmic dissolution and becomes liberated. Why not *Iswara* who is infinitely wiser and abler?

Q: *Do devas [angels] and pisachas [devils] exist similarly?*

A: Yes.[20]

Q: *These deities, what is their status relative to the Self?*

A: Siva, Ganapati and other deities like Brahma, exist from a human standpoint; that is to say, if you consider your personal self as real, then they also exist. Just as a government has its high executive officers to carry on the government, so has the creator. But from the standpoint of the Self all these gods are illusory and must themselves merge into the one reality.[21]

Q: *Whenever I worship God with name and form, I feel tempted to think whether I am not wrong in doing so, as that would be limiting the limitless, giving form to the formless. At the same time I feel I am not constant in my adherence to worship God without form.*

A: As long as you respond to a name, what objection could there be to your worshipping a God with name or form? Worship God with or without form till you know who you are.[22]

Q: *I find it difficult to believe in a personal God. In fact I find it impossible. But I can believe in an impersonal God, a divine force which rules and guides the world, and it would be a great help to me, even in my work of healing, if this faith were increased. May I know how to increase this faith?*

A: Faith is in things unknown, but the Self is self-evident. Even the greatest egotist cannot deny his own existence, that is to say, cannot deny the Self. You can call the ultimate reality by whatever name you like and say that you have faith in it or love for it, but who is there who will not have faith in his own existence or love for himself? That is because faith and love are our real nature.[23]

Q: *Should I not have any idea about God?*

A: Only so long as there are other thoughts in the Heart can there be a thought of God conceived by one's mind. The destruction of even that thought of God due to the destruction of all other thoughts alone is the unthought thought, which is the true thought of God.[24]

CHAPTER 20
Suffering and morality

The paradoxes inherent in theistic theories have engaged the minds of western theologians and philosophers for centuries. For example, if God is perfect, why is there evil in the world? Why does an omnipotent God allow suffering when he has the power to abolish it at a stroke?

Sri Ramana side-steps such conundrums by stating that the world, God and the individual who suffers are all inventions of the mind.

> All religions first postulate three principles, the world, the soul and God. To say that one principle alone appears as the three principles or that the three principles are always three principles is possible only as long as the ego exists.[1]

Instead of attributing suffering to the consequence of wrong actions or to the will of God, Sri Ramana taught that it only arises because we imagine that we are separate individuals interacting with each other and with the world. He said that wrong actions compound the suffering, and are therefore to be avoided, but they are not its original cause. It is the mind that creates the illusion of separateness and it is the mind that suffers the consequences of its illusory inventions. Suffering is thus a product and consequence of the discriminative mind; when the mind is eliminated, suffering is found to be non-existent.

Many questioners could relate to this idea on an individual level but they found it hard to accept that all the suffering in the world existed only in the mind of the person who perceived it. Sri Ramana was quite adamant about this and he repeatedly said that if one realises the Self one will know that all suffering, not just one's own, is non-existent. Taking this idea to its logical conclusion, Sri Ramana often said the most effective way of eliminating other people's suffering was to realise the Self.

This standpoint should not be interpreted to mean that Sri Ramana encouraged his followers to ignore the suffering of other people. On a more pragmatic level he said that prior to Self-realisation one should accept the reality of other people's suffering and take steps to relieve it whenever one comes across it. However, he also pointed out that such remedial actions would only be spiritually beneficial if they were done without the feeling that 'other people less fortunate than me are being helped' and without the feeling that 'I am performing these actions'.

On the whole, the question of what one should or should not do in the world was of little interest to Sri Ramana. He maintained the view that all conventional ideas about right and wrong were value-judgments made by the mind, and that when the mind ceases to exist, ideas about right and wrong also cease. Because of this he rarely spoke about the conventional canons of morality, and whenever he was pressed to offer an opinion on them, he would usually side-step the issue by saying that the only 'right action' was discovering the Self.

Q: *What do you consider to be the cause of world suffering? And how can we help to change it, (a) as individuals, or (b) collectively?*

A: Realise the real Self. It is all that is necessary.[2]

Q: *In this life beset with limitations can I ever realise the bliss of the Self?*

A: That bliss of the Self is always with you, and you will find it for yourself, if you would seek it earnestly. The cause of your misery is not in the life outside you, it is in you as the ego. You impose limitations on yourself and then make a vain struggle to transcend them. All unhappiness is due to the ego; with it comes all your trouble. What does it avail you to attribute to the happenings in life the cause of misery which is really within you? What happiness can you get from things extraneous to yourself? When you get it, how long will it last?

If you would deny the ego and scorch it by ignoring it, you would be free. If you accept it, it will impose limitations on you and throw you into a vain struggle to transcend them. To be the Self that you really are is the only means to realise the bliss that is ever yours.[3]

Q: *If truly there is neither bondage nor liberation, what is the reason for the actual experience of joys and sorrows?*

A: They appear to be real only when one turns aside from one's real nature. They do not really exist.[4]

Q: *Is the world created for happiness or misery?*

A: Creation is neither good nor bad; it is as it is. It is the human mind which puts all sorts of constructions on it, seeing things from its own angle and interpreting them to suit its own interests. A woman is just a woman, but one mind calls her 'mother', another 'sister', and still another 'aunt' and so on. Men love women, hate snakes, and are indifferent to the grass and stones by the roadside. These value-judgments are the cause of all the misery in the world. Creation is like a peepul tree: birds come to eat its fruit, or take shelter under its branches, men cool themselves in its shade, but some may hang themselves on it. Yet the tree continues to lead its quiet life, unconcerned with and unaware of all the uses it is put to. It is the human mind that creates its own difficulties and then cries for help. Is God so partial as to give peace to one person and sorrow to another? In creation there is room for everything, but man refuses to see the good, the healthy and the beautiful. Instead, he goes on whining, like the hungry man who sits beside the tasty dish and who, instead of stretching out his hand to satisfy his hunger, goes on lamenting, 'Whose fault is it, God's or man's?'[5]

Q: *If God is all why does the individual suffer for his actions? Are not the actions for which the individual is made to suffer prompted by him?*

A: He who thinks he is the doer is also the sufferer.

Q: *But the actions are prompted by God and the individual is only his tool.*

A: This logic is applied only when one suffers, but not when one rejoices. If the conviction prevails always, there will be no suffering either.

Q: *When will the suffering cease?*

A: Not until individuality is lost. If both the good and bad actions are his, why should you think that the enjoyment and suffering are yours alone? He who does good or bad, also enjoys pleasure or suffers pain. Leave it there and do not superimpose suffering on yourself.[6]

Q: *How can you say that suffering is non-existent? I see it everywhere.*

A: One's own reality, which shines within everyone as the Heart, is itself the ocean of unalloyed bliss. Therefore like the unreal blueness of the sky, misery does not exist in reality but only in mere imagination. Since one's own reality, which is the sun of *jnana* that cannot be approached by the dark delusion of ignorance, itself shines as happiness, misery is nothing but an illusion caused by the unreal sense of individuality. In truth no one has ever experienced any such thing other than that unreal illusion. If one scrutinises one's own Self, which is bliss, there will be no misery at all in one's life. One suffers because of the idea that the body, which is never oneself, is 'I'; suffering is all due to this delusion.[7]

Q: *I suffer in both mind and body. From the day of my birth I have never had happiness. My mother too suffered from the time she conceived me, I hear. Why do I suffer thus? I have not sinned in this life. Is all this due to the sins of past lives?*

A: You say the mind and body suffer. But do they ask the questions? Who is the questioner? Is it not the one that is beyond both mind and body? You say the body suffers in this life and ask if the cause of this is the previous life. If that is so then the cause of that life is the one before it, and so on. So, like the case of the seed and the sprout, there is no end to the causal series. It has to be said that all the lives have their first cause in ignorance. That same ignorance is present even now, framing this question. That ignorance must be removed by *jnana*.

'Why and to whom did this suffering come?' If you question thus you will find that the 'I' is separate from the mind and body, that the Self is the only eternal being, and that it is eternal bliss. That is *jnana*.[8]

Q: *I suffer from worries without end; there is no peace for me, though there is nothing wanting for me to be happy.*

A: Do these worries affect you in sleep?

Q: *No, they do not.*

A: Are you the very same man now, or are you different from him that slept without any worry?

Q: *Yes, I am the same person.*

A: Then surely those worries do not belong to you. It is your own fault if you assume that they are yours.[9]

Q: *When we suffer grief and complain and appeal to you by letter or mentally by prayer, are you not moved to feel what a pity it is that your child suffers like this?*

A: If one felt like that one would not be a *jnani*.[10]

Q: *We see pain in the world. A man is hungry. It is a physical*

*reality, and as such, it is very real to him. Are we to call it a dream
and remain unmoved by his pain?*

A: From the point of view of *jnana* or the reality, the pain you
speak of is certainly a dream, as is the world of which the pain is
an infinitesimal part. In the dream also you yourself feel hunger.
You see others suffering hunger. You feed yourself and, moved by
pity, feed the others that you find suffering from hunger. So long
as the dream lasts, all those hunger pains are quite as real as you
now think the pain you see in the world to be. It is only when you
wake up that you discover that the pain in the dream was unreal.
You might have eaten to the full and gone to sleep. You dream
that you work hard and long in the hot sun all day, are tired and
hungry and want to eat a lot. Then you get up and find your
stomach is full and you have not stirred out of your bed. But all
this is not to say that while you are in the dream you can act as if
the pain you feel there is not real. The hunger in the dream has to
be assuaged by the food in the dream. The fellow beings you
found so hungry in the dream had to be provided with food in
that dream. You can never mix up the two states, the dream and
the waking state. Till you reach the state of *jnana* and thus wake
out of this *maya*, you must do social service by relieving suffering
whenever you see it. But even then you must do it, as we are told,
without *ahamkara*, that is without the sense 'I am the doer', but
feeling, 'I am the Lord's tool.' Similarly one must not be conceited
and think, 'I am helping a man below me. He needs help. I am in a
position to help. I am superior and he inferior.' You must help the
man as a means of worshipping God in that man. All such service
too is for you the Self, not for anybody else. You are not helping
anybody else, but only yourself.[11]

Q: *In the case of persons who are not capable of long
meditation, will it not be enough if they engage themselves in
doing good to others?*

A: Yes, it will do. The idea of good will be in their heart. That
is enough. Good, God, love, are all the same thing. If the person
keeps continuously thinking of any one of these, it will be enough.
All meditation is for the purpose of keeping out all other
thoughts.[12]

Q: *So one should try to ameliorate suffering, even if one
knows that ultimately it is non-existent?*

A: There never was and never will be a time when all are
equally happy or rich or wise or healthy. In fact none of these

terms has any meaning except in so far as the opposite to it exists. But that does not mean that when you come across anyone who is less happy or more miserable than yourself, you are not to be moved to compassion or to seek to relieve him as best you can. On the contrary, you must love all and help all, since only in that way can you help yourself. When you seek to reduce the suffering of any fellow man or fellow creature, whether your efforts succeed or not, you are yourself evolving spiritually especially if such service is rendered disinterestedly, not with the egotistic feeling 'I am doing this', but in the spirit 'God is making me the channel of this service; he is the doer and I am the instrument.'[13]

If one knows the truth that all that one gives to others is giving only to oneself, who indeed will not be a virtuous person and perform the kind act of giving to others? Since everyone is one's own Self, whoever does whatever to whomever is doing it only to himself.[14]

Q: *There are widespread disasters spreading havoc in the world, for example famine and pestilence. What is the cause of this state of affairs?*

A: To whom does all this appear?

Q: *That won't do. I see misery everywhere.*

A: You were not aware of the world and its sufferings in your sleep but you are conscious of them now in your waking state. Continue in that state in which you were not afflicted by them. That is to say, when you are not aware of the world, its sufferings do not affect you. When you remain as the Self, as in sleep, the world and its sufferings will not affect you. Therefore look within. See the Self! Then there will be an end of the world and its miseries.

Q: *But that is selfishness.*

A: The world is not external. Because you identify yourself wrongly with the body you see the world outside, and its pain becomes apparent to you. But they are not real. Seek the reality and get rid of this unreal feeling.

Q: *There are great men, public workers, who cannot solve the problem of the misery of the world.*

A: They are ego-centred and that accounts for their inability. If they remained in the Self they would be different.

Q: *Why do not mahatmas help?*

A: How do you know that they do not help? Public speeches, physical activity and material help are all outweighed by the silence of *mahatmas*. They accomplish more than others.

Q: *What is to be done by us for ameliorating the condition of the world?*

A: If you remain free from pain, there will be no pain anywhere. The trouble now is due to your seeing the world externally and also thinking that there is pain there. But both the world and the pain are within you. If you look within there will be no pain.

Q: *God is perfect. Why did he create the world imperfect? The work shares the nature of the author. But here it is not so.*

A: Who is it that raises the question?

Q: *I – the individual.*

A: Are you apart from God that you ask this question?

So long as you consider yourself to be the body, you see the world as external and the imperfections appear to you. God is perfection. His work also is perfection. But you see it as imperfection because of your wrong identification.

Q: *Why did the Self manifest as this miserable world?*

A: In order that you might seek it. Your eyes cannot see themselves. Place a mirror before them and they see themselves. Similarly with creation.

'See yourself first and then see the whole world as the Self.'

Q: *So it amounts to this – that I should always look within.*

A: Yes.

Q: *Should I not see the world at all?*

A: You are not instructed to shut your eyes to the world. You are only to 'see yourself first and then see the whole world as the Self'. If you consider yourself as the body the world appears to be external. If you are the Self the world appears as *Brahman*.[15]

Q: *What is the best way to work for world peace?*

A: What is the world? What is peace, and who is the worker? The world is not in your sleep and forms a projection of your mind in your *jagrat* [waking state]. It is therefore an idea and nothing else. Peace is absence of disturbance. The disturbance is due to the arising of thoughts in the individual, which is only the ego rising up from pure consciousness.

To bring about peace means to be free from thoughts and to abide as pure consciousness. If one remains at peace oneself, there is only peace everywhere.

Q: *If it is a question of doing something one considers wrong, and thereby saving someone else from a great wrong, should one do it or refrain?*

A: What is right and wrong? There is no standard by which to judge something to be right and another to be wrong. Opinions differ according to the nature of the individual and according to the surroundings. They are again ideas and nothing more. Do not worry about them but get rid of thoughts instead. If you always remain in the right, then right will prevail in the world.[16]

Q: *Will not right conduct be enough to secure salvation?*

A: Salvation for whom? Who wants salvation? And what is right conduct? What is conduct? And what is right? Who is to judge what is right and what is wrong? According to previous *samskaras*, each one regards something or other as right. Only when the reality is known can the truth about right and wrong be known. The best course is to find out who wants this salvation. Tracing this 'who' or ego to its original source is the right conduct for everyone.

Q: *Will not the practice of good conduct [nitya karmas] lead to salvation? Several books state that it will.*

A: It is said so in books. Who denies that good conduct is good or that it will eventually lead you to the goal? Good conduct or *sat karma* purifies the *chitta* or mind and gives you *chitta suddhi* [pure mind]. The pure mind attains *jnana*, which is what is meant by salvation. So, eventually, *jnana* must be reached, that is, the ego must be traced to its source. But to those to whom this does not appeal, we have to say that *sat karmas* lead to *chitta suddhi*, and *chitta suddhi* will lead to right knowledge or *jnana*, and that in its turn gives salvation.[17]

Q: *What about motives? Are the motives for performing actions not important?*

A: Whatever is done lovingly, with righteous purity and with peace of mind, is a good action. Everything which is done with the stain of desire and with agitation filling the mind is classified as a bad action. Do not perform any good action [*karma*] through a bad means, thinking 'It is sufficient if it bears good fruit.' Because, if the means is bad, even a good action will turn out to be a bad one. Therefore, even the means of doing actions should be pure.[18]

Q: *Sankara says we are all free, not bound, and that we shall all go back to God from whom we have come as sparks from a fire. Then why should we not commit all sorts of sins?*

A: It is true we are not bound and that the real Self has no bondage. It is true that you will eventually go back to your source. But meanwhile, if you commit sins, as you call them, you will have to face the consequences of such sins. You cannot escape them. If a man beats you, then, can you say, 'I am free, I am not bound by these beatings and I don't feel any pain. Let him beat on'? If you can feel like that, you can go on doing what you like. What is the use of merely saying with your lips 'I am free'?[19]

Q: *It is said that the whole universe is God's play of consciousness and that everything is full of* Brahman. *Then why should we say that bad habits and bad practices should be discarded?*

A: Suppose there is some wound inside the human body. If you neglect it, on the assumption that it is only a small part of the body, it causes pain to the whole body. If it is not cured by ordinary treatment, the doctor must come, cut off the affected portion with a knife and remove the impurities. If the diseased part is not cut off it will fester. If you do not bandage it after operating, pus will form. It is the same thing with regard to conduct. Bad habits and bad conduct are like a wound in the body. Every disease must be given appropriate treatment.[20]

Q: *So one should adhere to the conventional codes of behaviour?*

A: Since the prescribed observances for self-discipline [*niyamas*] help one to a considerable extent, they are worthy to be accepted and followed. But if they are found to obstruct the superior practice of enquiry for true knowledge, give them up immediately as deficient.[21]

CHAPTER 21
Karma, *destiny and free will*

The theory of *karma* is common to many oriental religions. In its most popular form it states that there is a universal accounting system in which each individual must experience the consequences of all his actions [*karmas*]; good actions bring good results and bad actions inevitably result in suffering to the one who does them. The theory also states that the consequences of actions [also known as *karmas*] need not necessarily be experienced in the present life, they can be carried over into future lives. Because of this, several sub-divisions of *karma* have been postulated. The following classification which was used by Sri Ramana is common to many Hindu schools of thought:

1 *Sanchita karma* The store of *karmic* debts accumulated from previous births.
2 *Prarabdha karma* That part of one's *sanchita karma* which must be worked out in the present life. Because the law of *karma* implies determinism in human activities, *prarabdha* is often translated as destiny.
3 *Agami karma* New *karma* accumulated in the present lifetime which is carried forward into future lives.

Sri Ramana accepted the validity of the laws of *karma* but said that they were only applicable as long as a person imagined that he was separate from the Self. At this level (the level of the *ajnani*), he said that individuals will pass through a series of pre-ordained activities and experiences, all of which are the consequences of previous acts and thoughts. He occasionally even said that every act and experience in a person's life is determined at birth and that the only freedom one has is to realise that there is no one acting and no one experiencing. However, once one realises the Self there is no one left to experience the consequences of actions and so the whole structure of *karmic* laws then becomes redundant.

Sri Ramana regarded the law of *karma* as a manifestation of God's will. He said that prior to Self-realisation there is a personal

God, *Iswara*, who controls each person's destiny. It is *Iswara* who has ordained that everyone must suffer the consequences of his actions and it is *Iswara* who selects the sequence of activities that each person must undergo in each lifetime. One cannot escape from *Iswara*'s jurisdiction while one still identifies with the activities of the body. The only way to become free of his authority is to transcend *karma* completely by realising the Self.

Q: *Is it possible to overcome, even while the body exists, the* prarabdha karma *which is said to last till the end of the body?*

A: Yes. If the agent upon whom the *karma* depends, namely the ego, which has come into existence between the body and the Self, merges in its source and loses its form, how can the *karma* which depends upon it survive? When there is no 'I' there is no *karma*.[1]

Q: *It is said that* prarabdha karma *is only a small fraction of the* karma *accumulated from previous lives. Is this true?*

A: A man might have performed many *karmas* in his previous births. A few of these alone will be chosen for this birth and he will have to enjoy their fruits in this birth. It is something like a slide show where the projectionist picks a few slides to be exhibited at a performance, the remaining slides being reserved for another performance. All this *karma* can be destroyed by acquiring knowledge of the Self. The different *karmas* are the slides, *karmas* being the result of past experiences, and the mind is the projector. The projector must be destroyed so that there will be no further reflection and no further births and no deaths.[2]

Q: *Who is the projectionist? What is the mechanism which selects a small portion of the* sanchita karma *and then decides that it shall be experienced as* prarabdha karma?

A: Individuals have to suffer their *karmas* but *Iswara* manages to make the best of their *karmas* for his purpose. God manipulates the fruits of *karma* but he does not add or take away from it. The subconscious of man is a warehouse of good and bad *karma*. *Iswara* chooses from this warehouse what he sees will best suit the spiritual evolution at the time of each man, whether pleasant or painful. Thus there is nothing arbitrary.[3]

Q: *In* Upadesa Saram *you say that* karma *bears fruit by the ordinance of God [*karta*]. Does this mean that we reap the consequences of* karma *solely because God wills it?*

A: In this verse *karta* [God] means *Iswara*. He is the one who distributes the fruits of actions to each person according to his *karma*. That means that he is the manifest *Brahman*. The real *Brahman* is unmanifest and without motion. It is only the manifest *Brahman* that is named as *Iswara*. He gives the fruit to each person according to his actions [*karma*]. That means that *Iswara* is only an agent and that he gives wages according to the labour done. That is all. Without this *sakti* [power] of *Iswara*, this *karma* would not take place. That is why *karma* is said to be on its own, inert.[4]

Q: *The present experiences are the result of past* karma. *If we know the mistakes committed before, we can rectify them.*

A: If one mistake is rectified there yet remains the whole *sanchita karma* from former births which is going to give you innumerable births. So that is not the procedure. The more you prune a plant, the more vigorously it grows. The more you rectify your *karma*, the more it accumulates. Find the root of *karma* and cut it off.[5]

Q: *Does the* karma *theory mean that the world is the result of action and reaction? If so, action and reaction of what?*

A: Until realisation there will be *karma*, that is action and reaction. After realisation there will be no *karma* and no world.[6]

Q: *If I am not the body why am I responsible for the consequences of my good and bad actions?*

A: If you are not the body and do not have the idea 'I am the doer', the consequences of your good or bad actions will not affect you. Why do you say about the actions the body performs 'I do this' or 'I did that'? As long as you identify yourself with the body like that you are affected by the consequences of the actions, that is to say, while you identify with the body you accumulate good and bad *karma*.

Q: *But since I am not the body I am not really responsible for the consequences of good or bad actions.*

A: If you are not, why do you bother about the question?[7]

Q: *In some places it is stated that human effort is the source of all strength and that it can even transcend* karma. *In others it is said that it is all divine grace. It is not clear which of them is correct.*

A: Yes, some schools of philosophy say that there is no God other than the *karmas* of the previous birth, that the *karma* done in the present birth in accordance with the scriptures is known as *purushakara* [human effort], that the previous and present *karmas* meet for a head-on fight like rams and that the one that is weaker gets eliminated. That is why these people say that one should strengthen *purushakara*. If you ask such people what the origin of *karma* is, they say that such a question is not be raised as it is like the eternal question, 'Which is earlier, the seed or the tree?'

Debates such as this are mere arguments which can never arrive at the final truth. That is why I say first find out who you are. If one asks 'Who am I? How did I get this *dosha* [fault] of life?', the 'I' will subside and one will realise the Self. If one does this properly the idea of *dosha* will be eliminated and peace will be obtained. Why even obtained? The Self remains as it is.[8]

The essence of *karma* is to know the truth of oneself by enquiring 'Who am I, the doer, who begins to do *karmas*?' Unless the doer of *karmas*, the ego, is annihilated through enquiry, the perfect peace of supreme bliss, which is the result of *karma* yoga, cannot be achieved.[9]

Q: *Can people wipe out the consequences of their bad actions by doing* mantras *or* japa *or will they necessarily have to experience them?*

A: If the feeling 'I am doing *japa*' is not there, the bad actions committed by a man will not stick to him. If the feeling 'I am doing the *japa*' is there, the consequences of bad actions will persist.

Q: *Does not* punya *[merit accumulated from virtuous acts] extinguish* papa *[demerit accumulated from sinful acts]?*

A: So long as the feeling 'I am doing' is there, one must experience the result of one's acts, whether they are good or bad. How is it possible to wipe out one act with another? When the feeling that 'I am doing' is lost, nothing affects a man. Unless one realises the Self, the feeling 'I am doing' will never vanish. For one who realises the Self where is the need for *japa*? Where is the need for *tapas*? Owing to the force of *prarabdha* life goes on, but he who has realised the Self does not wish for anything.

Prarabdha karma is of three categories, *ichha*, *anichha* and *parechha* [personally desired, without desire and due to others' desire]. For the one who has realised the Self, there is no *ichha-prarabdha* but the two others, *anichha* and *parechha*, remain. Whatever a *jnani* does is for others only. If there are things to be done by him for others, he does them but the results do not affect him. Whatever be the actions that such people do, there is no *punya* and no *papa* attached to them. But they do only what is proper according to the accepted standard of the world – nothing else.[10]

Those who know that what is to be experienced by them in this life is only what is already destined in their *prarabdha* will never feel perturbed about what is to be experienced. Know that all one's experiences will be thrust upon one whether one wills them or not.[11]

Q: *The realised man has no further* karma. *He is not bound by his* karma. *Why should he still remain within his body?*

A: Who asks this question? Is it the realised man or the *ajnani*? Why should you bother what the *jnani* does or why he does anything? Look after yourself. You are now under the impression you are the body and so you think that the *jnani* also has a body. Does the *jnani* say he has a body? He may look to you as if he has a body and he may appear to be doing things with the body, as others do, but he himself knows that he is bodiless. The burnt rope still looks like a rope, but it can't serve as a rope if you try to bind anything with it. A *jnani* is like that – he may look like other people, but this is only an outer appearance. So long as one identifies oneself with the body, all this is difficult to understand. That is why it is sometimes said in reply to such questions, 'The body of the *jnani* will continue till the force of *prarabdha* works itself out, and after the *prarabdha* is exhausted it will drop off.' An illustration made use of in this connection is that of an arrow already discharged which will continue to advance and strike its target. But the truth is the *jnani* has transcended all *karmas*, including the *prarabdha karma*, and he is not bound by the body or its *karmas*.[12]

Not even an iota of *prarabdha* exists for those who uninterruptedly attend to the space of consciousness, which always shines as 'I am', which is not confined in the vast physical space, and which pervades everywhere without limitations. Such alone is the meaning of the ancient saying, 'There is no fate for those who reach or experience the heavens.'[13]

Q: *If a thing comes to me without any planning or working for it and I enjoy it, will there be no bad consequences from it?*

A: It is not so. Every act must have its consequences. If anything comes your way by reason of *prarabdha*, you can't help it. If you take what comes, without any special attachment, and without any desire for more of it or for a repetition of it, it will not harm you by leading to further births. On the other hand, if you enjoy it with great attachment and naturally desire for more of it, it is bound to lead to more and more births.[14]

Q: *According to the astrological science, predictions are made about coming events taking into account the influence of the stars. Is that true?*

A: So long as you have the feeling of egotism all that is true. When that egotism gets destroyed all that is untrue.

Q: *Does it mean that astrology won't be true in the case of those whose egotism is destroyed?*

A: Who is there left to say it won't be true? There will be seeing only if there is one who sees. In the case of those whose egotism is destroyed, even if they appear to see they do not really see.[15]

Destiny is the result of past action. It concerns the body. Let the body act as may suit it. Why are you concerned with it? Why do you pay attention to it? Should anything happen, it happens as the result of one's past actions, of divine will and of other factors.[16]

Q: *The present is said to be due to past* karma. *Can we transcend the past* karma *by our free will now?*

A: See what the present is. If you do this you will understand what is affected by or has a past or a future, what is ever-present and always free and what remains unaffected by the past or future or by any past *karma*.[17]

Q: *Is there such a thing as free will?*

A: Whose will is it? So long as there is the sense of doership, there is the sense of enjoyment and of individual will. But if this sense is lost through the practice of *vichara*, the divine will will act and guide the course of events. Fate is overcome by *jnana*, Self-knowledge, which is beyond will and fate.[18]

Q: *I can understand that the outstanding events in a man's life, such as his country, nationality, family, career or profession, marriage, death, etc., are all predestined by his* karma, *but can it be that all the details of his life, down to the minutest, have already been determined? Now, for instance, I put this fan that is in my hand down on the floor here. Can it be that it was already decided that on such and such a day, at such and such an hour, I should move the fan like this and put it down here?*

A: Certainly. Whatever this body is to do and whatever experiences it is to pass through was already decided when it came into existence.

Q: *What becomes then of man's freedom and responsibility for his actions?*

A: The only freedom man has is to strive for and acquire the *jnana* which will enable him not to identify himself with the body. The body will go through the actions rendered inevitable by *prarabdha* and a man is free either to identify himself with the body and be attached to the fruits of its actions, or to be detached from it and be a mere witness of its activities.[19]

Q: *So free will is a myth?*

A: Free will holds the field in association with individuality. As long as individuality lasts there is free will. All the scriptures are based on this fact and they advise directing the free will in the right channel.

Find out to whom free will or destiny matters. Find out where they come from, and abide in their source. If you do this, both of them are transcended. That is the only purpose of discussing these questions. To whom do these questions arise? Find out and be at peace.[20]

Q: *If what is destined to happen will happen, is there any use in prayer or effort or should we just remain idle?*

A: There are only two ways to conquer destiny or be independent of it. One is to enquire for whom is this destiny and discover that only the ego is bound by destiny and not the Self, and that the ego is non-existent. The other way is to kill the ego by completely surrendering to the Lord, by realising one's helplessness and saying all the time, 'Not I but thou, O Lord', giving up all sense of 'I' and 'mine' and leaving it to the Lord to do what he likes with you. Surrender can never be regarded as complete so long as the devotee wants this or that from the Lord. True surrender is love of God for the sake of love and nothing else, not even for the sake of liberation. In other words, complete effacement of the ego is necessary to conquer destiny, whether you achieve this effacement through self-enquiry or through *bhakti marga*.[21]

Glossary

advaita	Non-duality: also a subdivision of *vedanta* philosophy
ahamkara	Ego
aham-vritti	'I'-thought
ajapa	Unspoken and involuntary repetition of the name of God
ajata	Non-causality: see the introduction to chapter 21
ajnana	Ignorance, the opposite of *jnana*
ajnani	One who has not realised the Self
ananda	Bliss
Aparoksha Anubhuti	A work on Self-realisation attributed to Sankara
Arjuna	The recipient of Krishna's teachings in the *Bhagavad Gita*
Arunachala	The holy mountain in South India where Sri Ramana spent all his adult life
asana	Posture or seat: see the introduction to chapter 13
atman	The Self
atma-vichara	Self-enquiry
avidya	Ignorance
Bhagavad Gita	A portion of the *Mahabharata* in which Krishna, an incarnation of Vishnu, gives instructions to Arjuna
Bhagavata	Also called the *Bhagavatam*: a puranic work which recounts some of the life and teachings of Krishna
bhakta	Devotee
bhakti	Devotion
Blavatsky, H.P.	A Russian occultist, the founder of Theosophy
Brahma	The Hindu God who is the creator of the

universe; he is one of the three principal deities of Hinduism

Brahma-jnana	Knowledge of *Brahman*
Brahman	The impersonal absolute of Hinduism
Brindavan	A place in North India where Krishna once lived
Chaitanya	A sixteenth-century Hindu saint, well-known for his devotion to Krishna
chakras	Psychic centres in the body: see the introduction to chapter 13
chit	Consciousness
Courtallam	A small town in South India
Dattatreya	A sage whose name is mentioned in several *puranas*; little is known about his date or location, but the *advaitic* work *Avadhuta Gita* is attributed to him
dehatma buddhi	'I am the body' idea
dhyana	Meditation
diksha	Initiation
Ganapati	A Hindu God with an elephant head and a man's body; he is the son of Siva
Ganesa	See Ganapati
Gaudapada	Sankara's Guru's Guru, an early exponent of *ajata* and the author of a famous commentary (*karika*) on the *Mandukyopanishad*
gayatri	The most famous Vedic *mantra* – 'Let that adorable, full of light [God], enlighten us, who meditate on him'
Gita	See *Bhagavad Gita*
gunas	The three qualities of all manifestation – *sattva*, *rajas* and *tamas*: see the introduction to chapter 12
Iswara	The supreme personal God of Hinduism
Janaka	An Indian king: an account of his Self-realisation can be found in the *Ashtavakra Gita*
japa	Literally, 'muttering', but as an abbreviated form of *nama-japa* it means repetition of the name of God.
jivan mukta	One who is liberated while still alive

jivan mukti	Liberation while one is still alive
jnana	Knowledge of the Self: see the introduction to chapter 1
jnana drishti	The vision of knowledge
jnani	One who has realised the Self
Kailasa	A sacred mountain in the Himalayas where Siva is supposed to reside
kaivalya	The state of oneness
Kaivalya	The full title is *Kaivalya Navaneeta* and it is a Tamil text on *advaita*
karika	See Gaudapada
karma	There are three principal meanings:

    (1)   action,
    (2)   consequences of actions,
    (3)   destiny:

see the introduction to chapter 21

Kauravas	A family in the Mahabharata who were the chief antagonists of the Pandavas; Arjuna was one of the Pandavas and with Krishna's assistance the Kauravas were destroyed
kevala	Oneness
Krishna	An incarnation (*avatara*) of Vishnu
kundalini	Yogic power: see the introduction to chapter 13
laya	Literally it means 'dissolution', but when Sri Ramana uses it he is indicating a trance-like state in which the mind is temporarily in abeyance
leela	The play of God
mahatma	Great soul, great man or saint
mahavakyas	Literally it means 'great sayings'; more specifically it refers to four upanishadic quotations which affirm the reality of the Self:

    (1)   'That thou art',
    (2)   'I am *Brahman*',
    (3)   'This Self is *Brahman*',
    (4)   '*Prajnana* (consciousness) is *Brahman*'

Maha Yoga	A book on Sri Ramana's teachings: see bibliography
Malayalam	One of the vernacular languages of South India
Mandukyopanishad	One of the major *Upanishads*
mantras	Sacred words given to a disciple by a Guru: see the introduction to chapter 8
maya	Illusion
moksha	Liberation
mouna	Silence
muktas	Liberated ones
mukti	Liberation
nirvikalpa	No differences; *nirvikalpa samadhi* is the *samadhi* in which no differences are perceived: see the introduction to chapter 14
Parabrahman	The supreme *Brahman*
Panchadasi	A fourteenth-century work on *advaita vedanta*
papa	Sin, or the bad consequencs of bad acts
Patanjali	The author of the *Yoga Sutras* and the founder of *raja* yoga
prana	The vital energy that sustains the body
pranava	The *mantra om*
punya	Merit accumulated from good acts
Purusha Sukta	A portion of the *Rig Veda*; the *Rig Veda* is the oldest Hindu scripture
rajas	Activity
raja yoga	The system of yoga formulated by Patanjali: '*raja*' literally means 'royal'
Ramakrishna	A nineteenth-century Bengali saint
Ramanasramam	The ashram which grew up around Sri Ramana
sadhaka	Also spelt *sadhak*: a spiritual seeker
sadhana	Literally it translates as 'means', but in a more general sense it means 'spiritual practice'
Sadhana Panchakam	A work attributed to Sankara which gives advice to spiritual seekers
sadhu	A noble person or a spiritual seeker. However, Sri Ramana frequently used this

	term as a title for someone who has realised the Self.
sahaja	Natural
sakti	Power
samadhi	Sri Ramana used the term to mean a state in which one has a direct experience of the Self: see the introduction to chapter 14
samskaras	Innate tendencies
Sankara	Also called Sankaracharya: an eighth-century religious reformer and philosopher. He was the first to popularise the teachings of *advaita vedanta*
sastras	Scriptures
sat	Being
sat-chit-ananda	Being-consciousness-bliss
sat-sanga	Association with being, or, alternatively, being in the presence of someone who has realised the Self
sattvic	Pure: see the introduction to chapter 12
savikalpa	Literally 'with differences': Sri Ramana used the term to indicate a level of *samadhi* which one maintained by constant effort. See the introduction to chapter 14
Shirdi Sai Baba	An eccentric and charismatic spiritual teacher, widely known because of his supernatural powers. He died in 1918
siddhis	Supernatural powers
Siva	One of the three principal Hindu deities. Sri Ramana also used the word as a synonym for the Self
sloka	A verse in a Sanskrit scriptural work
soham	The affirmation 'I am he'
Sri, Srimad	Honorific prefixes
sushumna	A psychic channel in the spine: see the introduction to chapter 13
swarupa	Real form or real nature
Swarupanand	A seventeenth-century Tamil Guru
tamas	Inertia or sluggishness
Tamil	A South Indian language, Sri Ramana's mother-tongue
tapas	Usually this means meditation connected

	with the practice of personal self-denial or bodily mortification. However, *tapas* has many other meanings such as penance, religious austerity and heat.
Tattvaraya	A disciple of Swarupanand, a seventeenth-century Tamil Guru, and the author of several philosophical works in Tamil
Theosophical Society	A society founded by Mme Blavatsky in the nineteenth century to investigate the powers latent in man and to promote a universal brotherhood
Tiruvannamalai	A town about a mile from Sri Ramana's ashram
turiya	The fourth state
turyatita	Transcending the fourth
upadesa	Teachings
Upadesa Saram	A thirty verse Sanskrit poem composed by Sri Ramana
Upanishads	The concluding portions of the *Vedas* (the primary scriptural authority of Hinduism). The *Upanishads* are the texts from which all *vedanta* philosophy is derived
vada	Theory
Vaikuntha	The heaven of Vishnu
vasanas	Mental tendencies
vedanta	A metaphysical philosophy derived from the *Upanishadic* texts
Vedas	Four collections of scriptures dating from 2000 BC to 500 BC which are the ultimate source of authority for most Hindus
Vellore	A town fifty miles north of Sri Ramana's ashram
vichara	Self-enquiry
videha mukti	Liberated at the moment of death
Vidyaranya	The author of *Panchadasi*, a fourteenth-century work on *advaita*
Vishnu	One of the three principal deities of Hinduism. Vishnu periodically reincarnates in a human body
Vivekachudamani	An *advaitic* work attributed to Sankara. Nowadays most scholars think that it was

	written at least 200 years after he died
vritti	Modification, usually a mental modification
Who am I?	One of Sri Ramana's early written works which was based on some answers he gave in 1901
Yama	The Hindu God of death
Yoga Vasishtha	An *advaitic* text, attributed to Valmiki, in which the sage Vasishtha answers questions put by Rama, an incarnation of Vishnu
Yoga Sastra	Yoga scriptures
yugapat-srishti	Instantaneous creation

Notes and references

PART ONE   THE SELF

1 S. Om (tr.), *The Original Writings of Sri Ramana, Ulladu Narpadu Anubandham* benedictory verse.

CHAPTER 1   THE NATURE OF THE SELF

1 M. Venkataramiah (comp.), *Talks with Sri Ramana Maharshi*, p.123.
2 Muruganar, *Guru Vachaka Kovai*, vv.1036, 1034, 901, 438.
3 D. Mudaliar, *Day by Day with Bhagavan*, p.244.
4 M. Venkataramiah, op. cit., p.243.
5 Ibid., pp.110-11.
6 D Mudaliar, op. cit., p.296.
7 Ibid., p.155.
8 Muruganar, op. cit., v.1161.
9 T.N. Venkataraman (pub.), *Maharshi's Gospel*, p.15.
10 S. Nagamma, *Letters from Sri Ramanasramam* p.81.
11 Muruganar, op. cit., vv.1056, 422.
12 S. Natanananda, *Spiritual Instruction of Bhagavan Sri Ramana Maharshi*, p.20.
13 Muruganar, op. cit., vv.97, 99, 343.
14 D. Mudaliar, op. cit., p.88.
15 Ibid., p.65.
16 S. Nagamma, op. cit., pp.310-11.
17 'Who', *Maha Yoga*, p.202.
18 D. Mudaliar, op. cit., p.90.
19 Ibid., p.79.
20 Ibid., pp.90-1.
21 S. Nagamma, op. cit., p.196.
22 S. Natanananda, op. cit., p.21.
23 M. Venkataramiah, op. cit., p.402.
24 Ibid., p.31.
25 Muruganar, op. cit., v.1029.
26 M. Venkataramiah, op. cit., p.1.
27 T.N. Venkataraman, op. cit., p.72.

28   M. Venkataramiah, op. cit., pp.92-3.
29   Ibid., p.93.
30   Ibid., p.229.
31   Muruganar, op. cit., v.435.

CHAPTER 2   SELF-AWARENESS AND SELF-IGNORANCE

1   T.N. Venkataraman (pub.), *Maharshi's Gospel*, pp.31-2.
2   M. Venkataramiah (comp.), *Talks with Sri Ramana Maharshi*, pp.326-7.
3   Ibid., pp.91-2.
4   Ibid., pp.561-3.
5   T.N. Venkataraman, op. cit., pp.52-4.
6   S. Nagamma, *Letters from Sri Ramanasramam*, p.201.
7   D. Mudaliar, *Day by Day with Bhagavan*, p.287.
8   M. Venkataramiah, op. cit., pp.330-1.
9   D. Mudaliar, op. cit., p.74.
10   S. Cohen, *Guru Ramana*, p.63.
11   M. Venkataramiah, op. cit., p.6.
12   D. Mudaliar, op. cit., pp.79-80.
13   T.N. Venkataraman, op. cit., pp.86-7.
14   M. Venkataramiah, op. cit., p.4.
15   Muruganar, *Guru Vachaka Kovai*, v.779.
16   M. Venkataramiah, op. cit., pp.248-9.
17   Ibid., pp.128-9.
18   D. Mudaliar, op. cit., p.148.
19   M. Venkataramiah, op. cit., p.615.
20   Ibid., p.589.
21   Ibid., pp.564-5.
22   D. Mudaliar, op. cit., pp.15-16.
23   S. Nagamma, op. cit., p.130.

CHAPTER 3   THE *JNANI*

1   K. Sastri, *Sat-Darshana Bhashya*, p.xx.
2   T.N. Venkataraman (pub.), *Maharshi's Gospel*, pp.85-6.
3   S. Cohen, *Guru Ramana*, pp.101-2.
4   T.N. Venkataraman, op. cit., pp.60-2.
5   M. Venkataramiah (comp.), *Talks with Sri Ramana Maharshi*, p.217.
6   S. Cohen, op. cit., p.100.
7   S. Om (tr.), 'The Original Writings of Sri Ramana', *Ulladu Narpadu Anubandham*, v.32.
8   T.N. Venkataraman, op. cit., p.88.

9 M. Venkataramiah, op. cit., pp.349-50.
10 S. Om, *Guru Vachaka Kovai Urai*, p.360.
11 D. Mudaliar, *Day by Day with Bhagavan*, pp.189-90.
12 M. Venkataramiah, op. cit., pp.479-80.
13 K. Sastri, op. cit., pp.xxx-xxxi.
14 S. Nagamma, *Letters from Sri Ramanasramam*, p.147.
15 Ibid., pp.139-41.
16 M. Venkataramiah, op. cit., p.221.
17 S. Cohen, op. cit., pp.101-2.
18 D. Mudaliar, op. cit., p.144.
19 M. Venkataramiah, op. cit., p.393.
20 Ibid., p.3.
21 Ibid., p.53.
22 Ibid., p.534.

PART TWO   ENQUIRY AND SURRENDER

1 D. Mudaliar, *Day by Day with Bhagavan*, p.157.
2 M. Venkataramiah (comp.), *Talks with Sri Ramana Maharshi*, p.176.
3 Muruganar, *Guru Vachaka Kovai*, vv.722, 731.

CHAPTER 4   SELF-ENQUIRY – THEORY

1 M. Spenser, 'Sri Bhagavan's letter to Ganapati Muni', *The Mountain Path*, 1982, vol.19, p.96.
2 M. Venkataramiah (comp.), *Talks with Sri Ramana Maharshi*, p.25.
3 A. Osborne (ed.), *The Collected Works of Ramana Maharshi, Upadesa Saram*, vv.19, 17, 18, p.85.
4 M. Venkataramiah, op. cit., pp.232-3.
5 T.N. Venkataraman (pub.), *Maharshi's Gospel*, pp.83-5.
6 S. Cohen, *Guru Ramana*, p.46.
7 M. Venkataramiah, op. cit., pp.94-5.
8 Ibid., pp.154-5.
9 Muruganar, *Guru Vachaka Kovai*, vv.42, 613.
10 M. Venkataramiah, op. cit., p.574.
11 Ibid., pp.244-5.
12 S. Om (tr.), '*Ulladu Narpadu – Kalivenba*', *The Mountain Path*, 1981, vol.18, pp.220, 219.
13 S. Om (tr.), *The Path of Sri Ramana, Atmavidya Kirtanam*, v.2, p.45.
14 M. Venkataramiah, op. cit., p.357.
15 Muruganar, op. cit., v.756.
16 T.N. Venkataraman, op. cit., p.51.
17 Muruganar, op. cit., v.294.
18 M. Venkataramiah, op. cit., p.130.

CHAPTER 5   SELF-ENQUIRY – PRACTICE

1 S. Abhishiktananda, *The Secret of Arunachala*, p.73.
2 K. Sastri, *Sat-Darshana Bhashya*, pp.iii-iv.
3 T.N. Venkataraman (pub.), *Maharshi's Gospel*, p.87.
4 S. Om, *The Path of Sri Ramana*, pp.157, 159, 160, 163.
5 P. Brunton, *A Search in Secret India*, pp.156-7.
6 M. Venkataramiah (comp.), *Talks with Sri Ramana Maharshi*, pp.161-2.
7 Ibid., pp.571-2.
8 D. Mudaliar, *Day by Day with Bhagavan*, p.73.
9 T.N. Venkataraman, op. cit., p.43.
10 R. Swarnagiri, *Crumbs from his Table*, pp.25-7.
11 M. Venkataramiah, op. cit., pp.184-5.
12 Ibid., pp.463-4.
13 D. Mudaliar, op. cit., p.31.
14 M. Venkataraman, op. cit., p.163.
15 Ibid., p.27.
16 Muruganar, *Guru Vachaka Kovai*, v.399.
17 S. Cohen, *Guru Ramana*, p.91.
18 M. Venkataramiah, op. cit., p.145.
19 D. Mudaliar, op. cit., p.7.
20 M. Venkataramiah, op. cit., pp.582-3.
21 D. Mudaliar, op. cit., p.76.
22 T.N. Venkataraman, op. cit., p.50.
23 M. Venkataramiah, op. cit., p.550.
24 K. Sastri, op. cit., p.ix.
25 M. Venkataramiah, op. cit., p.470.
26 Ibid., pp.151-2.
27 Ibid., pp.332-3.
28 T.N. Venkataraman, op. cit., p.35.
29 Muruganar, op. cit., vv.433, 1232.

CHAPTER 6   SELF-ENQUIRY – MISCONCEPTIONS

1 S. Om (tr.), 'Ulladu Narpadu – Kalivenba', *The Mountain Path*, 1981, vol.18, p.217.
2 M. Venkataramiah (comp.), *Talks with Sri Ramana Maharshi*, p.162.
3 Ibid., pp.47-8.
4 Ibid., p.235.
5 D. Mudaliar, *Day by Day with Bhagavan*, p.68.
6 Ibid., pp.192-3.
7 M. Venkataramiah, op. cit., p.202.
8 Ibid., pp.306-7.

9 D. Mudaliar, op. cit., p.72.
10 K. Sastri, *Sat-Darshana Bhashya*, pp.viii-ix.
11 D. Mudaliar, op. cit., pp.280-1.
12 M. Venkataramiah, op. cit., pp.464-5.
13 K. Sastri, op. cit., pp.xvii-xix.
14 T.N. Venkataraman (pub.), *Maharshi's Gospel*, pp.73-4.
15 M. Venkataramiah, op. cit., p.378.
16 D. Mudaliar, op. cit., p.202.
17 M. Venkataramiah, op. cit., p.229.
18 Ibid., p.488.
19 'Who', *Maha Yoga*, p.197.
20 D. Mudaliar, op. cit., p.185.
21 G. Muni, *Sri Ramana Gita*, ch.5, v.2.
22 This description is given in *Ashtangahridayam*, the Hindu medical work cited earlier in the chapter.
23 M. Venkataramiah, op. cit., p.116.
24 Muruganar, *Guru Vachaka Kovai*, vv.251, 261, 257.

CHAPTER 7   SURRENDER

1 M. Venkataramiah (comp.), *Talks with Sri Ramana Maharshi*, p.285.
2 D. Mudaliar, *Day by Day with Bhagavan*, p.140.
3 Ibid., p.72.
4 Ibid., p.30.
5 M. Venkataramiah, op. cit., p.334.
6 Ibid., pp.322-3.
7 D. Mudaliar, op. cit., p.42.
8 M. Venkataramiah, op. cit., p.49.
9 Ibid., p.425.
10 Ibid., p.195.
11 Ibid., p.175.
12 S. Nagamma, *Letters from Sri Ramanasramam*, pp.181-3.
13 M. Venkataramiah, op. cit., p.69.
14 S. Nagamma, op. cit., pp.309-10.
15 Muruganar, *Guru Vachaka Vovai*, vv.974, 652, 655.
16 M. Venkataramiah, op. cit., p.219.
17 Ibid., p.133.
18 Ibid., p.69.
19 Muruganar, op. cit., vv.658, 657, 521, 520, 721, 1205, 472.
20 S. Nagamma, op. cit., p.18.
21 Muruganar, op. cit., v.683.
22 T.N. Venkataraman (pub.), *Maharshi's Gospel*, p.24.
23 D. Mudaliar, op. cit., p.157.
24 M. Venkataramiah, op. cit., pp.29-30.

PART THREE   THE GURU

1 S. Om, *The Path of Sri Ramana*, p.160.
2 A. Osborne, *Ramana Maharshi and the Path of Self Knowledge*, p.142.
3 P. Brunton, *Conscious Immortality*, p.35.

CHAPTER 8   THE GURU

1 T.N. Venkataraman (pub.), *Maharshi's Gospel*, pp.36-7.
2 S. Natanananda, *Spiritual Instruction of Bhagavan Sri Ramana Maharshi*, p.2.
3 D. Mudaliar, *Day by Day with Bhagavan*, p.169.
4 M. Venkataramiah (comp.), *Talks with Sri Ramana Maharshi*, pp.554-5.
5 'Who', *Maha Yoga*, p.193.
6 S. Natanananda, op. cit., pp.1-3.
7 S. Nagamma, *Letters from Sri Ramanasramam*, p.161.
8 M. Venkataramiah, op. cit., p.516.
9 Sri Ramana wrote several poems in praise of the mountain Arunachala. In some of the verses he specifically says that it was his Guru, his God and his Self.
10 S. Cohen, *Guru Ramana*, pp.67-8.
11 M. Venkataramiah, op. cit., p.46.
12 Ibid., p.404.
13 Ibid., p.392.
14 S. Nagamma, op. cit., p.75.
15 M. Venkataramiah, op. cit., pp.240-1.
16 Ibid., p.281.
17 Ibid., pp.20-1.
18 Ibid., p.242.
19 Muruganar, *Guru Vachaka Kovai*, vv.270, 248, 799, 800, 324, 290.
20 M. Venkataramiah, op. cit., p.208.
21 K. Sastri, *Sat-Darshana Bhashya*, p.v.
22 M. Venkataramiah, op. cit., p.80.
23 Ibid., p.124.
24 Ibid., p.33.
25 Ibid., p.114.
26 Ibid., p.181.
27 Ibid., p.183.
28 D. Mudaliar, *My Reminiscences*, p.106.
29 M. Venkataramiah, op. cit., p.5.
30 Ibid., p.136.

CHAPTER 9   SILENCE AND *SAT-SANGA*

1 S. Om (tr.), 'The Original Writings of Sri Ramana', *Ulladu Narpadu Anubandham*, vv.1-5.
2 T.N. Venkataraman (pub.), *Maharshi's Gospel*, p.16.
3 P. Brunton, *Conscious Immortality*, pp.141-2.
4 Muruganar, *Guru Vachaka Kovai*, v.286.
5 M. Venkataramiah (comp.), *Talks with Sri Ramana Maharshi*, p.402.
6 Ibid., p.501.
7 Ibid., pp.369-70.
8 D. Mudaliar, *Day by Day with Bhagavan*, pp.34-5.
9 M. Venkataramiah, op. cit., pp.200-1.
10 D. Mudaliar, op. cit., pp.145-6.
11 M. Venkataramiah, op. cit., pp.500-1.
12 Ibid., pp.74-5.
13 Ibid., p.528.
14 Ibid., p.135.
15 Ibid., p.177.
16 Ibid., p.123.
17 Ibid., p.572.
18 Ibid., p.247.
19 Ibid., p.318.
20 P. Brunton, op. cit., p.147.
21 M. Venkataramiah, op. cit., p.461.
22 Ibid., p.140.
23 Ibid., p.186.
24 D. Mudaliar, op. cit., pp.236-7.
25 M. Venkataramiah, op. cit., p.242.

PART FOUR   MEDITATION AND YOGA

1 S. Cohen, *Guru Ramana*, p.78.
2 Muruganar, *Guru Vachaka Kovai*, v.691.

CHAPTER 10   MEDITATION AND CONCENTRATION

1 P. Brunton, *Conscious Immortality*, p.176.
2 G. Muni, *Sri Ramana Gita*, ch.7, vv.26, 22.
3 S. Om, *The Path of Sri Ramana*, p.163.
4 M. Venkataramiah (comp.), *Talks with Sri Ramana Maharshi*, pp.144-5.
5 Muruganar, *Guru Vachaka Kovai*, vv.738-9.
6 M. Venkataramiah, op. cit., p.261.

7 Ibid., p.429.
8 Ibid., p.145.
9 Ibid., pp.255-6.
10 S. Natanananda, *Spiritual Instruction of Bhagavan Sri Ramana Maharshi*, p.13.
11 M. Venkataramiah, op. cit., pp.256-7.
12 Ibid., p.514.
13 Ibid., p.66.
14 S. Cohen, *Guru Ramana*, pp.73-4.
15 Ibid., p.76.
16 M. Venkataramiah, op. cit., p.337.
17 T.N. Venkataraman (pub.), *Maharshi's Gospel*, pp.81-2.
18 M. Venkataramiah, op. cit., pp.169-70.
19 Ibid., p.28.
20 Ibid., pp.518-19.
21 D. Mudaliar, *Day by Day with Bhagavan*, p.243.
22 M. Venkataramiah, op. cit., p.88.

CHAPTER 11   *MANTRAS AND JAPA*

1 T.N. Venkataraman (pub.), *Maharshi's Gospel*, p.25.
2 M. Venkataramiah (comp.), *Talks with Sri Ramana Maharshi*, p.417.
3 D. Mudaliar, *Day by Day with Bhagavan*, pp.146-7.
4 M. Venkataramiah, op. cit., pp.416-17.
5 D. Mudaliar, op. cit., p.147.
6 Muruganar, *Guru Vachaka Kovai*, v.707.
7 M. Venkataramiah, op. cit., p.376.
8 D. Mudaliar, op. cit., p.210.
9 Ibid., p.229.
10 S. Nagamma, *Letters from Sri Ramanasramam*, pp.202-3.
11 M. Venkataramiah, op. cit., p.296.
12 Ibid., pp.507-8.
13 T.N. Venkataraman, op. cit., p.25.
14 Muruganar, op. cit., vv.710, 709.
15 M. Venkataramiah, op. cit., pp.2-3.
16 S. Cohen, *Guru Ramana*, pp.75-6.
17 G. Muni, *Sri Ramana Gita*, ch.7, vv.10, 11.
18 M. Venkataramiah, op. cit., p.508.

CHAPTER 12   LIFE IN THE WORLD

1 R. Swarnagiri, *Crumbs from his Table*, p.43.
2 T.N. Venkataraman (pub.), *Maharshi's Gospel*, pp.7-8.

3 P. Brunton, *Conscious Immortality*, pp.130-1.
4 S. Nagamma, *Letters from Sri Ramanasramam*, pp.211-12.
5 M. Venkataramiah (comp.), *Talks with Sri Ramana Maharshi*, p.50.
6 Ibid., p.15.
7 Ibid., p.80.
8 S. Natanananda, *Spiritual Instruction of Bhagavan Sri Ramana Maharshi*, p.17.
9 P. Brunton, op. cit., pp.123-4.
10 Ibid., p.133.
11 Ibid., p.43. The question about Sri Aurobindo ashram comes from the original manuscript of the book. It was deleted from the published version.
12 Ibid., pp.139-40.
13 Ibid., p.31.
14 'Who', *Maha Yoga*, p.204.
15 S. Nagamma, op. cit., pp.175-6.
16 P. Brunton, op. cit., p.32.
17 Ibid., p.62.
18 M. Venkataramiah, op. cit., p.20.
19 P. Brunton, op. cit., pp.11-12.
20 S. Natanananda, op. cit., p.14.

CHAPTER 13   YOGA

1 M. Venkataramiah (comp.), *Talks with Sri Ramana Maharshi*, p.576.
2 Ibid., p.27.
3 Ibid., p.178.
4 D. Mudaliar, *Day by Day with Bhagavan*, pp.188-9.
5 *Chitta-vritti-nirodha* is the second *sutra* of Patanjali's *Yoga Sutras*.
6 'Who', *Maha Yoga*, p.194.
7 M. Venkataramiah, op. cit., pp.417-18.
8 Ibid., p.26.
9 S. Natanananda, *Spiritual Instruction of Bhagavan Sri Ramana Maharshi*, p.6.
10 M. Venkataramiah,, op. cit., p.134.
11 Muruganar, *Guru Vachaka Kovai*, v.701.
12 D. Mudaliar, op. cit., p.32.
13 Ibid., p.47.
14 S. Nagamma, *Letters from Sri Ramanasramam*, pp.373-4.
15 D. Mudaliar, op. cit., pp.14-15.
16 M. Venkataramiah, op. cit., p.366.
17 Ibid., pp.575-6.
18 R. Swarnagiri, *Crumbs from his Table*, pp.35-6.
19 'Who', op. cit., p.203.

20 M. Venkataramiah, op. cit., p.584.
21 Ibid., p.532.
22 Muruganar, op. cit., v.690.
23 S. Nagamma. op. cit., p.179.
24 M. Venkataramiah, op. cit., pp.599-600.
25 Ibid., p.414.
26 R. Swarnagiri, op. cit., pp.30-1.
27 T.N. Venkataraman (pub.), *Maharshi's Gospel*, p.34.
28 'Who', op. cit., pp.197-8.
29 T.N. Venkataraman, op. cit., p.34.
30 M. Venkataramiah, op. cit., p.484.

PART FIVE   EXPERIENCE

1 M. Venkataramiah (comp.), *Talks with Sri Ramana Maharshi*, pp.116-17.
2 Ibid., p.123.

CHAPTER 14   *SAMADHI*

1 M. Venkataramiah (comp.), *Talks with Sri Ramana Maharshi*, pp.357-8.
2 Muruganar, *Guru Vachaka Kovai*, v.898.
3 R. Swarnagiri, *Crumbs from his Table*, p.42.
4 S. Cohen, *Guru Ramana*, p.89.
5 Ibid., p.88.
6 Ibid., p.87.
7 D. Mudaliar, *Day by Day with Bhagavan*, p.116.
8 K. Sastri, *Sat-Darshana Bhashya*, pp.xi-xii.
9 M. Venkataramiah, op. cit., p.79.
10 S. Cohen, op. cit., pp.89-90.
11 S. Nagamma, *Letters from Sri Ramanasramam*, p.269.
12 Ibid., p.270.
13 S. Cohen, op. cit., p.90.
14 T.N. Venkataraman (pub.), *Maharshi's Gospel*, p.32.
15 Muruganar, op. cit., v.919.
16 M. Venkataramiah, op. cit., pp.381-2.
17 S. Cohen, op. cit., pp.86-7.
18 Muruganar, op. cit., vv.893, 174.
19 'Who', *Maha Yoga*, pp.202-3.
20 T.N. Venkataraman, op. cit., p.34.
21 S. Nagamma, op. cit., pp.239-40.
22 M. Venkataramiah, op. cit., p.121.

23 Muruganar, op. cit., v.895.

CHAPTER 15   VISIONS AND PSYCHIC POWERS

1 M. Venkataramiah (comp.), *Talks with Sri Ramana Maharshi*, p.357.
2 Ibid., p.550.
3 Ibid., pp.423-5.
4 D. Mudaliar, *Day by Day with Bhagavan*, pp.184-5.
5 M. Venkataramiah, op. cit., p.355.
6 Ibid., pp.278-9.
7 Ibid., p.442.
8 S. Nagamma, *Letters from Sri Ramanasramam*, p.46.
9 D. Mudaliar, op. cit., p.232.
10 K. Sastri, *Sat-Darshana Bhashya*, pp.xxii.
11 M. Venkataramiah, op. cit., p.552.
12 Muruganar, *Guru Vachaka Kovai*, v.1212.
13 M. Venkataramiah, op. cit., p.578.
14 Muruganar, op. cit., vv.219, 221, 222, 224.
15 S. Cohen, *Guru Ramana*, p.100.
16 M. Venkataramiah, op. cit., p.487.
17 Ibid., pp.17-18.

CHAPTER 16   PROBLEMS AND EXPERIENCES

1 T.N. Venkataraman (pub.), *Maharshi's Gospel*, p.33.
2 M. Venkataramiah (comp.), *Talks with Sri Ramana Maharshi*, p.314.
3 D. Mudaliar, *Day by Day with Bhagavan*, p.22.
4 S. Nagamma, *Letters from Sri Ramanasramam*, p.251.
5 D. Mudaliar, op. cit., p.193.
6 M. Venkataramiah, op. cit., p.129.
7 S. Cohen, *Guru Ramana*, p.39.
8 D. Mudaliar, op. cit., p.182.
9 P. Brunton, *Conscious Immortality*, p.202.
10 T.N. Venkataraman, op. cit., pp.43-4.
11 D. Mudaliar, op. cit., pp.237-8.
12 M. Venkataramiah, op. cit., p.179.
13 Ibid., p.55.
14 Ibid., p.549.
15 Ibid., pp.435-7.
16 D. Mudaliar, op. cit., p.198.
17 R. Swarnagiri, *Crumbs from his Table*, p.36.
18 D. Mudaliar, op. cit., pp.169-70.
19 M. Venkataramiah, op. cit., p.394.

PART 6   THEORY

1 P. Brunton, *Conscious Immortality*, p.195.

CHAPTER 17   CREATION THEORIES AND
THE REALITY OF THE WORLD

1 D. Mudaliar, *Day by Day with Bhagavan*, p.132.
2 S. Madhavatirtha, 'Conversations with the Maharshi', *The Mountain Path*, 1980, vol.17, p.211.
3 Muruganar, *Guru Vachaka Kovai*, vv.85-6.
4 D. Mudaliar, op. cit., p.149.
5 M. Venkataramiah (comp.), *Talks with Sri Ramana Maharshi*, pp.612-13.
6 Ibid., p.341.
7 Ibid., p.354.
8 Ibid., pp.36-7.
9 Ibid., p.432.
10 Ibid., p.41.
11 S. Cohen, *Guru Ramana*, p.65.
12 S. Nagamma, *Letters from Sri Ramanasramam*, p.94.
13 Muruganar, op. cit., vv.49, 50, 51, 52, 57.
14 T.N. Venkataraman (pub.), *Maharshi's Gospel*, pp.63-7.
15 S. Madhavatirtha, 'Conversations with Bhagavan', *The Mountain Path*, 1981, vol.18, pp.154-5.
16 S. Cohen, op. cit., pp.56-7.

CHAPTER 18   REINCARNATION

1 T.N. Venkataraman (pub.), *Maharshi's Gospel*, p.41.
2 Muruganar, *Guru Vachaka Kovai*, vv.874, 1122, Bhagavan 9.
3 M. Venkataramiah (comp.), *Talks with Sri Ramana Maharshi*, p.235.
4 Ibid., p.13.
5 Ibid., pp.191-2.
6 Ibid., p.55.
7 Ibid., p.121.
8 Ibid., p.40.
9 S. Cohen, *Guru Ramana*, p.44.
10 Ibid., pp.41-2.
11 M. Venkataramiah, op. cit., p.164.
12 D. Mudaliar, *Day by Day with Bhagavan*, p.263.
13 S. Cohen, op. cit., p.40.
14 T.N. Venkataraman, op. cit., p.27.

15 'Who', *Maha Yoga*, p.196.
16 M. Venkataramiah, op. cit., p.531.
17 D. Mudaliar, op. cit., p.221.
18 M. Venkataramiah, op. cit., p.602.

CHAPTER 19 THE NATURE OF GOD

1 T.N. Venkataraman (pub.), *Maharshi's Gospel*, pp.55-8.
2 M. Venkataramiah (comp.), *Talks with Sri Ramana Maharshi*, p.333.
3 Muruganar, *Guru Vachaka Kovai*, v.867.
4 M. Venkataramiah, op. cit., pp.610-11.
5 Ibid., p.102.
6 Muruganar, op. cit., vv.714-16.
7 Ibid., vv.105-9.
8 M. Venkataramiah, op. cit., pp.31-2.
9 Muruganar, op. cit., v.1191.
10 P. Brunton, *Conscious Immortality*, pp.7, 8, 10.
11 M. Venkataramiah, op. cit., p.268.
12 P. Brunton, op. cit., pp.180-1.
13 Ibid., p.187.
14 Muruganar, op. cit., vv.1098, 1099, 194, 195, 196.
15 S. Nagamma, *Letters from Sri Ramanasramam*, p.148.
16 Muruganar, op. cit., v.930.
17 M. Venkataramiah, op. cit., p.127.
18 P. Brunton, op. cit., p.7.
19 According to Hindu cosmology the whole of the manifest universe is periodically reabsorbed into the unmanifest *Brahman*. This absorption is known as *pralaya*.
20 M. Venkataramiah, op. cit., pp.34-5.
21 P. Brunton, op. cit., p.186.
22 R. Swarnagiri, *Crumbs from his Table*, p.44.
23 D. Mudaliar, *Day by Day with Bhagavan*, pp.242-3.
24 Muruganar, op. cit., v.1207.

CHAPTER 20 SUFFERING AND MORALITY

1 S. Om (tr.), *'Ulladu Narpadu – Kalivenba'*, *The Mountain Path*, 1981, vol.18, p.218.
2 M. Venkataramiah (comp.), *Talks with Sri Ramana Maharshi*, p.120.
3 T.N. Venkataraman (pub.), *Maharshi's Gospel*, pp.51-2.
4 S. Natanananda, *Spiritual Instruction of Bhagavan Sri Ramana Maharshi*, p.27.
5 S. Cohen, *Guru Ramana*, pp.47-8.

6 M. Venkataramiah, op. cit., pp.368-9.
7 Muruganar, *Guru Vachaka Kovai*, vv.952-4.
8 M. Venkataramiah, op. cit., pp.593-4.
9 'Who', *Maha Yoga*, p.192.
10 D. Mudaliar, *My Reminiscences*, pp.98-9.
11 D. Mudaliar, *Day by Day with Bhagavan*, pp.80-1.
12 Ibid., p.286.
13 D. Mudaliar, 1970, op. cit., pp.94-5.
14 Muruganar, op. cit., vv.807, 808.
15 M. Venkataramiah, op. cit., pp.226-8.
16 Ibid., p.428.
17 D. Mudaliar, 1977, op. cit., pp.304-5.
18 Muruganar, op. cit., vv.574, 573.
19 D. Mudaliar, 1977, op. cit., p.258.
20 S. Nagamma, *Letters from Sri Ramanasramam*, pp.151-2.
21 Muruganar, op. cit., v.791.

CHAPTER 21   *KARMA*, DESTINY AND FREE WILL

1 S. Natanananda, *Spiritual Instruction of Bhagavan Sri Ramana Maharshi*, p.21.
2 C. Aiyer, 'Quotations from the Maharshi', *The Mountain Path*, 1982, vol.19, p.23.
3 P. Brunton, *Conscious Immortality*, p.135. One portion of this quotation was inadvertently left out of the published version. The quotation given here is taken directly from the manuscript of the book.
4 S. Nagamma, *Letters from Sri Ramanasramam*, p.78.
5 M. Venkataramiah (comp.), *Talks with Sri Ramana Maharshi*, p.470.
6 Ibid., p.462.
7 D. Mudaliar, *Day by Day with Bhagavan*, p.222.
8 S. Nagamma, op. cit., p.171.
9 Muruganar, *Guru Vachaka Kovai*, v.703.
10 S. Nagamma, op. cit., p.65.
11 Muruganar, op. cit., v.150.
12 D. Mudaliar, op. cit., pp.295-6.
13 Muruganar, op. cit., v.697.
14 D. Mudaliar, *My Reminiscences*, p.63.
15 S. Nagamma, op. cit., pp.347-8.
16 M. Venkataramiah, op. cit., pp.159-60.
17 D. Mudaliar, 1977, op. cit., p.75.
18 S. Cohen, *Guru Ramana*, p.50.
19 D. Mudaliar, 1970, op. cit., pp.90-1.
20 M. Venkataramiah, op. cit., p.393.
21 D. Mudaliar, 1977, op. cit., p.230.

Bibliography

Abhishiktananda (1979), *The Secret of Arunachala*, New Delhi, ISPCK.

Aiyer, C.S. (1982), 'Quotations from the Maharshi', *The Mountain Path*, vol.19, p.23.

Brunton, P. (1980), *A Search in Secret India*, Bombay, BI Publications.

Brunton, P. (1984), *Conscious Immortality*, Tiruvannamalai, Sri Ramanasramam.

Cohen, S. (1980), *Guru Ramana*, Tiruvannamalai, Sri Ramanasramam.

Madhavatirtha, S. (1980), 'Conversations with the Maharshi', *The Mountain Path*, vol.17, p.211.

Madhavatirtha, S. (1981), 'Conversations with Bhagavan', *The Mountain Path*, vol.18, pp.153-5.

Mudaliar, D. (1970), *My Reminiscences*, Tiruvannamalai, Sri Ramanasramam.

Mudaliar, D. (1977), *Day by Day with Bhagavan*, Tiruvannamalai, Sri Ramanasramam.

Muni, G. (1977), *Sri Ramana Gita*, Tiruvannamalai, Sri Ramanasramam.

Muruganar, *Guru Vachaka Kovai*, unpublished translation by Sadhu Om, Tiruvannamalai.

Nagamma, S. (1973), *Letters from Sri Ramanasramam*, Tiruvannamalai, Sri Ramanasramam.

Natanananda, S. (1974), *Spiritual Instruction of Bhagavan Sri Ramana Maharshi*, Tiruvannamalai, Sri Ramanasramam.

Om, S. (1980), *Guru Vachaka Kovai (Urai)*, New Delhi, Sri Ramana Kendra.

Om, S. (1981a), *The Path of Sri Ramana, Part One*, Varkala, Kerala, Sri Ramana Kshetra.

Om, S. (1981b), '*Ulladu Narpadu – Kalivenba*', *The Mountain Path*, vol.18, pp.217-22.

Om, S. (tr.), 'The Original Writings of Sri Ramana', unpublished translation.

Osborne, A. (ed.) (1972), *The Collected Works of Ramana Maharshi*, London, Rider and Company.

Osborne, A. (1979), *Ramana Maharshi and the Path of Self Knowledge*, Bombay, BI Publications.

Sastri, K. (1975), *Sat-Darshana Bhashya*, Tiruvannamalai, Sri Ramanasramam.

Spenser, M. (1982), 'Sri Bhagavan's letter to Ganapati Muni', *The Mountain Path*, vol.19, pp.95-101.

Swarnagiri, R. (1981), *Crumbs from his Table*, Tiruvannamalai, Sri Ramanasramam.

Venkataraman, T.N. (pub.) (1979), *Maharshi's Gospel*, Tiruvannamalai, Sri Ramanasramam.

Venkataramiah, M. (comp.) (1978), *Talks with Sri Ramana Maharshi*, Tiruvannamalai, Sri Ramanasramam.

'Who' (1973), *Maha Yoga*, Tiruvannamalai, Sri Ramanasramam.

All books published by Sri Ramanasramam are available from Sri Ramanasramam, Tiruvannamalai, 606603, S. India.

Index

247

PENGUIN

ARKANA

NEW AGE BOOKS FOR MIND, BODY & SPIRIT

With over 200 titles currently in print, Arkana is the leading name in quality books for mind, body and spirit. Arkana encompasses the spirituality of both East and West, ancient and new. A vast range of interests is covered, including Psychology and Transformation, Health, Science and Mysticism, Women's Spirituality, Zen, Western Traditions and Astrology.

If you would like a catalogue of Arkana books, please write to:

Sales Dept. – Arkana
Penguin Books USA Inc.
375 Hudson Street
New York, NY 10014

Arkana Marketing Department
Penguin Books Ltd
27 Wrights Lane
London W8 5TZ

PENGUIN

ARKANA

NEW AGE BOOKS FOR MIND, BODY & SPIRIT

A SELECTION OF TITLES

Neal's Yard Natural Remedies
Susan Curtis, Romy Fraser and Irene Kohler

Natural remedies for common ailments from the pioneering Neal's Yard Apothecary Shop. An invaluable resource for everyone wishing to take responsibility for their own health, enabling you to make your own choice from homeopathy, aromatherapy and herbalism.

Zen in the Art of Archery   Eugen Herrigel

Few in the West have strived as hard as Eugen Herrigel to learn Zen from a Master. His classic text gives an unsparing account of his initiation into the 'Great Doctrine' of archery. Baffled by its teachings – that art must become artless, that the archer must aim at himself – he gradually began to glimpse the depth of wisdom behind the paradoxes. While many Western writers on Zen serve up secondhand slogans, Herrigel's hard-won insights are his own discoveries.

The Absent Father: Crisis and Creativity   Alix Pirani

Freud used Oedipus to explain human nature; but Alix Pirani believes that the myth of Danae and Perseus has most to teach an age which offers 'new responsibilities for women and challenging questions for men'. It is a myth that can help us face the darker side of our personalities and break the patterns inherited from our parents.

Power of the Witch   Laurie Cabot

In fascinating detail, Laurie Cabot describes the techniques and rituals involved in charging tools, brewing magical potions and casting vigorous, tantalizing spells. Intriguing and accessible, this taboo-shattering guide will educate and enlighten even the most sceptical reader in the ways of an ancient faith that has much to offer today's world.

Water and Sexuality   Michel Odent

Taking as his starting point his world-famous work on underwater childbirth at Pithiviers, Michel Odent considers the meaning and importance of water as a symbol.

PENGUIN

ARKANA

NEW AGE BOOKS FOR MIND, BODY & SPIRIT

A SELECTION OF TITLES

On Having No Head: Zen and the Rediscovery of the Obvious
D. E. Harding

'Reason and imagination and all mental chatter died down ... I forgot my name, my humanness, my thingness, all that could be called me or mine. Past and future dropped away...' Thus Douglas Harding describes his first experience of headlessness, or no self. This classic work truly conveys the experience that mystics of all ages have tried to put into words.

Self-Healing: My Life and Vision   Meir Schneider

Born blind, pronounced incurable – yet at 17 Meir Schneider discovered self-healing techniques that within four years led him to gain a remarkable degree of vision. In the process he discovered an entirely new self-healing system, and an inspirational faith and enthusiasm that helped others heal themselves. While individual response to self-healing is unique, the healing power is inherent in all of us.

Wa-Do   Dr Tran Vu Chi

Suitable for men and women of all ages, Wa-Do is a system of exercises especially designed to encourage good circulation, and improved breathing and posture and to relieve tension. Illustrated with easy-to-follow diagrams, *Wa-Do* will allow you to experience the pleasure of being alive and teach you how to be an attentive and understanding friend to your body.

The Universe is a Green Dragon   Brian Swimme

'The new scientific story of the universe's origin in the "Big Bang" has been told in popular terms before, but never like this. [It succeeds] in evoking a sense of wonder about the story's music, its poetry, its meaning in everyday life' – *San Francisco Chronicle*

PENGUIN
ARKANA

NEW AGE BOOKS FOR MIND, BODY & SPIRIT

A SELECTION OF TITLES

The Revised Waite's Compendium of Natal Astrology
Alan Candlish

This completely revised edition retains the basic structure of Waite's classic work while making major improvements to accuracy and readability. With a new computer-generated Ephemeris, complete for the years 1900 to 2010, and a Table of Houses that now allows astrologers to choose between seven house systems, it provides all the information on houses, signs and planets the astrologer needs to draw up and interpret a full natal chart.

Aromatherapy for Everyone   Robert Tisserand

The therapeutic value of essential oils was recognized as far back as Ancient Egyptian times. Today there is an upsurge in the use of these fragrant and medicinal oils to soothe and heal both mind and body. Here is a comprehensive guide to every aspect of aromatherapy by the man whose name is synonymous with its practice and teaching.

Tao Te Ching   The Richard Wilhelm Edition

Encompassing philosophical speculation and mystical reflection, the *Tao Te Ching* has been translated more often than any other book except the Bible, and more analysed than any other Chinese classic. Richard Wilhelm's acclaimed 1910 translation is here made available in English.

The Book of the Dead   E. A. Wallis Budge

Intended to give the deceased immortality, the Ancient Egyptian *Book of the Dead* was a vital piece of 'luggage' on the soul's journey to the other world, providing for every need: victory over enemies, the procurement of friendship and – ultimately – entry into the kingdom of Osiris.

Yoga: Immortality and Freedom   Mircea Eliade

Eliade's excellent volume explores the tradition of yoga with exceptional directness and detail. 'One of the most important and exhaustive single-volume studies of the major ascetic techniques of India and their history yet to appear in English' – *San Francisco Chronicle*

PENGUIN

ARKANA

NEW AGE BOOKS FOR MIND, BODY & SPIRIT

A SELECTION OF TITLES

Weavers of Wisdom: Women Mystics of the Twentieth Century
Anne Bancroft

Throughout history women have sought answers to eternal questions about existence and beyond – yet most gurus, philosophers and religious leaders have been men. Through exploring the teachings of fifteen women mystics – each with her own approach to what she calls 'the truth that goes beyond the ordinary' – Anne Bancroft gives a rare, cohesive and fascinating insight into the diversity of female approaches to mysticism.

Dynamics of the Unconscious: Seminars in Psychological Astrology II
Liz Greene and Howard Sasportas

The authors of The *Development of the Personality* team up again to show how the dynamics of depth psychology interact with your birth chart. They shed new light on the psychology and astrology of aggression and depression – the darker elements of the adult personality that we must confront if we are to grow to find the wisdom within.

The Myth of the Eternal Return: Cosmos and History Mircea Eliade

'A luminous, profound, and extremely stimulating work ... Eliade's thesis is that ancient man envisaged events not as constituting a linear, progressive history, but simply as so many creative repetitions of primordial archetypes ... This is an essay which everyone interested in the history of religion and in the mentality of ancient man will have to read. It is difficult to speak too highly of it' – Theodore H. Gaster in *Review of Religion*

The Second Krishnamurti Reader Edited by Mary Lutyens

In this reader bringing together two of Krishnamurti's most popular works, *The Only Revolution* and *The Urgency of Change*, the spiritual teacher who rebelled against religion points to a new order arising when we have ceased to be envious and vicious. Krishnamurti says, simply: 'When you are not, love is.' 'Seeing,' he declares, 'is the greatest of all skills.' In these pages, gently, he helps us to open our hearts and eyes.

NEW AGE BOOKS FOR MIND, BODY & SPIRIT

A SELECTION OF TITLES

A Course in Miracles
The Course, Workbook for Students and Manual for Teachers

Hailed as 'one of the most remarkable systems of spiritual truth available today', *A Course in Miracles* is a self-study course designed to shift our perceptions, heal our minds and change our behaviour, teaching us to experience miracles – 'natural expressions of love' – rather than problems generated by fear in our lives.

Fire in the Heart   Kyriacos C. Markides

A sequel to *The Magus of Strovolus* and *Homage to the Sun*, *Fire in the Heart* centres on Daskalos, the Cypriot healer and miracle-worker and his successor-designate Kostas. The author, who has witnessed much that is startling in his years with the two magi, believes humanity may today be on the verge of a revolution in consciousness 'more profound than the Renaissance and the Enlightenment combined.'

Arthur and the Sovereignty of Britain: Goddess and Tradition on the Mabinogion   Caitlín Matthews

Rich in legend and the primitive magic of the Celtic Otherworld, the stories of the *Mabinogion* heralded the first flowering of European literature and became the source of Arthurian legend. Caitlín Matthews illuminates these stories, shedding light on Sovereignty, the Goddess of the Land and the spiritual principle of the Feminine.

Shamanism: Archaic Techniques of Ecstasy   Mircea Eliade

Throughout Siberia and Central Asia, religious life traditionally centres around the figure of the shaman: magician and medicine man, healer and miracle-doer, priest and poet. 'Has become the standard work on the subject and justifies its claim to be the first book to study the phenomenon over a wide field and in a properly religious context' – *The Times Literary Supplement*

PENGUIN

ARKANA

NEW AGE BOOKS FOR MIND, BODY & SPIRIT

A SELECTION OF TITLES

Head Off Stress: Beyond the Bottom Line
D. E. Harding

Learning to head off stress takes no time at all and is impossible to forget – all it requires is that we dare take a fresh look at ourselves. This infallible and revolutionary guide from the author of *On Having No Head* – whose work C. S. Lewis described as 'highest genius' – shows how.

Shadows in the Cave   Graham Dunstan Martin

We can all recognize our friends in a crowd, so why can't we describe in words what makes a particular face unique? The answer, says Graham Dunstan Martin, is that our minds are not just computers: drawing constantly on a fund of tacit knowledge, we always *know* more than we can ever say. Consciousness, in fact, is at the very heart of the universe, and – like the earth itself – we are all aspects of a single universal mind.

The Magus of Strovolos: The Extraordinary World of a Spiritual Healer   Kyriacos C. Markides

This vivid account introduces us to the rich and intricate world of Daskalos, the Magus of Strovolos – a true healer who draws upon a seemingly limitless mixture of esoteric teachings, psychology, reincarnation, demonology, cosmology and mysticism, from both East and West. 'This is a really marvellous book ... one of the most extraordinary accounts of a "magical" personality since Ouspensky's account of Gurdjieff' – Colin Wilson

Meetings With Remarkable Men   G. I. Gurdjieff

All that we know of the early life of Gurdjieff – one of the great spiritual masters of this century – is contained within these colourful and profound tales of adventure. The men who influenced his formative years had no claim to fame in the conventional sense; what made them remarkable was the consuming desire they all shared to understand the deepest mysteries of life.

PENGUIN
ARKANA

NEW AGE BOOKS FOR MIND, BODY & SPIRIT

A SELECTION OF TITLES

When the Iron Eagle Flies: Buddhism for the West   Ayya Khema

'One of humanity's greatest jewels'. Such are the teachings of the Buddha, unfolded here simply, free of jargon. This practical guide to meaning through awareness contains a wealth of exercises and advice to help the reader on his or her way.

The Second Ring of Power   Carlos Casteneda

Carlos Castaneda's journey into the world of sorcery has captivated millions. In this fifth book, he introduces the reader to Dona Soledad, whose mission is to test Castaneda by a series of terrifying tricks. Thus Castaneda is initiated into experiences so intense, so profoundly disturbing, as to be an assault on reason and on every preconceived notion of life...

Dialogues with Scientists and Sages: The Search for Unity
Renée Weber

In their own words, contemporary scientists and mystics – from the Dalai Lama to Stephen Hawking – share with us their richly diverse views on space, time, matter, energy, life, consciousness, creation and our place in the scheme of things. Through the immediacy of verbatim dialogue, we encounter scientists who endorse mysticism, and those who oppose it; mystics who dismiss science, and those who embrace it.

The Way of the Sufi   Idries Shah

Sufism, the mystical aspect of Islam, has had a dynamic and lasting effect on the literature of that religion. Its teachings, often elusive and subtle, aim at the perfecting and completing of the human mind. In this wide-ranging anthology of Sufi writing Idries Shah offers a broad selection of poetry, contemplations, letters, lectures and teaching stories that together form an illuminating introduction to this unique body of thought.

PENGUIN

ARKANA

NEW AGE BOOKS FOR MIND, BODY & SPIRIT

A SELECTION OF TITLES

Being Intimate: A Guide to Successful Relationships
John Amodeo and Kris Wentworth

This invaluable guide aims to enrich one of the most important – yet often problematic – aspects of our lives: intimate relationships and friendships. 'A clear and practical guide to realization and communication of authentic feelings, and thus an excellent pathway towards lasting intimacy and love' – George Leonard

Real Philosophy: An Anthology of the Universal Search for Meaning
Jacob Needleman

It is only in addressing the huge, fundamental questions such as 'Who am I?' and 'Why death?' that humankind finds itself capable of withstanding the worst and abiding in the best. The selections in this book are a survey of that universal quest for understanding and are particularly relevant to the awakening taking place in the world today as old orders crumble.

The Act of Creation Arthur Koestler

This second book in Koestler's classic trio of works on the human mind (which opened with *The Sleepwalkers* and concludes with *The Ghost in the Machine*) advances the theory that all creative activities – the conscious and unconscious processes underlying artistic originality, scientific discovery and comic inspiration – share a basic pattern, which Koestler expounds and explores with all his usual clarity and brilliance.

Secrets of the Soil Peter Tompkins and Christopher Bird

In this long-awaited sequel to their bestselling *The Secret Life of Plants* Peter Tompkins and Christopher Bird explore the revolutionary methods of biodynamic agriculture introduced by the scientist–philosopher–mystic Rudolf Steiner. They show how Steiner's astonishing 'homeopathic' fertilizers and growing techniques have been used to revitalize previously barren areas and to achieve amazing feats of productivity.

PENGUIN

ARKANA

NEW AGE BOOKS FOR MIND, BODY & SPIRIT

A SELECTION OF TITLES

Working on Yourself Alone: Inner Dreambody Work
Arnold Mindell

Western psychotherapy and Eastern meditation are two contrasting ways of learning more about one's self. The first depends heavily on the powers of the therapist. *Process-oriented* meditation, however, can be used by the individual as a means of resolving conflicts and increasing awareness from within. Using meditation, dream work and yoga, this remarkable book offers techniques that you can develop on your own, allowing the growth of an individual method.

Neo-Astrology   Michel Gauquelin

Michel Gauquelin's Neo-Astrology is a frugal science that discards much of the traditional horoscope, and suggests that five planets only – Saturn, Jupiter, Mars, Venus and the Moon – affect us. This important work shows that the French psychologist and statistician may be pointing towards nothing less than a new model of the universe.

Homage to the Sun: The Wisdom of the Magus of Strovolos
Kyriacos C. Markides

Homage to the Sun continues the adventure into the mysterious and extraordinary world of the spiritual teacher and healer Daskalos, the 'Magus of Strovolos'. The logical foundations of Daskalos' world of other dimensions are revealed to us – invisible masters, past-life memories and guardian angels, all explained by the Magus with great lucidity and scientific precision.

The Eagle's Gift   Carlos Castaneda

In the sixth book in his astounding journey into sorcery, Castaneda returns to Mexico. Entering once more a world of unknown terrors, hallucinatory visions and dazzling insights, he discovers that he is to replace the Yaqui Indian don Juan as leader of the apprentice sorcerers – and learns of the significance of the Eagle.

PENGUIN

ARKANA

NEW AGE BOOKS FOR MIND, BODY & SPIRIT

A SELECTION OF TITLES

Herbal Medicine for Everyone   Michael McIntyre

'The doctor treats but nature heals.' With an increasing consciousness of ecology and a move towards holistic treatment, the value of herbal medicine is now being fully recognized. Discussing the history and principles of herbal medicine and its application to a wide range of diseases and ailments, this illuminating book will prove a source of great wisdom.

The Tarot   Alfred Douglas

The puzzle of the original meaning and purpose of the Tarot has never been fully resolved. An expert in occult symbolism, Alfred Douglas explores the traditions, myths and religions associated with the cards, investigates their historical, mystical and psychological importance and shows how to use them for divination.

Views from the Real World   G. I. Gurdjieff

Only through self-observation and self-exploration, Gurdjieff asserted, could man develop his consciousness. To this end he evolved exercises through which awareness could be heightened and enlightenment attained. *Views from the Real World* contains his talks and lectures on this theme as he travelled from city to city with his pupils. What emerges is his immensely human approach to self-improvement.

Riding the Horse Backwards   Arnold and Amy Mindell

Arnold Mindell is the originator of perhaps the most inspiring 'school' of healing we have in the West now, process work, and in this running narrative of one of his workshops, which he gave with Amy Mindell at the Esalen community in the United States, we're taken to the heart of the magic.